Dynamic Teaching of Russian

Dynamic Teaching of Russian: Games and Gamification of Learning explores the theory and practice of gamification in language education, with a special focus on Russian, offering an in-depth theoretical account of the psychology of games and their practical application to language teaching.

This edited collection brings together diverse perspectives from an international pool of contributors. Topics covered include hands-on game-like activities, play, and games to enrich the Russian-language classroom that can be used with both adult and young Russian-language learners worldwide. The chapters use case studies to showcase innovative approaches that can be used in the language classroom to both motivate learners and improve the outcomes of teaching Russian.

This book will appeal to lecturers, tutors, teachers, and all other educators of Russian in subject areas of Russian studies, Slavonic studies, language learning, and foreign language acquisition.

Svetlana V. Nuss is an editor and teacher educator affiliated with the University of Alaska and Grand Canyon University, USA.

Vita V. Kogan is an assistant professor in Russian at University College London, UK.

Routledge Russian Language Pedagogy and Research

Series Editor: Svetlana V. Nuss
University of Alaska, USA

Routledge Russian Language Pedagogy and Research brings together edited volumes on the advances in the research and pedagogy of teaching the Russian language. Written by experts from across the world, the series brings together diverse schools of thought and serves as an inclusive discussion forum showcasing state-of-the-art advances in teaching and researching Russian.

Task-Based Instruction for Teaching Russian as a Foreign Language
Edited by Svetlana V. Nuss and Wendy Whitehead Martelle

Student-Centred Approaches to Russian Language Learning
Insights, Strategies, and Pandemic Adaptations
Edited by Svetlana V. Nuss and Cynthia L. Martin

Dynamic Teaching of Russian
Games and Gamification of Learning
Edited by Svetlana V. Nuss and Vita V. Kogan

For more information about this series please visit: www.routledge.com/Routledge-Russian-Language-Pedagogy-and-Research/book-series/RLPR

Dynamic Teaching of Russian

Games and Gamification of Learning

Edited by Svetlana V. Nuss
and Vita V. Kogan

Series Editor: Svetlana V. Nuss

LONDON AND NEW YORK

First published 2024
by Routledge
4 Park Square, Milton Park, Abingdon, Oxon OX14 4RN

and by Routledge
605 Third Avenue, New York, NY 10158

Routledge is an imprint of the Taylor & Francis Group, an informa business

© 2024 selection and editorial matter, Svetlana V. Nuss and Vita V. Kogan; individual chapters, the contributors

The right of Svetlana V. Nuss and Vita V. Kogan to be identified as the authors of the editorial material, and of the authors for their individual chapters, has been asserted in accordance with sections 77 and 78 of the Copyright, Designs and Patents Act 1988.

All rights reserved. No part of this book may be reprinted or reproduced or utilised in any form or by any electronic, mechanical, or other means, now known or hereafter invented, including photocopying and recording, or in any information storage or retrieval system, without permission in writing from the publishers.

Trademark notice: Product or corporate names may be trademarks or registered trademarks, and are used only for identification and explanation without intent to infringe.

British Library Cataloguing-in-Publication Data
A catalogue record for this book is available from the British Library

ISBN: 978-1-032-43980-8 (hbk)
ISBN: 978-1-032-43747-7 (pbk)
ISBN: 978-1-003-36972-1 (ebk)

DOI: 10.4324/9781003369721

Typeset in Times New Roman
by Apex CoVantage, LLC

Contents

List of contributors   *vii*
Preface   *viii*
SVETLANA V. NUSS

Terminology   *x*
Acknowledgments   *xii*

PART I
Pedagogy of teaching language with games and gamification   1

1 Teaching language with games: research, practice, and cohesion of pedagogy   3
SVETLANA V. NUSS

2 Gamification and game-based learning: an overview and application to language teaching   17
VITA V. KOGAN

PART II
Impacting speaking and beyond: up the teaching game   37

3 Mingling games for beginner learners of L2 Russian   39
DARIA KOTELNIKOVA AND ELENA BOGOMOLOVA

4 Trivia games for student-centered learning in the Russian-language classroom   67
MARIA KHOTIMSKY

PART III
Building language structures through games   79

5 The use of authentic games in teaching L2 Russian grammar   81
   ANNA LEONTYEVA AND EKATERINA SCHNITTKE

6 Learning motion verbs through a board game: insights from a cognitive linguistics perspective   107
   MARIA BONDARENKO

7 Game-based learning in L2 Russian classrooms: interaction, multimodality, and practical suggestions   138
   OLESIA PAVLENKO AND DMITRII PASTUSHENKOV

PART IV
Winning creative language at creative play   153

8 Ludic acts of language acquisition: role, dialogue, and stage for L2 Russian oral proficiency   155
   E. SUSANNA WEYGANDT

9 "I like brown, eyes, potatoes": gamified poetry for beginners   177
   POLINA PEREMITINA

10 Playing at conversation: chatbots in Russian language teaching   189
   DARIA DORNICHEVA AND SANDRA BIRZER

PART V
Are the games worth the candle?   209

11 Playing while learning: are the games worth the candle? Reflections on practice and future directions   211
   VITA V. KOGAN AND SVETLANA V. NUSS

Index   *230*

Contributors

Sandra Birzer, Otto-Friedrich-Universität Bamberg, Germany

Elena Bogomolova, Brookes International IB School, Saint Petersburg, Russia

Maria Bondarenko, University of Montreal, Canada; University of Heidelberg, Germany

Daria Dornicheva, Otto-Friedrich-Universität Bamberg, Germany

Maria Khotimsky, Massachusetts Institute of Technology, USA

Vita V. Kogan, University College London, UK

Daria Kotelnikova, Derzhavin Institute, Saint Petersburg, Russia

Anna Leontyeva, Higher School of Economics, Moscow, Russia

Svetlana V. Nuss, University of Alaska, USA

Dmitrii Pastushenkov, Harvard University, USA

Olesia Pavlenko, Kent State University, USA

Polina Peremitina, University of Illinois at Chicago, USA

Ekaterina Schnittke, Higher School of Economics, Moscow, Russia

E. Susanna Weygandt, Sewanee: The University of the South, USA

Preface

Is *teaching language with games* a sound pedagogical practice or just another *mug's game*? This volume not only answers this question but also shows teachers how to *up their instructional game*, as it solidifies the *use of games and gamified instruction* as one of the desirable elements of student-centered teaching. The book builds on the discourse of human-centeredness in language education, previously developed in the edited collection *Student-Centered Approaches to Russian Language Teaching: Insights, Strategies, and Adaptations* and conceptualized in its editorial chapters.

Dynamic Teaching of Russian: Games and Gamification of Learning lends further pedagogical evidence to the human-centered discourse in the field of teaching morphologically rich languages initiated by the Routledge series on Russian Language Pedagogy and Research. It presents a collection of pedagogical cases detailing the use of games and gamification strategies in teaching L2 Russian.

Visualizing language learning as more student- and human-centered means visualizing L2 instruction built on high-impact instructional strategies that encourage and nurture learner autonomy and self-efficacy, foster classroom community, and inspire enjoyment of learning. It also means paying attention to the efforts of L2 teachers to diversify their pedagogical expertise. These efforts often translate into adopting new tools, materials, and teaching strategies.

Trying something new often involves changing habitual ways of teaching, which in turn translates into large amounts of time and energy being invested by teachers to investigate, get acquainted with, choose, and eventually adopt new elements of instruction. It is critical that such changes happen cohesively and not fragmentize and disbalance an already-complex teaching process. This volume's mission is to help teachers of Russian as a foreign language do just that – introduce more games and joy into their practice more cohesively.

No matter what we discuss in education, it seems the conversation is always about *nature and nurture*. This volume is a good example, its contributing authors holding pedagogical beliefs that can be positioned at different places of the nature/nurture continuum of the language acquisition theory debate. In relation to language acquisition, this continuum can be visualized as framed by its polar points of *teacher-directed presentation and practice* on one end and *unregulated and unassisted learning through the natural exposure of the learner to the language* on the other.

The pedagogical cases of this volume's chapters, while distant from the continuum's extreme points and informed by various theoretical positions, nevertheless converge on the idea of meaningful language creation by students, with much attention paid to mastering language structures. This, of course, explains the differences in the authors' motivations and the variety of choices of how the games they offer are used in instruction. Our reader is certainly free to take these games and gamification strategies and create their own dynamics in integration practices.

This collection of contextualized theory and best teaching practices of game-based instruction of L2 Russian is published in the spirit of sharing with teachers of many other morphologically rich languages who have a smaller research and practice base to work with. These teachers, too, may benefit from getting acquainted with game-based and gamified instructional practices solidly grounded in theory that worked well for teachers of L2 Russian.

It is our hope that this book will help teachers of RFL *up their instructional game*. We publish it with expectations that this resource would aid the teachers' creativity and professional growth as they implement a student-centered shift of instruction. It will save them personal time while bringing more joy and professional satisfaction into their lives and the lives of their students.

Most importantly, we publish this volume for you, our students, so that your *big game* – the time you spend learning Russian – is worth every candle!

Svetlana V. Nuss

Terminology

Applied linguistics is a fast-developing field with strong academic publishing traditions and a fluid terminology base – a sign of healthy growth. The following terms are used in the volume:

Educational game: any structured form of play that serves an educational function in addition to entertainment.
Gamification: integration of game mechanics into the educational process; an umbrella term that combines various motivational affordances (e.g., competition, rewards, and the introduction of rules). Educational activities that include such elements are called *gamified activities*.
GBL: *game-based learning* is an approach to teaching that employs games to support the learning process.
L1: the first language acquired by a learner; may or may not be shared by learners and the teacher.
L2: a language of study. Often referred to as *L2* in academic literature, the language of study may, in fact, be the third or fourth language the learner is acquiring in addition to their L1. In this volume, *L2* is used interchangeably with the term *target language*.
Language acquisition: the process of acquiring language in an instructional setting. Acknowledging the deeply nuanced discussion of *learning* and *acquisition* in SLA, for the purposes of this volume, *language learning* and *L2 language acquisition* are used interchangeably unless noted otherwise.
Learner-centered and student-centered: the terms *student-centered* and *learner-centered* are used as synonyms. Student-centered education is viewed here as equally important for both K–12 and tertiary settings; therefore, they are addressed as one *learning environment*.
RFL: *Russian as a foreign language* refers to the context where Russian, being the target language of study, is not the dominant language of the country where it is being acquired by learners.
RHL: *Russian as a heritage language* refers to the Russian language as a part of the learner's linguistic background when Russian is spoken in the family as the learner is growing up in a country where Russian is not a dominant language.

RSL: *Russian as a second language* refers to the context where Russian, being the target language of study, is the dominant language of the country where it is being acquired by the learner(s).

Shared language: a language spoken by both the students and the teacher. The earners and the teacher may or may not have a common language they share.

SLA: *Second language acquisition* refers to the field of study and the process of acquiring an additional – and not necessarily second for the learner – language.

Target language: a language of study. In this volume, *target language* is used interchangeably with the term *L2*.

Teacher: the term *teacher* is used to refer to any educator who practices teaching with learners of any age.

Acknowledgments

Dynamic Teaching of Russian: Games and Gamification of Learning continues the line of premier academic publications in Routledge's series on Russian Language Pedagogy and Research. The volume we offer to the reader was created by the efforts of many, but first and foremost its contributing authors. Their dedication to the profession, pedagogical talent, and academic scholarship is no short of admirable. Their ideas helped build a unique resource and a much-needed addition for the field of Russian language teaching. You are an inspiration!

Sandra Birzer, Elena Bogomolova, Maria Bondarenko, Daria Dornicheva, Maria Khotimsky, Vita V. Kogan, Daria Kotelnikova, Anna Leontyeva, Svetlana V. Nuss, Dmitrii Pastushenkov, Olesia Pavlenko, Polina Peremitina, Ekaterina Schnittke, E. Susanna Weygandt.

Ensuring the highest quality of academic scholarship would not be possible without the help of a competitively selected team of peer reviewers. We are grateful for their generous contribution of time, effort, and professional expertise. Without a doubt, their questions and suggestions helped strengthen the content of the book in a myriad of ways: sharpen ideas, focus narration, and ultimately, make the volume shine:

Kirstin Bebell, independent scholar, USA
Olena Chernishenko, American University, ICA, USA
Steven Clancy, Harvard University, USA
Nadezhda A. Dubinina, Saint Petersburg State University, Russia
Lidia Gault, University of Wisconsin–Madison, USA
Daniel Martín González, Universidad Complutense de Madrid, Spain
SHI Haoting, Ritsumeikan University, Japan
Valentina Ilić, University of Belgrade, Serbia
Anna Ivanov, Harvard University, USA
Natallia Kabiak, University of Melbourne, Australia
Natalya Khokholova, YTIT Lewis University Cyracom, USA
Elizaveta Levina, University of Southern California, USA

Maxim Likhanov, ITMO University, Saint Petersburg, Russia
Evelina Mendelevich, New York University, USA
Jill Neuendorf, Georgetown University, USA
Christina Nuss, Heidelberg University, Germany
Dmitrii Pastushenkov, Harvard University, USA
Olesia Pavlenko, Kent State University, USA
John Pendergast, West Point, USA
James Joshua Pennington, independent scholar, USA
Maria Gatti Racah, Università Ca' Foscari Venezia, Italy
Vladyslava Reznyk, Akademeia High School, Warsaw, Poland
Wolfgang Stadler, Innsbruck University, Austria
Rachel Stauffer, University of Illinois Urbana-Champaign, USA
Mara Sukholutskaya, East Central University, USA
Anastassia Zabrodskaja, Tallinn University, Estonia

We are thankful to Samantha Vale Noya, Commissioning Editor, Taylor & Francis Group, for her foresight, superior knowledge of the industry, and supportive spirit. We are also grateful to Tassia Watson, Editorial Assistant in the Language Learning division at Routledge, for her timely communication, professionalism, and proactive support. The editors also wish to thank Routledge's three anonymous proposal reviewers, whose comments and suggestions were instrumental in shaping this volume.

We would like to express our deepest appreciation to Nicholas Brazones, MA candidate at the University of Maryland, for his efficient editorial assistance work, dedication, and expertise throughout this project. The editors are especially grateful to Christina Nuss, MA candidate at Heidelberg University, Germany, for her exemplary attention to detail, knowledge of the field, and overall excellence in building a comprehensive index for this book.

Part I

Pedagogy of teaching language with games and gamification

Chapter 1

Teaching language with games
Research, practice, and cohesion of pedagogy

Svetlana V. Nuss

CHAPTER SUMMARY

This chapter establishes the need for pedagogical cohesion in the integration of games into the instruction of Russian as a foreign language (RFL). The chapter offers an overview of meta-meta-research in general education that may help teachers shape their approaches to instruction. It offers a scale of reference and considers various influences of student achievement. The chapter points out the imbalance in the way research and teaching practice approach the integration of games in instruction with the dominance of the digital component in research to the detriment of analog games and the role of the teacher. It provides teachers with practical considerations of balancing research and practice when designing student experiences and implementing games in language teaching. The chapter discusses the volume's contributions based on the context of instruction, the kind of games and gamified teaching they offer, the affordances of various games, and the student-centered nature of teaching language with games. In conclusion, it argues for the necessity of shifting the instruction of RFL to be more human-centered and empathy-driven.

КРАТКОЕ СОДЕРЖАНИЕ ГЛАВЫ

Данная глава посвящена обзору сборника и представляет собою введение в его предмет – обучение русскому языку как иностранному (РКИ) посредством интеграции игр и игровой механики. Представлена база эмпирических исследований в области образования с мета-мета-анализом данных о категориях влияния на достижения учащихся. В главе поднимается вопрос о дисбалансе исследовательской деятельности и нужд практики преподавания с включением игр и преобладании цифровой составляющей в исследованиях в ущерб практике и недостаточной теоретизации и концептуализации работы нецифровых игр и роли учителя в выстраивании обучения с применением игр. В главе подвергается анализу данный сборник на предмет образующих его глав и подходов их авторов к преподаванию РКИ посредством игр и игровых технологий с точки зрения контекста практики, содержания и формы предлагаемых игр и технологий, особенностей их применения и глубинную личностно ориентированную, студентоцентричную природу такого подхода к организации учебного процесса. Выдвигается и обосновывается принцип необходимости развития теоретической и практической базы преподавания РКИ посредством игровых технологий, их потенциала в преобразовании обучения иностранным языкам в более студентоцентричное и продвижения обсуждения этого вопроса в контексте преподавания РКИ.

Sound language pedagogy *vs.* the game of chance

When examined more closely, the conversation about the *use of games in education* is reminiscent of the *use of technology in education*: eventually, *technology* was reined in and *pedagogy* dominated the landscape. The *technology* took its appropriate place as a device in service of the advancement of pedagogical aims. Today, the proverbial pedagogical horse is driving the technology cart (Sankey, 2020) in more places and more often (Tsui & Tavares, 2021), with each influencing and propelling the other. Time and again, when the initial excited embrace of a new tool in teaching loosens its hold, stakeholders circle back to a common understanding of the preeminence of pedagogical grounding. We then choose to abandon our *game of chance* – a frenzied inclusion of assorted disconnected instructional tools – and start disciplining ourselves to define our whys, whats, and hows of using these tools with regard to their pedagogical validity in our pursuit of impacting student learning.

While there is no shortage of assorted individual games available to teachers of world languages today, with new volumes mushrooming the second and foreign language education landscape (Bolen, 2021; DiGiacomo, 2018; Kaznyshkina [Казнышкина], 2019; Leontyeva [Леонтьева], 2018; Nurmukhamedov & Sadler, 2020; Razin & Kingisepp [Разин & Кингисепп], 2018), pedagogy has yet to extend its reign over their classroom integration: there is a distinct need for more rigorous pedagogical priming and reasoning when it comes to teaching language with games (Cornillie et al., 2012; York et al., 2021). The leading role of sound language pedagogy should help streamline the imbalanced use of games in the field of language teaching today, which, in turn, is a part of larger issues of cohesion of instruction and supplementation of the core curriculum.

In the instruction of RFL, two recent volumes published by the Routledge series on Russian Language Pedagogy and Research share exemplary practices of curriculum development and supplementation in the field of teaching RFL. Systematic in nature, they reflect serious and innovative pedagogical effort (e.g., the chapters by Mendelevich; Nimis et al.; and Zheltoukhova featured in Nuss and Whitehead Martelle (2022a) and chapters by Anderson and Sokolova et al. from Nuss and Martin's volume on student-centered teaching practices of RFL). An instance of cooperative planning and instructional co-design, involving the cooperation of eight premier institutions (unprecedented in its scale for the teaching of Russian in the United States), took place recently within a multi-university partnership: 29 students from the Russian Flagship programs of those eight colleges and universities came together to play a co-curricular interinstitutional online game of *Что? Где? Когда?* [What? Where? When?] (Godwin-Jones et al., 2022). The fundamental pedagogical advances I describe here don't "just happen" on their own – they are results of a changed frame of mind that triggered a change in the teaching practice. This can only happen when teachers come from a place of empathy for their students, engage in deep professional reflection, and dare to come out of the tightening cocoon of their comfort zone and create a new learning reality for their students. Pedagogy must be cultivated.

Balancing research and practice of teaching languages with games

Even though games have been a prominent feature in the educational practice of second language acquisition (SLA), upon careful review, research on using games to teach languages is surprisingly imbalanced. While one might assume that research follows the needs of practice and reflects the distribution of classroom practices, a review of the available research reveals that this is not the case. With analog games in language teaching practice overwhelmingly outweighing the use of computer-mediated games, research has been limited in scope to the games in digital environment (York et al., 2021), favoring game design over its pedagogy (Cornillie et al., 2012). Indeed, the sheer number of terms associated with games in digital contexts is a playing field of its own (Thanyawatpokin & York, 2021).

That research is often divorced from the pedagogy of teaching is not a new topic of conversation in the field of SLA (Sato & Loewen, 2019; Nuss, 2022c), and the relationship between research- and practice-based discourse of teaching language with games today is indisputably far from encouraging. The research is taken with anything but pedagogy, and on the rare occasions where studies are actually being conducted in the classroom,

> only a few of them provide any details about pedagogical practices. . . . These are not trivial details. If the vision of games transforming education is to be realized, and if using games in the classroom is to become normalized, it will be done so by *teachers*. Thus, research must turn its focus towards the language classroom and how games can be integrated into curricula, and how educators can teach with games . . . with teachers as the "main character" in research that investigates the use of games for language learning.
> (York et al., 2021, p. 1,165)

While educators have traditionally regarded games as a favorable form of instruction enjoyable to students and teachers alike, research of their impact on second language acquisition has been inconclusive, although it has made promising claims (see Kogan, Chapter 2 of the present volume, for an overview). The wide variety of game structures and compositions, contexts, and demographics of participants and their personalities have hindered attempts to produce decisive empirical evidence of the efficacy of games in RFL (Vandercruysse et al., 2012).

Similar confounds are cited in reviews of the research on the *gamification* of learning in digital contexts, which have demonstrated mixed success at best (Majuri et al., 2018). Gamification is particularly criticized for its manipulative nature (York et al., 2022). Reviews point to a large body of research with null or mixed results in addition to the share of favorable reports, especially noting an almost-complete absence of controls in conducted research and the challenges in quantifying the effect of each feature of gamification, much less than their combined or grouped effect (Majuri et al., 2018, p. 16). *Gamification* is a widely accepted educational design feature (the gamification movement started around 2010) that aims to produce and support desirable psychological and behavioral outcomes in teaching. It accomplishes this by employing the same experiences people enjoy when playing games. It is, therefore, an umbrella term that combines various motivational affordances found in games, including such features as progress, status bars, leaderboards, rankings, points, scores, badges, trophies, challenges, quests, missions, tasks, and more.

Designing student learning experiences: integration of research

Designing student learning experiences to reflect the most recent and accurate research findings is one of the aspirations of language teachers. When we study research literature, it starts transforming our thinking and the overall instructional frame of mind, which, in turn,

> shapes classroom instruction through teachers' willingness to change their current pedagogical mindset and implement new practices to benefit the learner. The individual's pedagogical background and intuition become the catalyst and the medium that transform research findings into specific instructional approaches.
> (Nuss, 2022a, p. 18)

This is one way pedagogy is cultivated.

Powerful insights and learning design ideas may come from non-language-specific education research. I will now invite the reader to take a glance at one of the most comprehensive databases and educational research collections to date. Taking the world of education by storm, Hattie's meta-meta-analysis (a synthesis of previously conducted meta-analyses) of over 270 influencers of student achievement (ongoing research, first publicized in Hattie, 2009) involves 300 million students to date and spans over 1,800 meta-analyses, comprising 90,000+ individual studies (Hattie & Hamilton, 2020). Each of the 270 influencers' impact is calculated as effect size (d), with $d = 0.40$, representing an average of all effect sizes (also referred to as a year's worth of growth for a year's worth of input). Cohen's d value of 0.20 is interpreted as having a small 0.50 medium and 0.80 large effect size. According to these data (Hattie, 2015), just about anything we do in education "works" to advance student learning, with very few influences falling below 0, for example, *boredom* with the effect size of $d = -49$. For educators aspiring to exhilarate student learning, the desirable influences would have values greater than 0.50 (Cohen, 1988). Games, *per se*, are not represented in this ranking as a separate category; however, there are several influences that are relevant to our discussion.

Games are directly addressed in Hattie's index in reference to **gaming and simulations** (implementations using technologies). Their effect size is calculated to be $d = 0.34$, indicating digital *gaming and simulations* overall to be a small but impactful influence on student achievement. By designing student learning experiences with the integration of games and gamification, we can build in the features proven to help learning and minimize those that inhibit it. Not appearing in the top positions of the most impactful instructional strategies, games nevertheless certainly can contribute to learning when they fight **boredom** $d = -49$ and ignite **engagement** (beliefs, attributes, and disposition) with an effect size of 0.56.

Being aware of the "big" data in this set may help teachers channel their instructional efforts and use the precious instructional time more productively. For example, knowing the effect sizes of **motivation** and **reducing anxiety** $d = 0.42$ builds an understanding that while these are important areas contributing to student success and should be addressed with learners, they are not the most impactful influences of student achievement. **As teachers, we must develop priorities and attend to the most impactful influences in designing instruction to advance student achievement**. The idea is not new. In his review of scholarship on "old problems" and "new solutions" for teaching grammar spanning several decades, Pawlak (2021) speaks of the need for teachers to be selective when it comes to aligning their instruction with the research findings, especially highlighting the fact that while important to scholars and thought advancement overall, research findings often have little meaning for practice: "when studies are carried out, the point of departure is seldom a concern emanating from real classroom" (Pawlak, 2021, p. 892). **The needs of a particular group of students should be the decisive factor** when educators build a balanced and cohesive system of supports and consider various influences for this purpose. The bigger datasets provide a bird's-eye view of what works best and thus would make sense to be prioritized in practice. I will discuss some of these data in the following paragraphs.

Integrating games into instruction opens doors of opportunity for nurturing several high-impact proficiency-building practices which, when present as sound features of the design in the organization of student learning, demonstrate the following impact: **deliberate practice** with $d = 0.82$ (learning strategies), **summarization** and **effort** with $d = 0.79$ each (learning strategies), **vocabulary programs** with $d = 0.62$ (reading, writing, and the arts). I also highlight the prominence of **rehearsal and memorization** (learning strategies) with $d = 0.74$, an affordance that can be amply supplied by games. The authors of this volume specifically mention *rehearsal and memorization* in several accounts (Bondarenko, Chapter 6; Leontyeva & Schnittke, Chapter 5; Weygandt, Chapter 8). Special attention is devoted to the concept of *deliberate practice* via games as well (Khotimsky, Chapter 4; Kotelnikova & Bogomolova, Chapter 3; Peremitina, Chapter 9).

Helping students access and comprehend the content in the target language, as well as be productive and effectively function in the context of their learning, can take many forms, from illustrating the process or a concept with images to chunking information, asking specific questions, and offering elaborations or highlighting theme-related parts of the text and creating graphic representations – ***scaffolding*** (teaching/instructional strategies) $d = 0.82$ embodies a result of a well-orchestrated intentional effort and mindful support of learning. Elements of scaffolding are discussed in this volume as well (Bondarenko, Chapter 6; Dornicheva & Birzer, Chapter 10; Pavlenko & Pastushenkov, Chapter 7; Weygandt, Chapter 8).

Anyone who has tried to play even the simplest of games with a group of learners (and, better yet, shared in the experience of playing a game as a participant and a language learner) appreciates the necessity of clear directions and well-defined expectations: predictably impactful, the effect size of ***teacher clarity*** (teacher attributes) is $d = 0.75$. There is a good reason that the authors of this volume speak to it in just about every chapter and invested much effort in perfecting the directions to the games they detail here in multiple class sessions. In fact, game directions featured in the volume's chapters can be considered to be a special gift the authors of this volume offer to the field of teaching RFL.

While each of the data categories I discuss here requires specific conversation in the context of language learning, some preliminary conclusions point to specific design features that can be used in creating an instructional frame for game integration. As we just witnessed, teaching is not about "What works?" anymore; today, responsible teaching is about "What works best?" The main value of examining large-scale educational data is in its ability to disrupt the borders of professional silos where we may unintentionally get enclosed without even realizing it.

Another review of empirical evidence I bring to the reader's attention is **devoted specifically to educational games** and comes from a study unique in its scope – a bright combination of a quantitative and qualitative large-scale research effort. In their comparative meta-analysis and meta-thematic analysis of efficiency of educational games, Talan and colleagues (2020) are more positive in the estimate of the documented evidence of how games influence learning. With the 1,920 studies conducted in the last 15 years in their original pool and 154 studies eventually meeting their strict selection criteria, this study is one of the most wide-scope research efforts of game-based teaching today. Talan et al. (2020) summarize results of multiple studies where games impacted problem-solving and critical thinking, student creativity, memory, knowledge retention, and recall; cognitive abilities (analogy, processing speed, and deductive reasoning); perceptual attention and mental rotation skills; and spatial skills, ultimately leading to higher cognitive gains (p. 4). They also report on a steady stream of research of the positive impact games can have on affective components of learning we are used to seeing in language education research, such as motivation, attitudes, engagement, self-efficacy, self-esteem, social recognition, and anxiety, as well as a newly developed interest regarding innovative thinking, collaboration, information and technology literacy, and productivity.

Interestingly, in relation to the subjects of study, Talan and colleagues observed the largest effect size of game-based learning on foreign language learning with the effect size of $g = 0.87$, while the overall impact of games on student achievement was reported to be $g = 0.67$, qualifying game-based learning as a potentially medium-high influence on student achievement. Another intriguing finding is the impact of non-digital games boasting the highest of all effect size $g = 0.90$, making non-digital games the champion of game-based learning and a worthy ally in language teaching practice. It seems to make no difference whether the games are used incrementally or systemically (the terms are used consistent with definitions from Nuss & Whitehead Martelle, 2022a) – the impact remains the same. The overall recommendation of the study is that based on the synthesized quantitative and qualitative evidence, the educators already "have justified reasons to make games, whether digital or not, an indispensable and integrated part of our curricula" (Talan et al., 2020, p. 24).

Such larger sets of data allow the permeance of ideas in the teaching profession and become meaningful points of reference for its distinct and often disconnected fields. They may transform our thinking and help create an overarching frame of mind that guides our instructional choices. In doing so, such references mediate teachers' willingness to change their current pedagogical mindset and consider adopting or seeking out new practices, transforming specific facts of research findings into instructional approaches, and waking professional curiosity. As I have stated in Nuss (2022a) and reiterate in this chapter, **pedagogy must be cultivated**. Teaching is a profession (a recent discussion of it is summarized in Goodwin et al., 2022), and teaching RFL should also be professionalized (Anderson et al., 2020; Martin & Nuss, 2022b; Nuss, 2022a; Spasova & Welsh, 2020; Whitehead Martelle & Nuss, 2022). This conversation is prominent in the field of teaching Russian and not going away anytime soon: professional competencies of teachers of RFL must come to the foreground of future field discussions. It is not enough to write new textbooks (although creating modern RFL textbooks is still as important as ever); it is just as important that, as a field, we *cultivate the inner teacher* in our faculty in all contexts, nurture it, and continuously strive to grow – to the greatest benefit of our students.

Game-based pedagogy of teaching Russian as a foreign language: setting the stage

The volume's composition – analog games *vs.* digital or technology-mediated games – reflects the main trends in the integration of games for language learning, where the use of analog games outweighs that of technology-mediated games (based on the representation of games detailed in Nurmukhamedov & Sadler, 2020, and analyzed in York et al., 2021). I note that most of the analog games offered in this book can be adjusted to online teaching, both synchronous and asynchronous.

The research vector, however, diverges from the current trends in language teaching practices, concentrating primarily on digital and video games (see Kogan, Chapter 2 of the present volume, and Gee and Gao, 2022, for an overview of the most recent research). There are strong voices advocating for more research on the *pedagogy of games*, with the broadened research agenda aiming to include games outside of digital scope and concentrate on the role of the teacher (York et al., 2021). Such research would benefit greatly from ethnographic accounts and case studies detailing what the pedagogy of language learning with games may look like in various teaching contexts, akin to the ones collected in this volume.

Instructional aids and tools serve pedagogy in the teaching process; they are employed by teachers to solve problems of practice and get integrated into the instruction based on the elaborate framework of pedagogical considerations – starting with the can-dos and visualization of the end product, leading with standards, verifying direction via best assessment practices, adjusting the sails, and taking learning to the next cycle through reflection. The volume features examples of how instructional practices are first conceptualized within a pedagogical frame of thought and then manifested in a learning tool framed as a game, play, or gamified approach.

Each chapter presented in this book is grounded in the theoretical underpinnings of its game-based pedagogic events, with authors engaging in thorough professional reflection as they identify and review the literature on the subject. Hence, this **volume presents a unique collection of SLA literature reviews on various specific kinds of game-based language teaching:**

> **Trivia games** (Khotimsky, Chapter 4), **mingle games** and activities (Kotelnikova & Bogomolova, Chapter 3), **video games and traditional games** (Pavlenko & Pastushenkov, Chapter 7), use and adaptations of **authentic games** (Leontyeva & Schnittke, Chapter 5), a unique Russian-language-specific **author-produced board game** (Bondarenko, Chapter 6), **use of a poetry kit** in developing writing (Peremitina, Chapter 9), the use of **drama and deep play** (Weygandt, Chapter 8), and integration of **chatbots** (Dornicheva & Birzer, Chapter 10); the general **state of the art of teaching language with games** (Kogan, Chapter 2), a **cohesive pedagogy and design of learning** with games (Nuss, Chapter 1), and volume's lessons and **emerging perspectives**
>
> (Kogan & Nuss, Chapter 11).

All the games and gamification elements offered by the authors were originally conceived as a means of replacing the mundane and often energy-draining practice drills of various morphological features of the Russian language. The authors were also driven to give their students meaningful speaking opportunities. Such aspirations in teachers often come from the place of empathy and understanding of the challenges faced by learners. For me, it took witnessing a strong emotional response coming from learner dissatisfaction with self that was driven by a perceived lack of rate of progress in learning Russian and sympathy for their feelings.

Russian, as a morphologically rich language, certainly gives learners plenty of opportunities to be dissatisfied with their progress and to get discouraged on their journey to proficiency: from the number of errors in case markings and other morphology-related choices (see Nuss, 2022a, for a review of research on L2 Russian morphology acquisition) to uncertainties of the shifting stressed syllables and the (ever-present in language learning) figurative language, linguistic and pragmatic dynamics of various registers, not to mention Russian phonetics and prosody. Learner dissatisfaction can also be unintentionally provoked by the imbalanced instructional practices of well-meaning educators who, with one hand, encourage student risk-taking and, with the other, punish this supposedly welcome behavior with punitive grading and evaluation practices (Martin & Nuss, 2022b).

In the coming pages, the reader will witness how powerful teachers' creative efforts can be in making language instruction more student-centered. Such practice, ideally, takes into account students' social-emotional qualities and connections, gives students choices, and brings meaning to learning as it fosters student agency and encourages students to "honor the process of learning and value deeper understanding and expertise" (Nuss, 2022b, p. 26). Such student-centeredness makes the learning environment more humane and organic overall by shifting learners' attention away from the stress-inducing pressure to produce correct forms to enjoyment and satisfaction of making and expressing meaning, as it encourages and rewards learner risk-taking (Martin & Nuss, 2022b). This doesn't mean we ignore the accuracy of output; it simply sends learners the message that producing, noticing, and correcting errors is a normal and expected part of growing their language. Scaffolding input and output with the help of games and elements of gamification contributes to a vibrant atmosphere in our classrooms by effectively minimizing boredom, learner anxiety, and monotonous drills, with the hope of eventually squishing them out of our virtual and face-to-face L2 Russian classrooms for good. This will also help us turn the tide from "*Russian is hard*" to "*Russian is fun!*" which may even bring more students into our RFL classrooms.

Diversity of games and their integration in L2 Russian

In terms of (non)systemic implementation, the games can be integrated into the class flow *systemically*, when a syllabus or a program is built and sequenced using game-based instruction, or *incrementally*, when games are used as episodes of instruction, more or less cohesively integrated into an otherwise non-game-based curriculum, to include the use of games for assessment (definitions are based on Nuss and Whitehead Martelle's original classification (2022a, pp. 1 and 7–8) for the use of tasks in teaching). **Most of the chapters feature incremental instruction of Russian with games, with some detailing systematic implementation** (Bondarenko, Chapter 6; Weygandt, Chapter 8).

An encouraging feature of this volume is the **considerable number of games for students with low levels of proficiency**. Beginner learners warrant special consideration when it comes to morphologically rich languages, bearing in mind that every advanced speaker was once a beginner learner, but not every beginner learner becomes an advanced speaker. This bestows a special responsibility upon teachers of beginner learners, as program vitality largely depends on how readily students enroll in subsequent courses. Considering the profound impact beginner courses may have on the vigor and strength of language learning programs, it is with special joy that we showcase a large number of games that can be used with learners at early stages of language proficiency: Bondarenko, Chapter 6; Khotimsky, Chapter 4; Kotelnikova and Bogomolova, Chapter 3; Leontyeva and Schnittke, Chapter 5; Pavlenko and Pastushenkov, Chapter 7; and Peremitina, Chapter 9. In fact, almost every game featured in the volume can be either used as is or scaffolded and adjusted for beginners.

Implementing games in foreign language instruction takes **laser-sharp focus on the structure and purpose of the game** (focus on chatbots in Dornicheva and Birzer, Chapter 10; mingling games in Kotelnikova and Bogomolova, Chapter 3; authentic games in Leontyeva and Schnittke, Chapter 5; traditional analog as well as video games in Pavlenko and Pastushenkov, Chapter 7), **on the curriculum** (semantic labeling in verbs of motion in Bondarenko's board game, Chapter 6; use of poetry in developing writing in Peremitina, Chapter 9), and **on the student** (content-based student needs driving choices in Khotimsky's trivia games, Chapter 4; deep play influence on the community of learners, student choice, and focus on student role on stage in Weygandt, Chapter 8). The **role of the teacher** is explored in all chapters and, additionally, explicitly analyzed in the editorial chapters (Kogan and Nuss, Chapter 11; Kogan, Chapter 2; Nuss, Chapter 1).

Shifting instruction: the spirit and vision of human-centered, empathy-driven education

Integrating games in the class flow allows for the implementation of many qualities desired in language teaching: games offer an opportunity to practice and develop learners' ability to use targeted structures in real-time interactions, can offer opportunities for spaced repetition, and provide plenty of comprehensible input; they have an outcome that is greater than the use of language as such, providing plenty of opportunities for input flood (frequent use of a language pattern in a text conceived broadly). Games can be used as focused communication or form-trapping tasks when the use of a certain language structure is unavoidable (Ellis, 2003) and as a low-stakes formative assessment, as well as provide learners with multiple exposures and meaningful use of target language structures in context. The context in a student-centered environment can be chosen in such a way that it is relevant and of high interest to students, filling conversations with meaning and charging them with emotion.

Human- and student-centered learning and teaching environment doesn't just happen; I imagine it appearing out of thin air. This thin air is woven by the spirit of responsible pedagogy and the intellectual thought that envisions a better future for humanity. As educators, we can choose to teach with empathy, touching the hearts of

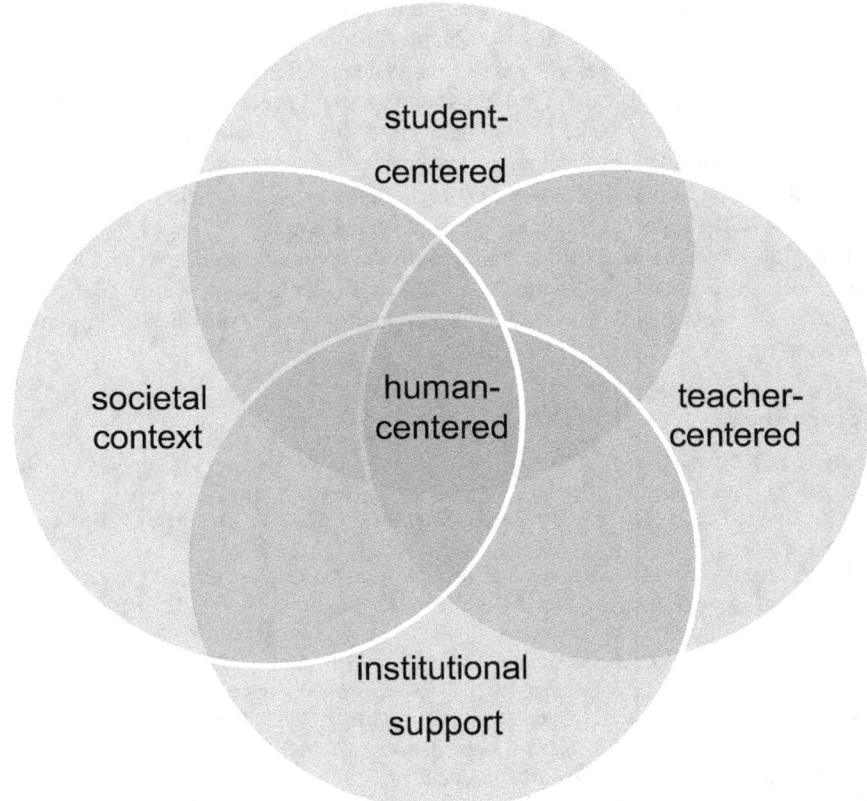

Figure 1.1 Vision of human-centered, equity-focused education.

those to whom this future belongs – today's students. Education is a twofold process where both students and teachers have a role to play and can positively impact the learning environment and society at large, so that everyone involved achieves their full potential. The dichotomy of polarizing thinking of us/them – teachers/students – belongs in the past. When students are empowered agents of their learning, education becomes about us – together – a journey of mutual aspirations and growth.

> In the end, student-centeredness is a mindset, not a technique, approach, or process, driven by its key element – empathy. Modeling it and disseminating accounts of practices in search of student-centeredness is of utmost importance, as it matters to so many: the teachers, the students, the institutions, and the society at large. Where the interests of all four converge, we come close to a human-centered environment that serves all.
>
> (Martin & Nuss, 2022a, p. 202)

When teachers aspire to develop a well-balanced instructional practice, the needs and goals of learners are the decisive factors in planning instruction. In such an approach to teaching, games can serve to advance proficiency and respond to certain language learning needs of students with surgical precision. These games are integrated not just for the sake of playing a game – they are strategically employed. It is my deep conviction that games and elements of gamification are uniquely positioned for adding to the *human-friendly* dynamics in L2 Russian classrooms, a conviction well-supported by the chapters of this volume.

I would like to thank the three anonymous reviewers as well as Nicholas Brazones, Maxim Likhanov, Christina Nuss, Olesia Pavlenko, and Wendy Whitehead Martelle for their insightful comments and editing suggestions. All remaining shortcomings are, of course, my own.

References

Anderson, C., Mikhailova, J., & Tumarkin, A. (2020). Russian language readiness in graduate teaching assistants: Implications for teaching and learning. In E. Dengub, I. Dubinina, & J. Merrill (Eds.), *The art of teaching Russian* (pp. 72–94). Georgetown University Press.

Bolen, J. (2021). *ESL technology games, activities, and resources: 59 ways to implement tech in a language learning classroom* (Teaching English as a second or Foreign language). Bolen.

Cohen, J. (1988). *Statistical power analysis* (2nd ed.). Erlbaum.

Cornillie, F., Thorne, S. L., & Desmet, P. (2012). Games for language learning: From hype to insight? *ReCALL, 24*(3), 243–256. https://doi.org/10.1017/S0958344012000134

DiGiacomo, M. (2018). *ESL games for the classroom: 101 interactive activities to engage your students with minimal prep*. Rockridge Press.

Ellis, R. (2003). *Task-based language learning and teaching*. Oxford University Press.

Gee, E., & Gao, Y. (2022). Digital game-mediated language learning for adults. *Adult Literacy Education, 4*(1), 67–73 http://doi.org/10.35847/EGee.YGao.4.1.67

Godwin-Jones, M., Murphy, D., & Evan-Romaine, K. (2022). Language, culture, and community: Fostering learning through an interinstitutional online game. *The FLTMAG*, January 5, n.p.

Goodwin, B., Rouleau, K., Abla, C., Baptiste, K., Gibson, T., & Kimball, M. (2022). *The new classroom instruction that works: The best research-based strategies for increasing student achievement*. ACSD.

Hattie, J. (2015). The applicability of Visible learning to higher education. *Scholarship of Teaching and Learning in Psychology, 1*(1), 79–91. https://doi.org/10.1037/stl0000021

Hattie, J., & Hamilton, A. (2020). *As good as gold? Why we focus on the wrong drivers in education*. Corwin Press.

Kaznyshkina, I. [Казнышкина, И.] (2019). *Communicative games for teaching Russian as a Foreign language* [Коммуникативные игры на уроках русского языка как иностранного]. Russkij Yazyk [Русский Язык].

Leontyeva, A. L. [Леонтьева, А. Л.] (2018). *50 games in Russian language lessons* [50 игр на уроках русского языка: Учебное пособие]. Russkij jazyk, Kursy [Русский язык, Курсы].

Majuri, J., Koivisto, J., & Hamari, J. (2018). Gamification of education and learning: A review of empirical literature. May 2018. *The 2nd international GamiFIN conference.* Pori, Finland, May 21–23, 2018.

Martin, C., & Nuss, S. (2022a). Student-centered teaching of Russian: From principles to practice. In S. Nuss & C. Martin (Eds.), *Student-centered approaches to student-centered approaches to Russian language teaching: Insights, strategies, and adaptations.* Routledge.

Martin, C., & Nuss, S. (2022b). Reflections on practice, additional considerations, and the importance of institutional support for teachers. In S. Nuss & C. Martin (Eds.), *Student-centered approaches to student-centered approaches to Russian language teaching: Insights, strategies, and adaptations.* Routledge.

Nurmukhamedov, U., & Sadler, R. (Eds.) (2020). *New ways in teaching with games.* TESOL Press.

Nuss, S. (2022a). Morphology acquisition research meets instruction of L2 Russian: A contextualized literature review. In S. Nuss & W. Martelle (Eds.), *Task-based instruction for teaching Russian as a Foreign language* (pp. 15–35). Routledge. https://doi.org/10.4324/9781003146346-2

Nuss, S. (2022b). History of student-centeredness, its modern vision in education, and what this means for teaching L2 Russian today. In S. Nuss & C. Martin (Eds.), *Student-centered approaches to student-centered approaches to Russian language teaching: Insights, strategies, and adaptations.* Routledge.

Nuss, S. (2022c). TBLT in L2 Russian pedagogy. In S. Nuss & W. Martelle (Eds.), *Task-based instruction for teaching Russian as a Foreign language* (pp. 7–13). Routledge. https://doi.org/10.4324/9781003146346-1

Nuss, S., & Whitehead Martelle, W. (Eds.). (2022a). *Task-based instruction for teaching Russian as a Foreign language.* Routledge. https://doi.org/10.4324/9781003146346

Nuss, S., & Whitehead Martelle, W. (2022b). Task-based instruction for teaching Russian as a Foreign language: Perspectives and practice. In S. Nuss & W. Whitehead Martelle (Eds.), *Task-based instruction for teaching Russian as a Foreign language.* Routledge. https://doi.org/10.4324/9781003146346-1

Pawlak, M. (2021). Teaching foreign language grammar: New solutions, old problems. *Foreign Language Annals, 54,* 881–896. https://doi.org/10.1111/flan.12563

Razin, A., & Kingisepp, L. [Разин, А., и Кингисепп, Л.] (2018). *"Everyone plays!" 101 communication games for teachers of Russian as a Foreign language* [*"Играют все!" 101 коммуникативная игра для учителей русского языка как иностранного*]. Keelekeskus. https://gamekeskus.ee/ru/kursused/elektronnaja-kniga-igrajut-vse/

Sankey, M. (2020). Putting the pedagogic horse in front of the technology cart. *Journal of Distance Education in China, 5,* 46–53. https://doi.org/10.13140/RG.2.2.17755.21288

Sato, M., & Loewen, S. (2019). Do teachers care about research? The research–pedagogy dialogue. *ELT Journal, 73*(1), 1–10. https://doi.org/10.1093/elt/ccy048

Spasova, S., & Welsh, C. (2020). Mixing it up with blended learning. In E. Dengub, I. Dubinina, & J. Merrill (Eds.), *The art of teaching Russian* (pp. 405–430). Georgetown University Press.

Talan, T., Doğan, Y., & Batdi, V. (2020). Efficiency of digital and non-digital educational games: A comparative meta-analysis and a meta-thematic analysis. *Journal of Research on Technology in Education, 52*(4), 474–514. http://doi.org/10.1080/15391523.2020.1743798

Thanyawatpokin, B., & York, J. (2021). Issues in the current state of teaching languages with games. In M. Peterson, K. Yamazaki, & M. Thomas (Eds.), *Digital games and language learning: Theory, development and implementation* (pp. 260–280). Bloomsbury Academic.

Tsui, A. B. M., & Tavares, N. J. (2021). The technology cart and the pedagogy horse in online teaching. *English Teaching and Learning, 45*(1), 109–118. https://doi.org/10.1007/s42321-020-00073-z.

Vandercruysse, S., Vandewaetere, M., & Clarebout, G. (2012). Game-based learning: A review on the effectiveness of educational games. In M. M. Cruz-Cunha (Ed.), *Handbook of research on serious games as educational, business and research tools* (pp. 628–647). IGI Global. http://doi.org/10.4018/978-1-4666-0149-9.ch032

Whitehead Martelle, W., & Nuss, S. (2022). TBLT in Russian classrooms: Reflections on practice and future directions. In S. Nuss & W. Whitehead Martelle (Eds.), *Task-based instruction for teaching Russian as a foreign language* (pp. 206–217). Routledge. https://doi.org/10.4324/9781003146346-13

York, J., deHaan, J., Childs, M., & Collins, M. (2022). How is gamification like being trapped in the Matrix? And what is the "real-world" of game-based learning? *Digital Culture & Education, 14*(3), 35–54. Accessed December 28, 2022. www.digitalcultureandeducation.com/volume-14-3

York, J., Poole, F. J., & deHaan, J. W. (2021). Playing a new game – An argument for a teacher-focused field around games and play in language education. *Foreign Language Annals, 54*(4), 1164–1188. https://doi.org/10.1111/flan.12585

Chapter 2

Gamification and game-based learning
An overview and application to language teaching

Vita V. Kogan

CHAPTER SUMMARY

This chapter provides an overview of the use of games in education, the theory behind it, and the current trends in application to second language (L2) learning. The chapter opens with a brief historical overview of gamification as a new pedagogical paradigm, the theoretical underpinnings of this trend, and the challenges that educators encounter when applying game principles and mechanics to teaching. The concepts of game and gamification are then defined, followed by the description of several foundational game mechanics (game elements that support player engagement). The second part of the chapter is dedicated to the application of games in second and foreign language teaching and learning. We discuss the existing gap between the theory and practice of game design with a few examples of how this gap has been successfully bridged by recent studies in L2 Russian. The chapter concludes with a discussion of specific benefits that the gamified L2 classroom presents and accentuate the relevance of this new approach to teaching L2 Russian.

Краткое содержание главы

В данной главе представлен краткий обзор использования игр в образовательном контексте, лежащая в основе этого теория и современные тенденции в применении игр к обучению иностранным языкам. Глава открывается кратким обзором геймификации (адаптации игровых методов к неигровым процессам) как новой педагогической парадигмы, теоретических основ этой тенденции и проблем, с которыми сталкиваются педагоги при применении игровых принципов в обучении. Далее следуют определения игры и геймификации, сопровождаемые описанием наиболее частотных игровых механик (элементов игры, которые вовлекают игрока в процесс). Вторая часть главы посвящена применению игр непосредственно в обучении иностранным языкам. Обсуждается существующий разрыв между теорией и практикой с примерами того, как этот разрыв успешно преодолевается недавними исследованиями в области преподавания русского языка как иностранного (РКИ). В заключение систематизируются конкретные преимущества, которые предоставляет геймификация курсов иностранного языка, и подчеркиваются потенциальные достоинства этого нового подхода в изучении РКИ.

Gamification as a new educational paradigm

Brief historical overview

The term "gamification" first appeared in the business world in the 2010s and defined game design elements that helped promote engagement in non-game environments (Deterding et al., 2011; Werbach & Hunter, 2012a). Zichermann and Linder (2010) were among the first to describe a game-based model of marketing where leveraging points, completing challenges for rewards, and featuring top players increased customer engagement and helped build sustainable communities of product fans. Soon after, gamification became a popular tool for transforming social behaviors and educating the general public on a range of subjects: from improving employee health behavior (Caminal, 2012) to enhancing the experience of banking transactions (Iliev-Piselli et al., 2011). One fascinating example of social behavior change through gamification is the Piano Stairs project created by Volkswagen Sweden as an ad campaign that aimed to inspire pedestrians to use stairs as opposed to elevators on their way outside the subway. An overwhelming number of commuters preferred stairs to the elevator on this day, from toddlers to dogs. Unfortunately, the long-term gains were not captured, and it is yet to be established whether the novelty would wear off after a few days of using the Piano Stairs or a similar gamified approach. A lack of empirical evidence is the leitmotif of the gamification theory criticism, but a growing body of research studies demonstrates positive results in large sample groups (e.g., Knight et al., 2010; Osipov et al., 2015), providing strong initial support to theoretical claims and anecdotal accounts.

Are games suitable for the language classroom?

There are several reasons that gamification is an effective **tool for changing behaviors and learning**. The characteristics of learning and playing games are closely related: curiosity, persistence, risk-taking, reward, attention to detail, problem-solving, and interpretation (Klopfer et al., 2009). There are two prominent types of learning theories that guide the use of games in education: behavioral theories and constructivist theories of learning.

Games through the behavioral and constructivist lenses

Behavioral theories of learning approach a **game as a stimulus**, to which the player responds, and depending on whether the response was right or wrong, the player is either rewarded or not. For example, in the mobile game *Angry Birds*, the player is rewarded with a highly satisfying scream whenever a pig is killed (the game's goal). A reward for the right response could present itself as a happy tune or applause, which further stimulates positive emotions in the player. Correspondingly, the wrong response triggers negative game feedback (e.g., a sad tune or sad emoticons). Such games rely on the "drill and practice principle" and are perfect for pedagogical activities, such as quizzes, point-and-click activities, and basic computation operations (Rugelj & Rugelj, 2021).

The games based on constructivist theories of learning rely on the **learner's active role and engagement of higher cognitive skills**, such as creating, evaluating, and analyzing. Such games are problem-based, lifelike, and immersive. The immersive aspect of games implies components of interactivity, narrativity, and flow and is critical for good game design: it engages and motivates (Czikszentmihalyi, 1990; De Freitas & Oliver, 2006). A representative example of a constructivist game is *Monopoly*, in which players take on roles, interact with each other, follow a predetermined narrative, and solve complex problems.

Neuropsychology of playing games

From a neuropsychological perspective, games are the optimal portal to **brain plasticity**. When we play, our brain releases endogenous opioids – the type of chemicals that calm the body and make the prefrontal cortex less rigid (Siviy & Panksepp, 2011). The prefrontal cortex is the part of the brain responsible for planning and control; when its circuits are engaged and more flexible, we can see and explore new opportunities to interact with the environment. In other words, the prefrontal cortical plasticity helps us test the scenarios and roles we would otherwise ignore. The resulting playful mindset – allowing yourself to expand the number of outcomes one is willing to entertain – expands our capabilities over time and makes learning happen. The cognitive potential of an animal can be predicted by the duration of its play stage in childhood (Burghardt, 2005). Humans are playing champions often extending play into adolescence and later years (and many never give up playing).

One distinctive quality of playing behavior that is also conducive to learning is that **play takes place in a low-stake environment** that reduces stress and allows us to embrace novel things without the fear of failure (that being said, gaming can be very competitive, but as teachers, we can create a low-stake environment). The emotional component of play is another powerful mechanism of learning, as it supports the long-term retrieval from memory (Habgood & Ainsworth, 2011). Neuropsychological studies show that emotional events are remembered better than neutral events, thanks to the part of the brain called the amygdala, which enhances the function of the memory system (Dolcos et al., 2004).

Gamification of learning

Once the benefits of gaming had been recognized in business and other social settings, it was about time gamification arrived at universities, together with research into how to incorporate game-based mechanics and thinking into academic curricula (Berkling & Thomas, 2013; O'Donovan et al., 2013; Fitz-Walter et al., 2011; York et al., 2019). Gamification has been adopted to support learning in a variety of educational contexts and subjects: participatory learning, collaboration, self-guided study, completion of assignments, assessment paradigms, exploratory approaches, and practices strengthening student creativity and retention (Caponetto et al., 2014). The rationale behind gamification is that by adding game elements to learning activities, it is possible to create immersion in a way similar to what happens in games (Codish & Ravid, 2015). Thus, we can engage learners in a productive learning experience and, more generally, change their behavior in a desirable way (Holman et al., 2013). The teacher now plays a more discrete role, their impact is predominantly formative, applicative, and interactive – of counseling and guidance. Generally speaking, researchers and practitioners recognize two ways to use games in education: (1) game-based learning, or using games alongside the curriculum, and (2) gamification, or adding game mechanics to enhance a non-game environment (Al-Azawi et al., 2016; Figueroa-Flores, 2016; Karagiorgas & Niemann, 2017). We will come back to this classification later in the chapter.

Methodology of game-based and gamified learning

Although there is a trend of growing agreement on the instructional potential of games, the field is faced with a lack of methodologies and tools to design games and support the analysis and assessment of game-based and gamified learning. There is a pressing need to understand why some seemingly well-designed games do not interest learners while others deliver remarkable learning outcomes. Dichev et al. (2019, 2020) argue that contextual factors are critical for designing effective gamified environments. They divide such contextual factors into motivators (acquiring useful skills, engaging with interesting problems) and de-motivators (boring content, a high level of difficulty). For example, cumbersome long game instructions might serve as a powerful de-motivator to try a game. It is also rather underwhelming to play a game that does not provide an adequate level of challenge. The authors argue that to maximize the effectiveness of games and gamified activities, the games should be tailored to learners' individual differences, such as perceived activity value and perceived abilities. In other words, learners should find a game useful and challenging but not overwhelming. If the tailoring is not done properly, games fail to engage and provide desirable learning outcomes. Thus, a teacher has to make a series of important decisions on what, when, and how to incorporate games to fit the learner – the process summarized under the term *game design* (Landers et al., 2018). At the heart of this process is a user-centered approach characterized by the focus on learners' needs and objectives.

The balance between engagement and pedagogy is also acknowledged as being of critical importance to the success of gamification. In fact, getting a balance between the demands of good game design with the requirements to measure and show learning outcomes has driven much of the conceptual work in the field (Bellotti et al., 2013; Boughzala et al., 2013; Kirkley et al., 2011). To be effective, motivational tactics have to support instructional goals. A game can be entertaining, but unless it engages the learner in the instructional purpose and content, it will not promote learning. Moreover, Arnab et al. (2015) observed that at times the principles of learning and gameplay can be conflicting. To translate pedagogical intents to low-level game mechanics, they present a non-exhaustive list of pedagogical goals extracted from a wide range of learning theories (group work, peer coaching) and how these goals can be realized through specific game mechanics (competition, cooperation). According to the authors, the consistent mapping between the two will ensure the effectiveness of a given game or gamified activity, so games are not implemented just to pay tribute to a fashionable trend.

Gamification vs. games

So far in this chapter, the terms "game" and "gamification" have been used interchangeably, yet they are not always the same thing. Gamification is a broader concept and is not restricted to the idea of using games; rather, it encapsulates the principles that structure gamified environments. Hamari et al. (2014) define *gamification* as the phenomenon of creating gameful experiences. Werbach (2014) refers to gamification as the process of making activities more game-like. The concept of gamification might be familiar to many parents who routinely gamify the day-to-day activities of their young children to motivate completion. For example, mealtime frequently turns into taking each spoon to support family members' well-being: *ложечка за маму, ложечка за папу* [take a spoonful for mommy, take a spoonful for daddy]. According to various accounts, such an activity cannot be defined as a game because it employs a limited repertoire of game mechanics, namely, two – "epic context and higher purpose" and "goal direction." In other words, the child is convinced that they participate in an important task and the next step is measurable and doable. Games are typically more restrictive, assuming more game mechanics and more constraints on the players' actions. Granted, at times it is hard to draw a clear line between gamification and games (Becker, 2021). For the current volume, it is not essential to separate one from another; rather, it is more practical to know that specific game mechanics can be used on their own without introducing a full-scale game to the learners. For example, the teacher can integrate one of the game mechanics – "safe failure" (discussed later) – into the assessment pattern: the students are given a chance to retake the exam if they are not happy with the grade. It does not transform the assessment into a game, but it can be done if more game mechanics are added: competition, predefined roles, epic context, awards, etc. This way, the assessment becomes a full-scale game – a treasure hunt or an escape room. Following are more examples of game mechanics that can be effortlessly incorporated into the academic curriculum to seize the benefits of gamification.

Manageable obstacles

Providing the right level of challenge to the students – when a task is neither too hard nor too easy – is essential for generating a state of flow, defined as a focused mental state conducive to productivity (Czikszentmihalyi, 1990). There are several ways to accomplish this in academic settings. For example, the teacher can structure the content of the course in terms of complexity (e.g., level 1, level 2) and allow students to customize their learning path by selecting the task that reflects their skill level. "Homework menu" is another example of this mechanic: students pick and choose from the teacher-defined selection of textbook activities that they can accomplish at home. Computerized adaptive testing is another game-like tool that can ensure that the test's difficulty adapts to the taker's performance. It is now easy to build adaptive tests on Moodle and other e-learning platforms.

Direct vivid feedback

Obstacles are enjoyable when the challenge is feasible and when students are supported by a vivid real-time report of their progress. Frequent feedback in a variety of formats – quantitative and qualitative evaluations, peer and self-assessment, teacher and extramural advice – helps students identify their areas of weaknesses and strengths early in the course. Gamified environments have a range of tools to render acquired knowledge visual and measurable: for example, collecting the learned concepts into a personal "knowledge backpack" or building a portfolio of accomplished tasks and projects.

Epic context and higher purpose

McGonigal (2011) observes, "We want to be estimated in the eyes of others for what we have done that really matters" (p. 45). Most of the games incorporate a mission to give players a sense of purpose and to inspire the best effort. Working on projects that contribute to a real cause – for example, reaching out to the local communities to fill a need gap (e.g., translating to Russian a brochure for a local museum, helping a community of senior Russian expatriates navigate paperwork in English) – would constitute a highly rewarding activity for most students. In this example, service-based learning (more about this pedagogical approach in Jacoby (2015)) meets gamification, and often, the resulting projects are hard to define as games. Such "epic" projects contribute to real-world professional experience and can be collaborative projects or individual missions.

Strong social connectivity

Prosocial emotions are a subset of positive emotions that get generated when we interact with our social network. The brain releases feel-good chemicals – neurotransmitters – when we synchronize our actions with others (Reddish et al.,

2013; Tunçgenç & Cohen, 2016). Peer teaching, tandem learning, and competitions are ways for students to engage with each other and learn effectively. That being said, peer interaction can be a source of anxiety as well. Adams and Oliver (2019) discuss potential caveats in great detail, with the main conclusion that it is the teacher's responsibility to create a comfortable, supportive environment where learners could socialize and interact safely. Noticeably, there is still much to learn on how to facilitate teamwork and interaction in *online spaces*.

Safe failure

Unlike real-life experiences, games have a guaranteed safety net, which makes "dangerous" situations safe but exciting. In an academic setting, failure is seldom encouraged, yet it is a critical part of learning. Cultivating an intelligent risk culture is one of the key components of the gamified classroom. It means giving students a second chance, incorporating an alternative system of assessment alongside standard grades, rewarding for mistakes, and emphasizing group as opposed to individual contributions (for more information on the application of productive failure in pedagogy, see the works of Manu Kapur).

These are just a few examples of how game mechanics can be incorporated into the academic curriculum without an extensive effort to create a full-scale game. Moreover, game design does not necessarily have to be among the teacher's foremost skills – many educational games already exist and can be easily adapted to a specific classroom and course.

Gamification of language learning

Theory and practice gap

In the past years, games have been increasingly deployed to enhance learning across a wide range of domains (Connolly et al., 2012). As language educators, we are primarily concerned with how games and game mechanics can be applied to the language classroom and if the same benefits apply to language learning. Even though a growing body of research demonstrates that games do present opportunities for language learning by providing exposure to the target language, comprehensive input and purposeful output, meaningful interaction, and authentic world-like language tasks, it is still to be determined which linguistic environments benefit the most. Is it better to play alone or together? Are speaking games more effective than writing ones? To answer these questions, a number of researchers are working to develop a comprehensive theoretical framework to describe, categorize, and analyze the type of target language used in games (Biber & Conrad, 2019; Reinhardt, 2019). Although their efforts advance us forward, the theory has to be validated by practice: "without a bidirectional, collaborative, constructive dialogue, L2 researchers may conduct studies that are irrelevant to and out of touch with real-world teaching issues" (Sato & Loewen, 2022, p. 506). In this regard, case studies of the actual implementation of games and game mechanics in the language classroom are of particular importance.

Instructed language learning is a complex, dynamic, multifaceted system, with many of its components interacting and changing in unpredictable ways. Today's favorite game might easily turn into students' nightmare tomorrow. Looking closer at just one component of the educational environment – learner's motivation – shows us how unreliable and fluctuating real-life learning can be. A learner's motivation is not a stable personal characteristic; rather, it is a continuum influenced by a myriad of factors, to the point that some researchers propose to call it *situated* motivation (Ushioda, 2009). Day-to-day learning is full of complex, unforeseen variables and often cannot benefit from generalized claims produced in the homogenous static environment of laboratory experiments. This volume is an effort to look into the actual language classroom and to see how gamification fits this dynamic and complex landscape.

State of research

It does not help that most research on game-based language learning has been developing within the **computer-assisted learning (CALL)** context, narrowing the scope of possible research questions. However, often it means that research studies are conducted with learners playing alone at home. Within CALL, researchers are most interested in the effects of authentic (meant for native speakers: for example, *Sims*) video games on L2 outcomes, and a separate line of research is concerned with open educational platforms, such as *Duolingo* and *Busuu*. Authentic video games are praised for their reduced anxiety effects (Hwang et al., 2017), improved communication skills (Wu et al., 2014), exposure to rich sources of the target language (Berns et al., 2013), and access to conditions conducive to peer learning (Sylvén & Sundqvist, 2012). Simulation games in particular have been a major subject of investigation (Peterson, 2010; Wang, 2019) for offering a highly engaging virtual reality where players are presented with language learning opportunities through their exposure to game content. Calvo-Ferrer (2017) observes that due to the repetitive, highly contextualized, and visually supported nature of simulation games, they are particularly effective for language acquisition. For example, in the *Sims* video game series, a player can create people with unique personalities (sims), build their home and work environment, travel between locations, and interact with other players' sims. Currently, the game is available in English, German, French, Russian, Polish, and Swedish.

The second theme in L2 gamification research is **open educational platforms**. They are built specifically for language learning and incorporate various game mechanics (reward points, achievement, badges, difficulty levels) to motivate the users. Osipov et al. (2015) introduced one such platform – *i2istudy* – to study L2 English, German, Russian, and Spanish. They investigated the platform's effectiveness by measuring the number of users and the time the users spent learning languages. Even though the average time of connection was not long – about

15 minutes per session – the most active users spent hours learning a new language. Osipov et al. (2015) concluded that gamification worked and adequately motivated language learners. Most recently, Hou et al. (2022) demonstrated similar results with the *Revita* language learning system that aims at intermediate to advanced learners of Italian, German, Finnish, Kazakh, Mandarin, Russian, and Swedish. *Revita* employs feedback, adaptive difficulty levels, and social interaction as its main mechanics. The authors tracked 600 learners of Russian from various universities around the globe and reported increased learning gains across all skills among the most active users.

It is possible that language learners in these studies improve simply because of the practice time and not because of specific game mechanics. In other words, the learners could equally succeed with a traditional method (e.g., following a textbook), given the same amount of time to study. Junttila et al. (2022) investigated this question with an L2 English phonetic game that focused on mastering challenging sound contrasts. They had two groups of children: one group playing a digital language learning game, *Say it again, kid!* and another group learning the same L2 sounds in a non-game environment. The practice time was kept the same across both conditions, and the only difference between the groups was the presence or the absence of gamification. The results showed that the employed game mechanics (appealing graphics, autonomy to explore the content, and feedback rewards) triggered learning and the associated brain plasticity. These results were significantly different from the non-game group, who did not demonstrate the same positive learning effects. The next question the authors put forward (for future research) is which game mechanics contribute to the most learning.

It is important to keep in mind that most of these studies are static snapshots of learners' progress in laboratory settings as opposed to a longitudinal study in a complex environment, such as the language classroom. Such studies predominantly focus on L2 English and the United States/United Kingdom as the participant pool (Shortt et al., 2021). Another downside is that it is hard for teachers to recreate and integrate the same approaches into a real curriculum. For instance, Zheng et al. (2015) designed a two-hour quest-play game in English between a Japanese student and a native speaker of English to investigate vocabulary gains. Neville et al. (2009) conducted a three-day game to study vocabulary retention, transfer, and attitudes toward the game material. Neither of the proposed settings would be suitable for a typical university-level language course that meets two to three hours per week and has about 30 students. Zhou (2016) summarizes the issue: emphasis on laboratory settings and generalizability often precludes teachers as researchers.

Games in the context of teaching L2 Russian

It is not, however, implied that teachers do not use games. Language games are a well-established pedagogical vehicle, with favorite classics including role-plays and tabletop games of bingo, Scrabble, and crosswords. There are a substantial number of books and articles dedicated to the methodology of game-based teaching and step-by-step instructions on how to implement games into the language classroom (e.g., Langran & Purcell, 1994). In Russian lingo-didactic literature, games have been praised for their adaptability and positive vibes for decades. For example, Derkach and Shcherbak (1991) emphasize the fact that games can be organized with different forms of pedagogical work and audiences, which helps address specific aspects of a linguistic system and diversify the learning process. Stronin (2001) believes that the main advantage of games is that they prepare language learners for communication and spontaneous speech – a key methodological struggle in instructed L2 learning. Stronin (2001) divides educational games into (1) preparatory games that help practice narrow grammatical, lexical, and phonetic points, and (2) creative games that contribute to the development of spontaneous speech. In this regard, **games can function as pedagogical tasks** – stepping stones that help learners accomplish real-world tasks (Sasayama, 2022). These reports are rarely accompanied by evidence of measurable learning outcomes, and the fundamental question of learning transfer remains: Did the students learn anything? Thus, while gamification research collects data from outside of real classrooms in the laboratory and simulated settings, the real learning is unexplored, leaving us with anecdata – evidence based on personal experience or observation rather than systematic research and analysis.

Several attempts to provide a window into contemporary applications of games and – importantly – the corresponding evidence of learning have been presented recently in the literature on the instructed Russian-language acquisition. Nimis et al. (2022) described a series of gamified simulations implemented with intermediate learners of Russian in a language immersion program and presented quantifiable learning outcomes. The typical immersion programs in the context they describe last for two to three weeks and allow the learners to participate in several simulations. Such simulations, the re-enactment of real-life scenarios, are essentially extended role-plays, in which the learners are assigned predefined parts and objectives. **In game terminology, these are narrative games**, with the most common mechanics being "epic context and higher purpose" and "social connectivity." In Nimis et al. (2022), one example of a gamified simulation is *the Russian immigration process*: the students act as immigrants crossing the Russian border and dealing with relevant (not exclusively linguistic) tasks. The resulting learning outcomes were measured both qualitatively (via teachers' holistic evaluation and students' self-assessment) and quantitatively with a computerized Oral Proficiency Interview (OPIc). Nimis et al. (2022) report that, on average, nearly half of all learners improve by at least one sublevel on the ACTFL (the American Council of Teachers of Foreign Languages) proficiency scale. Such a proficiency leap is particularly impressive at the intermediate levels and higher. As Mendelevich (2022) observes, "motivating students to expand their vocabulary and its application is often more challenging than getting them started [to study another language] in the first place" (p. 172). To overcome this challenge, in her study, Mendelevich uses a simulation game that, similarly to *Sims*, requires players to take on fictional identities and create a living space in a virtual communal apartment [коммуналка]. The gains in vocabulary were evaluated with essays written at the end of each thematic unit throughout the semester. Mendelevich (2022) observed that the learners began using the acquired vocabulary creatively, constructing personal meaning and expanding the semantic maps beyond the course material. A self-assessment survey confirmed these observations: the learners reported acquiring a wide range of vocabulary and registers, which, according to them, would not be possible in traditional classroom settings. They also felt more motivated and engaged throughout the semester.

A pedagogical rationale: why play?

Many of the gamification benefits discussed earlier would apply to language learning the same way they would to learning mathematics or history. Yet there are a few concepts that seem to make games a particularly suitable tool for the language classroom.

Meaningful interaction

During a game, learners have to use language as a tool to accomplish something: to provide a correct answer to a clue in a crossword puzzle or to claim railway routes connecting cities in *Ticket to Ride*. Meaningful use of language comes with a sociocultural and interpersonal significance that learners have to navigate. For example, crossword clues, besides the language, bring information about the target culture and community. The interaction in a group game will require players to relate to each other and manipulate language based on the interlocutor's knowledge. Even the simplest games (*bingo*, *Scrabble*) introduce layers of contextual richness that the most carefully constructed exercise does not have. Barnes (1976) showed how in a science game, two learners began developing their interpersonal relationship through language in addition to the primary goal of solving the puzzle. This additional linguistic discourse – laughing at each other's mistakes, making jokes, and helping each other – organically grew out of what was meant to be a purely problem-solving task. The teacher did not instruct students to establish a common linguistic space – it happened naturally. Interestingly, shared L1 does not necessarily preclude learners from effective communication – on the contrary, learners who are familiar with each other and share common characteristics might generate richer output (Pastushenkov, 2022).

Interaction does not have to always consist of language production and pair/group settings. Single-player games are great examples of how a learner can meaningfully interact with language and benefit from the pragmatic knowledge that comes with it. For example, in building games for one player such as *Деревни* [*Villages*] or *Город Мечты* [*City of Dreams*], learners have to deal with socially situated language: they experience and explore the functional uses of language as they solve complex problems (e.g., hiring craftsmen for one's village while taking into account the professions that the village already has). Just like input-based tasks (R. Ellis, 2001), games for one player are optimal for beginner learners, especially in languages with a rich morphosyntactic structure, such as Russian.

Meaningful interaction can also be a powerful facilitator, helping the learner to decipher the language system by providing relevant contexts and clues (Long, 2015). In Bruner (1983), a mother and a child play a game of peekaboo, in which a toy is repeatedly hidden and reappears as the mother says, "It is coming, it is coming . . . here it is!" The illustration of the process helps the child make sense of the verbal progressive forms used.

Focus of form

Games are restrictive by definition: the player has to follow a set of rules, giving them only limited access to resources (see Weygandt, this volume, for a reflection of this notion). Thus, games create a natural environment for language learners, who are also somewhat restricted in their linguistic resources. Game-imposed restrictions provide opportunities for comprehensive input, adjusting it to the learner's proficiency level and also allowing for reduced (yet meaningful) output.

The restrictive nature of games also makes them an optimal tool for focusing on form. Such focus can be implicit when a specific linguistic feature is made more noticeable to learners. It can be done by the means of repetition, as in the game *Have You Ever*, where the same question (*Have you ever eaten an insect? Have you ever been to a wedding?*) and a corresponding grammatical form is recycled at each player's turn. It can also be done by isolating a target feature and building a set of activities around it, as in *bingo*, where calling numbers is the central point of the game. The *explicit* focus on form is also available during the game – the teacher can pause the game and draw learners' attention to a particular aspect of language. Van den Branden (2016) proposed several techniques that the teacher might employ within the context of ongoing activity: the teacher can ask questions, provide feedback on the student's written and oral input, or simply explain a novel concept and model optimal performance. For example, the teacher can pause the game *Monopoly* and review the declension of the word "rubles" with various numbers (one ruble, two rubles . . .), then return to playing the game.

Lastly, focusing on the language is possible after the game has been completed. York (2020, p. 256) proposes the following steps in playing a board game while focusing on form:

1 Learn to play the chosen game.
2 Play the game, record the spoken audio, and transcribe the audio as a homework activity.
3 Analyze transcriptions and watch native English speakers play the same game, noticing any useful expressions.
4 Replay the game, record, and transcribe.

5 Reanalyze gameplay, compare gameplay sessions for changes in output, and create a report about the game (good points, bad points, English usage, etc.).

This sequence has multiple opportunities for implicit and explicit foci on form. Certainly, the post-game analysis does not have to be as involved as in York (2020); it might consist of a short discussion of challenging linguistic features that surfaced during the game. Here, York (2020) brings up another valuable point of games – they can be replayed several times, with each time directing the student's attention to a different aspect of language.

Feedback

Feedback is one of the fundamental elements of games. From L2 research, we also know that corrective feedback – the type of feedback provided to a learner that contains evidence of learner error – is a powerful tool for language learning and, in particular, grammar learning (Russell & Spada, 2006). One advantage of games is that corrective feedback is no longer the sole responsibility of the teacher. In *bingo*, the game flow will be naturally interrupted if the player calls out the numbers incorrectly. Other players would make sure the mistake is attended to and corrected (*Did you say 30 or 13? Can you repeat that, please?*). That being said, certainly, the teacher can offer explicit corrections that could be (or not) further gamified: for example, using a whistle or a sad tune every time a player mispronounces a specific form.

Speaking anxiety and identity

In the 60s and early 70s, Guiora et al. conducted a series of famous experiments to demonstrate that consuming alcohol improves L2 speaking fluency. In this regard, Guiora (1972) coined the term "language ego," a self-representation of one's linguistic capacity that has rigid boundaries and relaxes after alcohol consumption or hypnoses. In their earlier work, Guiora et al. observed that "language behavior is a unique and complex attribute of man, not only in the evolutionary sense but in the developmental psychological history of each individual" (Guiora et al., 1969). An L2 learner, to a certain extent, takes on a new identity, which comes with (quite naturally) impoverished linguistic abilities. This new identity constitutes what Norton Pierce (1995) calls "a site of struggle" and causes many L2 learners anxiety and distress. Since then, several researchers have investigated L2 speaking anxiety and how it limits language learning (most recently, Ozdemir and Papi (2022)).

Games have several properties that alleviate and, at times, eliminate L2 speaking anxiety. First of all, games generate a state of flow (discussed earlier) that provides concentrated engagement and motivation to overcome speaking anxiety. Secondly, some games allow learners to use alternative identities as symbolic masks that temporarily release the associated performance distress. For example, in an extended version of the popular party game *Mafia*, the characters (detective, doctor, barman) act in a certain way, which allows the learner to shift their attention from their own identity to that of this new, imaginary character. The learner can now act as somebody else and is no longer "responsible" for their language repertoire.[1]

The game affordances previously described come particularly useful in the acquisition of L2 Russian. In comparison to, for instance, Romance languages, Russian is largely isolated from most countries where it is acquired as L2. The opportunities to practice it in a socially and culturally authentic context remain rather limited. Games that bring relevant, ample cultural and pragmatic environments – such as *Странометр: Города России* [*Countrymeter: Cities of Russia*] or *Покорители Космоса* [*Space Conquerors*] or even charades – fill the existing gap. Another crucial aspect of Russian as an L2 is an elaborate morphosyntactic structure (see Nuss (2022) for an in-depth discussion), which requires significant time and attention resources dedicated to automatization. Games with repetitive elements (e.g., *Pizza Snowball*) and game repetition are suitable solutions to recycle target grammatical forms without students becoming bored. The feedback loops that games contain also ensure focus on form. Lastly, speaking anxiety in L2 Russian – an immense challenge for many native speakers of non-Slavic languages – is alleviated through the game-induced state of flow.

Connections

In this chapter, I sought to demonstrate the learning potential of games – in education and, specifically, in language learning. No matter how effective they can be, games are not sufficient on their own in facilitating language acquisition. To fully benefit from games, the acquired skills have to be transferred from the learning environment into real life. Therefore, games should be integrated into a larger cycle of learning, with the final objective of such learning taking place outside the classroom. In this volume, the reader will see multiple examples of how this is done. The following case studies are grounded in reflection, practice, and research. As gamification and associated methodology continue to expand, it appears that more action research studies will become increasingly influential in shaping the future research agenda in this area. With the majority of work focused on video games and the EFL context, we need to broaden the existing research base to include a variety of game genres and languages. This volume is among the first steps in this direction.

Note

1 See Pastushenkov (2022) for a detailed description and materials of *Mafia* adapted to L2 Russian.

References

Adams, R., & Oliver, R. (2019). *Teaching through peer interaction*. Routledge.
Al-Azawi, R., Al-Faliti, F., & Al-Blushi, M. (2016). Educational gamification vs. game-based learning: Comparative study. *International Journal of Innovation, Management, and Technology*, 7(4), 132–136.

Arnab, S., Lim, T., Carvalho, M. B., Bellotti, F., de Freitas, S., Louchart, S., Suttie, N., Berta, R., & De Gloria, A. (2015). Mapping learning and game mechanics for serious games analysis. *British Journal of Educational Technology, 46*, 391–411. http://doi.org/10.1111/bjet.12113

Barnes, D. (1976). *From communication to curriculum*. Penguin.

Becker, K. (2021). What's the difference between gamification, serious games, educational games, and game-based learning? *Academia Letters, 209*.

Bellotti, F., Kapralos, B., Lee, K., Moreno-Ger, P., & Berta, R. (2013). Assessment in and of serious games: An overview. *Advances in Human-Computer Interaction, 1*, 1–11. http://doi.org/10.1155/2013/136864

Berkling, K., & Thomas, C. (2013, September). Gamification of a software engineering course and a detailed analysis of the factors that lead to its failure. In *2013 international conference on interactive collaborative learning (ICL)* (pp. 525–530). IEEE.

Berns, A., Gonzalez-Pardo, A., & Camacho, D. (2013). Game-like language learning in 3-D virtual environments. *Computers & Education, 60*(1), 210–220.

Biber, D., & Conrad, S. (2019). *Register, genre, and style*. Cambridge University Press.

Boughzala, I., Bououd, I., & Michel, H. (2013). Characterization and evaluation of serious games: A perspective of their use in higher education. *Proceedings of the 46th Hawaii international conference on system sciences (HICSS)* (pp. 844–852), Maui, USA. IEEE. http://doi.org/10.1177/1753193412469127

Bruner, J. S. (1983). *Child's talk*. Cambridge University Press.

Burghardt, G. M. (2005). *The genesis of animal play: Testing the limits*. MIT Press.

Calvo-Ferrer, J. R. (2017). Educational games as stand-alone learning tools and their motivational effect on L2 vocabulary acquisition and perceived learning gains. *British Journal of Educational Technology, 48*(2), 264–278.

Caminal, R. (2012). The design and efficiency of loyalty rewards. *Journal of Economics & Management Strategy, 21*(2), 339–371. http://doi.org/10.1111/j.1530-9134.2012.00334.x

Caponetto, I., Earp, J., & Ott, M. (2014, October). Gamification and education: A literature review. In *European conference on games based learning* (Vol. 1, p. 50). Academic Conferences International Limited.

Codish, D., & Ravid, G. (2015). Detecting playfulness in educational gamification through behavior patterns. *IBM Journal of Research and Development, 59*(6), 6–14.

Connolly, T. M., Boyle, E. A., MacArthur, E., Hainey, T., & Boyle, J. M. (2012). A systematic literature review of empirical evidence on computer games and serious games. *Computers & Education, 59*(2), 661–686.

Czikszentmihalyi, M. (1990). *Flow: The psychology of optimal experience*. Harper & Row.

De Freitas, S., & Oliver, M. (2006). How can exploratory learning with games and simulations within the curriculum be most effectively evaluated? *Computers & Education, 46*(3), 249–264.

Derkach, A. A., & Shcherbak, S. F. (1991). *Pedagogicheskaja jevristika: Iskusstvo ovladenija inostrannym jazykom* [Педагогическая эвристика: Искусство овладения иностранным языком]. Pedagogika.

Deterding, S., Dixon, D., Khaled, R., & Nacke E. L. (2011, May). Gamification: Toward a definition. *Proceedings of the gamification workshop (CHI 2011)* (pp. 12–15), Vancouver, Canada. http://gamification-research.org/wp-content/uploads/2011/04/CHI11_Workshop_Gamification.pdf

Dichev, C., Dicheva, D., & Irwin, K. (2019). Towards activity-centered gamification design. In *Proceedings of the 2019 IEEE international conference on teaching, assessment, and learning for engineering* (TALE 2019). IEEE.

Dichev, C., Dicheva, D., & Irwin, K. (2020). Gamifying learning for learners. *International Journal of Educational Technology in Higher Education, 17*(1), 1–14.

Dolcos, F., LaBar, K. S., & Cabeza, R. (2004). Interaction between the amygdala and the medial temporal lobe memory system predicts better memory for emotional events. *Neuron, 42*(5), 855–863.

Ellis, R. (2001). Non-reciprocal tasks, comprehension, and second language acquisition. In M. Bygate, P. Skehan, & M. Swain (Eds.), *Researching pedagogic tasks second language learning, teaching and testing* (pp. 49–74). Longman.

Figueroa-Flores, J. F. (2016). Gamification and game-based learning: Two strategies for the 21st-century learner. *World, 3*(2), 507–522.

Fitz-Walter, Z., Tjondronegoro, D., & Wyeth, P. (2011, November). Orientation passport: Using gamification to engage university students. In *Proceedings of the 23rd Australian computer-human interaction conference* (pp. 122–125), Canberra, Australia. Association for Computing Machinery. https://dl.acm.org/doi/proceedings/10.1145/2071536

Guiora, A. Z. (1972). Construct validity and transpositional research: Toward an empirical study of psychoanalytic concepts. *Comprehensive Psychiatry, 13*(2).

Guiora, A. Z., Taylor, L. C., & Brandwin, M. A. (1969). A contribution to the psychology of second language behavior. In *Proceedings of the XVIth international congress of applied psychology*. Swets and Zeitlinger.

Habgood, M. J., & Ainsworth, S. E. (2011). Motivating children to learn effectively: Exploring the value of intrinsic integration in educational games. *The Journal of the Learning Sciences, 20*(2), 169–206. http://doi.org/10.1080/10508406.2010.508029

Hamari, J., Koivisto, J., & Sarsa, H. (2014). Does gamification work? – A literature review of empirical studies on gamification. In *the 47th Hawaii international conference on system sciences* (pp. 3025–3034). Hawaii. http://doi.org/10.1109/HICSS.2014.377

Holman, C., Aguilar, S., & Fishman, B. (2013). GradeCraft: What can we learn from a game-inspired learning management system? *Third international conference on learning analytics and knowledge, 2013* (pp. 260–264). ACM.

Hou, J., Katinskaia, A., Furlan, G., Kylliäinen, I. P., & Yangarber, R. (2022). Applying gamification incentives in the Revita language-learning system. In *Proceedings of the 13th international conference on language resources and evaluation*. LREC.

Hwang, G. J., Hsu, T. C., Lai, C. L., & Hsueh, C. J. (2017). Interaction of problem-based gaming and learning anxiety in language students' English listening performance and progressive behavioral patterns. *Computers & Education, 106*, 26–42.

Iliev-Piselli, M. M., Fadjo, C. L., & Lee, J. J. (2011). Bank-It: A mobile financial literacy game. *Proceedings of the 7th international conference on games learning society conference* (pp. 260–262), Pittsburgh, PA, United States. ETC Press. https://dl.acm.org/doi/proceedings/10.5555/2206376?id=31

Jacoby, B. (2015). *Service-learning essentials: Questions, answers, and lessons learned*. Jossey-Bass.

Junttila, K., Smolander, A. R., Karhila, R., Giannakopoulou, A., Uther, M., Kurimo, M., & Ylinen, S. (2022). Gaming enhances learning-induced plastic changes in the brain. *Brain and Language, 230*, 105124.

Karagiorgas, D. N., & Niemann, S. (2017). Gamification and game-based learning. *Journal of Educational Technology Systems, 45*(4), 499–519.

Kirkley, J. R., Duffy, T. M., Kirkley, S. E., & Kremer, D. L. H. (2011). Implications of constructivism for the design and use of serious games. In S. Tobias & J. D. Fletcher (Eds.), *Computer game and instruction* (pp. 371–394). Information Age Publishing.

Klopfer, E., Osterweil, S., & Salen, K. (2009). *Moving learning games forward*. The Education Arcade.

Knight, J. F., Carley, S., Tregunna, B., Jarvis, S., Smithies, R., de Freitas, S., Dunwell, I., & Mackway-Jones, K. (2010). Serious gaming technology in major incident triage training: A pragmatic controlled trial. *Resuscitation, 81*(9), 1175–1179.

Landers, R. N., Tondello, G. F., Kappen, D. L., Collmus, A. B., Mekler, E. D., & Nacke, L. E. (2018). Defining gameful experience as a psychological state caused by gameplay: Replacing the term "Gamefulness" with three distinct constructs. *International Journal of Human Computing Studies, 127*, 81–94.

Langran, J., & Purcell, S. (1994). *Language games and activities. Network 2: Teaching languages to adults*. Centre for Information on Language Teaching and Research.

Long, M. H. (2015). *Second language acquisition and task-based language teaching*. John Wiley & Sons.

McGonigal, J. (2011). *Reality is broken: Why games make us better and how they can change the world*. Penguin Press.

Mendelevich, E. (2022). Kommunalka: Virtual space as a platform for task-based learning. In *Task-based instruction for teaching Russian as a Foreign language* (pp. 171–189). Routledge.

Neville, D., Shelton, B., & McInnis, B. (2009). Cybertext redux: Using digital game-based learning to teach L2 vocabulary, reading, and culture. *Computer Assisted Language Learning, 22*(5), 409–424.

Nimis, S., Krylova, N. V., & Fedoseeva, I. (2022). Task-based learning in the "grand simulation" context: Six principles for success from isolated immersion programs. In *Task-based instruction for teaching Russian as a Foreign language* (pp. 121–134). Routledge.

Norton Pierce, B. (1995). Social identity, investment, and language learning. *TESOL Quarterly, 29*(1), 9–31.

Nuss, S. V. (2022). Morphology acquisition research meets instruction of L2 Russian: A contextualized literature review. In *Task-based instruction for teaching Russian as a Foreign language* (pp. 15–35). Routledge.

O'Donovan, S., Gain, J., & Marais, P. (2013). A case study in the gamification of a university-level games development course. *Proceedings of the South African institute for computer scientists and information technologists conference* (pp. 242–251), East London, South Africa. Association for Computing Machinery. https://dl.acm.org/doi/proceedings/10.1145/2513456

Osipov, I. V., Nikulchev, E., Volinsky, A. A., & Prasikova, A. Y. (2015). Study of gamification effectiveness in online e-learning systems. *International Journal of Advanced Computer Science and Applications, 6*(2), 71–77.

Ozdemir, E., & Papi, M. (2022). Mindsets as sources of L2 speaking anxiety and self-confidence: The case of international teaching assistants in the US. *Innovation in Language Learning and Teaching, 16*(3), 234–248.

Pastushenkov, D. (2022). Task-based peer interaction in Russian as a second/Foreign language classes. In *Task-based instruction for teaching Russian as a Foreign language* (pp. 152–170). Routledge.

Peterson, M. (2010). Computerized games and simulations in computer-assisted language learning: A meta-analysis of research. *Simulation & Gaming, 41*(1), 72–93.

Reddish, P., Fischer, R., & Bulbulia, J. (2013). Let's dance together: Synchrony shared intentionality and cooperation. *PLoS ONE, 8*(8).

Reinhardt, J. (2019). Gameful L2 learning. In *Gameful second and foreign language teaching and learning* (pp. 101–139). Palgrave Macmillan.

Rugelj, M. Š., & Rugelj, J. (2021). Gamification in the study of mathematics for engineering students. *Proceedings of the 20th special interest group in mathematics (SEFI)* (pp. 57–62), Kristiansand, Norway. SEFI. https://www.sefi.be/wp-content/uploads/2021/09/Maths-Proceedings_final.pdf

Russell, J., & Spada, N. (2006). The effectiveness of corrective feedback for the acquisition of L2 grammar. *Synthesizing Research on Language Learning and Teaching, 13*, 133–164.

Sasayama, S. (2022). Why task? Task as a unit of analysis for language education. In M. Ahmadian & M. Long (Eds.), *The Cambridge handbook of task-based language teaching (Cambridge Handbooks in language and linguistics)* (pp. 55–72). Cambridge University Press. http://doi.org/10.1017/9781108868327.004

Sato, M., & Loewen, S. (2022). The research – practice dialogue in second language learning and teaching: Past, present, and future. *The Modern Language Journal, 106*(3), 509–527.

Shortt, M., Tilak, S., Kuznetcova, I., Martens, B., & Akinkuolie, B. (2021). Gamification in mobile-assisted language learning: A systematic review of Duolingo literature from the public release of 2012 to early 2020. *Computer Assisted Language Learning*, 1–38.

Siviy, S. M., & Panksepp, J. (2011). In search of the neurobiological substrates for social playfulness in mammalian brains. *Neuroscience & Biobehavioral Reviews, 35*(9), 1821–1830.

Stronin, M. F. [Стронин, М. Ф.] (2001). *Obuchayushchiye igry na uroke angliyskogo yazyka*. [*Обучающие игры на уроке английского языка*]. Просвещение [Prosveschenie].

Sylvén, L. K., & Sundqvist, P. (2012). Gaming as extramural English L2 learning and L2 proficiency among young learners. *ReCALL, 24*(3), 302–321.

Tunçgenç, B., & Cohen, E. (2016). Movement synchrony forges social bonds across group divides. *Frontiers in Psychology, 7*, 782.

Ushioda, E. (2009). A person-in-context relational view of emergent motivation, self, and identity. In Z. Dörnyei & E. Ushioda, (Eds.), *Motivation, language identity and the L2 self* (pp. 215–228). Multilingual Matters.

Van den Branden, K. (2016). The role of teachers in task-based language education. *Annual Review of Applied Linguistics, 36*, 164–181.

Wang, J. (2019). ClassroomIntervention for integrating simulation games into language classrooms: An exploratory study with the SIMs 4. *CALL-EJ, 20*(2), 101–127.

Werbach, K. (2014). (Re) Defining gamification: A process approach, persuasive technology. *Lecture Notes in ComputerScience, 8462*, 266–272.

Werbach, K., & Hunter, D. (2012a). *For the win: How game thinking can revolutionize your business*. Wharton Digital Press.

Wu, C. J., Chen, G. D., & Huang, C. W. (2014). Using digital board games for genuine communication in EFL classrooms. *Educational Technology Research and Development, 62*(2), 209–226.

York, J. (2020). Pedagogical considerations for teaching with games: Improving oral proficiency with self-transcription, task repetition, and online video analyses. *Ludic Language Pedagogy, 2*, 225–255.

York, J., deHaan, J., & Hourdequin, P. (2019). It's your turn: EFL teaching and learning with tabletop games. In *Innovation in language teaching and learning* (pp. 117–139). Palgrave Macmillan.

Zheng, D., Bischoff, M., & Gilliland, B. (2015). *Vocabulary learning in massively multiplayer online games: Context and action before words*. Educational Technology Research Development. http://doi.org/10.1007/s11423-015-9387-4

Zhou, Y. (2016). Digital vocabulary competition as a motivator for learning in CFL classrooms. *Journal of Technology and Chinese Language Teaching, 7*(2), 1–22.

Zichermann, G., & Linder, J. (2010). *Game-based marketing: Inspire customer loyalty through rewards, challenges, and contests*. John Wiley & Sons.

Part II

Impacting speaking and beyond

Up the teaching game

Chapter 3

Mingling games for beginner learners of L2 Russian

Daria Kotelnikova and Elena Bogomolova

CHAPTER SUMMARY

Students tend to evaluate their progress in language classes based on the development of their speaking skills; however, meaningful speaking activities and tasks are not always provided in the core curriculum. Our review of the studies on teaching modern languages shows that speaking accuracy and fluency can be facilitated by mingling games that involve peer–peer communication. Further analysis indicates that in teaching Russian as an additional language, the beneficial effects of games and cooperative learning on language acquisition have been documented. At the same time, there is still a lack of research on the impact of mingling games in Russian-language acquisition. In our practice of teaching Russian to non-native speakers, we used mingling games widely and not only received positive feedback from students but also noted significant advances in their language proficiency. The chapter offers a variety of ways mingling games could be used in teaching Russian to improve speaking skills at the beginner level and details specific high-, low-, and no-prep examples of mingling games for teaching L2 Russian.

КРАТКОЕ СОДЕРЖАНИЕ ГЛАВЫ

Устная речь остается одним из самых востребованных и в то же время сложных аспектов в обучении русскому языку как неродному, хотя во многих случаях студенты (как взрослые, так и подростки) оценивают свой прогресс в изучении языка на основе развития своих разговорных навыков. Проведя исследование работ по обучению иностранным языкам, мы пришли к выводу, что *mingling games*, основанные на общении с одногруппниками, способствуют улучшению грамотности и беглости речи. Дальнейший анализ литературы показал, что в преподавании русского языка уже несколько десятилетий изучается вопрос о благотворном влиянии игр и командной работы на процесс и результаты обучения. Несмотря на отсутствие большого количества научных работ по использованию *mingling games* непосредственно в преподавании русского языка как неродного, в нашей педагогической практике мы широко применяли *mingling games*, получая положительные отзывы студентов. В этой главе показаны различные способы использования *mingling games* с целью улучшения разговорных навыков студентов, изучающих русский язык на начальном уровне.

Why mingling games?

In the past decade, we have witnessed a significant shift in the development of teaching resources of Russian as a foreign language (RFL) for adults and young learners to communicative approach in language learning: for example, *Точка Ру.* [Tochka Ru.] *Russian course* (Dolmatova & Novacac [Долматова и Новакак], 2017); *Русский сувенир* [*Russian souvenir*] Mozelova, 2019), *Привет, Россия!* [*Hello Russia!*] (Nakhabina [Nakhabina] et al., 2020; Сорока [*Magpie*] (Averi, 2017). Nevertheless, many course books for beginner learners rely heavily on focus on formS as opposed to focus on form (Long, 1988),[1] emphasizing discrete grammar rules and fill-in-the-blanks exercises, with basic vocabulary introduced through pictures or simple texts. To facilitate the development of speaking skills and to create situations when students at the beginner level are communicating, it is essential to use additional communicative activities. Those could be found in separate textbooks, for example, *Playing on Words: Games and Activities for a Russian Language Classroom* (Kolesova & Kharitonov [Колесова и Харитонов], 2011) and *Communicative Games in Russian language lessons* (Kaznishkina, [Казнишкина], 2019). The challenge of using such supplementary materials is finding the communicative games that would fit the target vocabulary and grammar patterns and would not create extra cognitive load by introducing too many new words and structures (Robinson, 2005). We suggest considering mingling games as an effective and versatile tool, as they could be created and adapted by teachers to any learning content even at the beginner level and serve the purpose of turning the target grammar and vocabulary into speaking practice.

What are mingling games?

We follow the description of *mingling games* given by Borzova [Борзова] (2014), who defines them as face-to-face activities where students walk around the classroom and talk to each other in pairs or small groups. She states that mingling games are usually based on the information, experience, or opinion gap and therefore stimulate motivation for natural, meaningful communication in the target language.

In this respect, mingling games are close to the method of activation of personal and collaborative potential [*метод активизации возможностей личности и коллектива*] proposed by Kitaygorodskaya in the 1980s for teaching foreign languages in intensive courses. The method included, among other principles, the principle of cooperative learning, the principle of personal communication, and the principle of gamification of the learning process (Kitaygorodskaya [Китайгородская], 1986).

In our review of the literature on the subject, we note that there is no commonly accepted equivalent in the Russian language to the notion of "mingling games/activities" and that most scholars use the English term in their papers written in Russian. We also noticed the gap in literature on the use of mingling games in teaching RFL. Therefore, in our chapter, we mostly generalize the data confirming the benefits of mingling games for teaching other foreign languages and the effectiveness of gamification in general in teaching Russian.

Effectiveness of mingling games

Mingling games help recycle vocabulary and grammar structures in a natural way. Asonova [Асонова] (2013) highlights that learning grammar in Russian language is often approached by teachers as a priority, especially at the beginner level. She emphasizes the importance of shifting the focus from that of cramming grammar rules to meaningful use of language to address students' needs to actively participate in communication. Asonova believes that games facilitate the development of speaking accuracy and fluency from early stages of language learning. Chou (2014) notes that almost all young learners in the group where research was conducted positively responded to the use of games to help both memorize vocabulary items and increase their vocabulary size.

Table 3.1 Comparison of traditional work in pairs with mingling games

Asking questions from the list in pairs (mini dialogues)	Mingling games
Students talk to one partner, who might not be willing to speak at length or has few ideas to share.	Students talk to multiple partners, which increases the chances to have a longer, meaningful conversation with one of them.
Students ask each question once, which is often not enough to practice vocabulary and grammar.	Recycling the language with multiple partners improves speaking accuracy.
Students might lack the motivation to communicate due to lack of confidence in their language abilities.	The spirit of competition (e.g., talking to as many people as possible) motivates students to talk as much as they can, creates a positive class dynamic, and can offer an opportunity to stretch, giving students more energy.
When interacting with one partner, students often stay at the same place, which could be tiring, especially in long classes.	
Adult learners in language schools often do not interact with each other outside the classroom and might feel awkward engaging with peers as part of the class.	Improve the social connectivity between group's members and offer opportunities to engage with the peers they would normally not to.

Mingling games offer students more speaking time and introduce a variety of speaking partners within a given period of time, which is essential when working with large groups. In their book *Учимся учить* [*Learning to Teach*], Akishina and Kagan [Акишина и Каган] (2002) suggest using pair and group work alongside spontaneous dialogues to maximize students' speaking time. Mingling games were proved effective for speaking interaction by Mufidah and Fitriani (2022), who used mingling games to teach speaking in large groups.

Mingling games reduce the stress of making mistakes and speaking in front of others, as interaction takes place in changing pairs and is monitored by a teacher without interfering for the on-spot error correction. Karsudianto (2020) reports that more than 80% of students improved their self-confidence in speaking activities as a result of using mingling games in instruction for English learners.

Form-focused mingles help students achieve accuracy and confidence in speaking when they repeat multiple times a short pre-checked utterance. The repetition monotony is brightened by the constant change of partners. The positive effects of task repetition on the accuracy and fluency of speaking in a foreign language were explored by Ahmadian (2012).

Meaning-focused/scenario mingles focus on developing reading comprehension and listening skills along with speaking since they are accompanied by the texts on role-play cards and involve general and detailed reading comprehension. Swain concludes that students' engagement in peer dialogues improves all language skills (reading, writing, listening, and speaking) (Swain et al., 2002).

To implement mingling games successfully, it is essential to remember that mingles should be a logical part of a chain of tasks intended to achieve a learning goal, rather than a pure entertainment feature or a time filler (Borzova, 2014).

Our experience of using mingling games to teach RFL convinced us of their effectiveness for students of L2 Russian. In the following two sections, we will provide guidelines on how to create and use different mingling games in the Russian-language classroom at the beginner level. We use the classification of mingling games offered by Borzova (2014), who suggests that depending on the stage of the learning process and the lesson aim, mingling games can focus on (a) language – form-focused mingling games (often in a communicative disguise), where students practice the target vocabulary and grammar in short communicative situations – or (b) meaning – meaning-focused mingles, where students use the information from the provided texts to solve a communicative task.

Form-focused mingling games

The first set of mingling games is aimed at recycling target vocabulary and grammar patterns through multiple repetitions in situations that simulate real-life communication. With less than 20 minutes of preparation time, these games are easily adapted to any academic content and could supplement any coursebook. All form-focused games should only include familiar vocabulary studied within the course; no new vocabulary is recommended (Ponkratova et al. [Понкратова и др.], 2017).

From our experience of working with groups of adults and young learners, mingling games have certain advantages compared to traditional work in pairs summarized in Table 3.1

Find the person who

Brief description

Students get a checklist and walk around the room, trying to find a person who has characteristics from the checklist. The goal is to talk to as many people as possible within the time limit and to put the names of students who answered affirmatively by each of the characteristics (Folse, 2006). The winner of the game is either the person who finished interviewing first or the one who managed to talk to the greatest number of people in a given time. (See Appendix A for a sample worksheet.) Table 3.2 provides a planning activity map for *Find the Person Who* mingle.

Important

1   There should be a limited number of grammar constructions to be practiced in each game (not more than three per game).
2   To promote speaking, the teacher should emphasize the importance of replying in full sentences rather than just saying "yes" or "no."

Table 3.2 "Find the Person Who" activity route map

Stage	Comments	Time	Teacher involvement/ interaction pattern
1. Before the lesson: preparation	a. Select 5–10 vocabulary items students are familiar with. Ideally, they should all be used within the same grammar pattern. b. If time allows, make a worksheet (see a sample in Appendix A). If not, see 2b.	5–10 min.	Teacher
2. In-class: lead-in, preparation for the activity	a. Revise the target vocabulary preselected for the activity. b. If there was no time to make a worksheet, write all target vocabulary on the board and ask students to copy them to make a checklist in their notebooks.	5–10 min.	Teacher-centered T – Ss

(Continued)

Table 3.2 (Continued)

Stage	Comments	Time	Teacher involvement/ interaction pattern
3. Setup: instructions and example	a. Explain that the class is going to do an interview game. Students need to find a person to match each of the items in the checklist (hand out the checklists if done in advance or ask students to use their notes from stage 2b as a checklist). To complete the task, students have to interview everyone in class until they find a person who does that activity or has that characteristic. b. Model the activity with a student. Draw students' attention to the target grammar pattern or changes in the vocabulary (e.g., cases, singular-plural forms).	5–10 min.	Teacher-centered T – Ss
4. Run the activity	a. Ask students to stand up and start the game. b. If there is an uneven number of people, the teacher might choose to join in. Alternatively, walk around the classroom, monitoring the language, and encourage students to change partners.	10–15 min.	Student-centered, S – S
5. Closing of the activity: analyzing results	When students have interviewed everyone, go through the answers in the worksheets and announce the winner. To work on speaking further, the teacher can organize: • Whole-class discussion, by pointing at various students and asking the rest of the class to tell everything they found out about this person.	5 min.	Student-centered T – S or S – S

Stage	Comments	Time	Teacher involvement/ interaction pattern
6. Follow-up	• Small-group discussion, by asking students to compare and summarize the results of the questionnaire in groups of 4–5 students. If the teacher notices any mistakes while monitoring the mingling activity, they could write these mistakes on the board and ask students to comment on them.	2 min.	Teacher-centered T – S

Note: T = teacher, and S = student(s).

Differentiation and extension

1 In classes with lower language proficiency, it is more efficient if students write all questions in the worksheet before they start interviewing each other. This way, the teacher can check the accuracy of the target grammar and word choice. This also improves spelling and involves different mechanisms of memorizing (e.g., Manchón et al., 2019).
2 Students with higher language proficiencies might want to ask additional follow-up questions while interviewing each other to get more information about the characteristics in the checklist.

Matching pairs

Table 3.3 "Matching Pairs" activity route map

Stage	Comments	Time	Teacher involvement/ interaction pattern
1. Before the lesson: preparation	The preparation stage is of crucial importance. Select vocabulary items and prepare cards, pictures, sentences, or texts. There should be one card for each student, two identical copies of each card. Prepare an extra set of two cards to use for modeling.	10–20 min.	Teacher

(*Continued*)

Table 3.3 (Continued)

Stage	Comments	Time	Teacher involvement/ interaction pattern
2. In-class: lead-in, preparation for the activity	Revise the vocabulary needed for the activity.	5 min.	Teacher-centered T – Ss
3. Setup: instructions, examples	a. Explain that students will go around the class trying to find a person who has the same card. b. Hand out the cards and ask students to look at them without showing them to anyone. c. Model the activity with a student. Draw students' attention to the target grammar pattern or changes in the vocabulary.	5–15 min.	Teacher-centered T – Ss
4. Run the activity	a. Ask students to stand up and start the game. b. If there is an uneven number of people, the teacher has to join in as one of the participants. c. The winner is the one who finds the matching partner first, or you can choose to continue the game until all the pairs are made.	10–15 min.	Student-centered S – S
5. Closing of the activity: analyzing results	Once the pairs are made, ask students to comment on what question/information helped them to find their partner.	5 min.	Student-centered S – S
6. Follow-up	If the teacher notices any language mistakes, they might want to write them on the board and discuss with the students.	2 min.	Teacher-centered T – S

Brief description

Students get cards with a picture or a text. They go around the classroom to find a person who has an identical card. To complete the task, students should ask and answer questions about their cards, but they cannot show them. The winners are two students who find their matching partner first.

Types of tasks

Words and simple images. For this type of task, each card should contain a familiar word in Russian or in students' native/common language[2] or an image (this makes the task more complicated). Students can ask each other, "Это . . . ?"

"У тебя . . . ?" (Appendix B). This task aims at recycling and revising vocabulary along with the simple sentence structure. The task can be used at the beginning of the course for vocabulary revision, or later, as the course progresses, as a warm-up.

Visual. Pictures or photos displaying real-life situations, people, places, or actions are used to develop paraphrasing, predicting, and contextual guessing skills to improve speaking fluency (accuracy is not of a major focus here) and develop paraphrasing, predicting, and contextual guessing skills. Students ask questions about details on the picture, which suggests that students should be familiar with such grammatical concepts as gender, number, colors, and basic verbs. The pictures should be chosen to match the semantic topic studied at the moment. The activity is more interesting and challenging if the offered set of visuals looks similar in general and differs in detail.

Sentences. This type of task suggests in-depth work on sentence structure and question words focusing mostly on speaking accuracy. The set of sentences offered should be on the studied topics, similar in structure, containing different key vocabulary. When talking to each other, students can ask general and special questions. The teacher should double-check if students are familiar with the question words necessary to find matching sentences (Appendix C).

Texts. A standard reading comprehension activity from a textbook can be transformed into a mingling game if it is composed of several extracts separated without the loss of meaning (e.g., different people express their opinion). Students receive one text, read it, and then go around the classroom to find the person who has the same text, asking and answering comprehension questions. The teacher can add "tabooed" words/questions to make the task more challenging. Table 3.3 provides a detailed overview of *Matching Pairs* mingle activity.

Differentiation and extension

1 Students of lower language proficiency can write all the questions they are going to ask before they start interviewing each other. The teacher can monitor the accuracy of grammar.
2 When working with sentences, the teacher can ask students to write similar sentences that say something about students' personalities or hobbies (depending on the topic covered in class).
3 When working with texts, a variety of post-reading activities could be offered, for example, comparing or retelling the texts.

Live dominoes

Brief description

This is the easiest game to play; it aims at recycling vocabulary and can be used from the second lesson on or when students have learned the alphabet and first words. This mingling game is an adaptation of a well-known game of dominoes, in which players have to match other players' tiles according to the number of pips on each tile. The difference is that each student gets only one domino tile, and they have to walk around the class looking for a match to make a live chain (Appendix D).

Important

1 The teacher can use standard domino tiles or make their own paper "tiles" with target vocabulary.
2 Tiles can either have images or words/texts.

Differentiation and extension

1 If domino cards have pictures, students of lower language proficiency might find it useful to first write down a corresponding word on their card.
2 When the chain is created, put all the dominoes on the table or hang on the board and give students a minute to memorize the words. Then ask students to write down the sequence in their notebooks from memory.

Table 3.4 "Live dominoes" activity route map

Stage	Comments	Time	Teacher involvement/ interaction pattern
1. Before the lesson: preparation	Select the key vocabulary and prepare domino tiles (e.g., paper index cards) equal to the number of students in class.	15 min.	Teacher
2. In-class: lead-in, preparation for the activity	Revise the vocabulary needed for the activity.	5 min.	Teacher-centered T – Ss
3. Setup: instruction, examples	a. Explain to the students that they will go around the class trying to find two people who have dominoes matching their domino tile, one match for each end of the tile. b. Hand out dominoes and ask students to look at them without showing them to others. c. Model activity with one student. Draw students' attention to the target grammar pattern or changes in the vocabulary.	5 min.	Teacher-centered T – Ss

Stage	Comments	Time	Teacher involvement/ interaction pattern
4. Run the activity	a. Ask students to stand up and start the game. Students should ask and answer simple questions, for example, *У тебя есть . . . ?* b. When the matching part is found, students can either continue the game moving together (this would add an element of fun) or remember the partners and line up when everyone has found their matches.	10 min.	Student-centered, Teacher out of sight S – S
5. Closing of the activity: analyzing results	When the full chain is created, ask students to open their domino cards and check if they are standing in the correct order.	2 min.	Student-centered S – S
6. Follow-up	If the teacher notices any mistakes in the target language during the game, they might write them on the board and discuss with students after the game is finished.	2 min.	Teacher-centered T – S

Meaning-focused or scenario mingling games

Mingling games in this section are created with carefully chosen vocabulary and grammar patterns that are suitable for beginner students. They are based on information gaps and aim to facilitate speaking fluency skills (Long, 1980). Besides speaking, the role cards with information about characters used in this game promote close reading. The comprehension of the written text develops organically as students ask each other questions about their characters. The meaning-focused games in this section are based on the tasks from the coursebook for beginners *Класс!* [*Class!*] (Kotelnikova & Bogomolova [Котельникова и Богомолова], 2019). Some of these games are presented in the book as reading comprehension tasks. But from our experience of turning these reading tasks into mingling games, the latter has distinct advantages. Table 3.5 compares reading comprehension tasks and mingling games.

All three meaning-focused mingling games we describe in this section follow a similar route. Table 3.6 provides an outline of these mingles.

Table 3.5 Comparison of reading tasks and meaning-focused mingling games

Reading comprehension activity	Meaning-focused mingling games
Each student has to read an entire text to complete reading comprehension activities; therefore, the majority of the class time is spent on reading, which leaves little time for speaking.	Each student has to read only a portion of a text, which allows for more speaking time.
Students might not always be motivated to read long texts about people or situations not related to their life and lack the motivation to read for details.	Students take on the role of a person described in a role card. This contributes to the increased motivation to understand the text in detail, which translates in greater involvement in speaking.

Table 3.6 Meaning-focused mingling games route map

Stage	Comments	Time	Teacher involvement/ interaction pattern
1. Before the lesson: preparation	a. Look through the texts for any new words your students might not know. b. Print out the role cards and interview lists to be filled in. c. If there are more students than the role cards, the class could be split into groups that will play separately, or two students can get one card and work together.	2 min.	Teacher
2. In-class: prepare for the activity	a. If needed, introduce new vocabulary. b. Revise any target vocabulary and grammar patterns.	5 min.	Teacher-centered T – Ss
3. Setup: lead-in, instruction, example, reading	a. Discuss introductory questions to raise the level of interest and motivation. b. Announce the topic of the game and give a brief description. b. Hand out the role cards and give enough time for students to read through them. Encourage students to work with dictionaries or ask questions if something is not clear.	15 min.	Teacher-centered T – Ss

Stage	Comments	Time	Teacher involvement/ interaction pattern
	c. Model the activity with a student. Write possible questions on the board so that students can easily refer to them during the game.		
4. Run the activity	a. Ask students to stand up. Start the game. b. Monitor the discussion without interfering for error correction. Help students with formulating questions and answers if needed. Take notes of errors in the target language.	15–25 min.	Student-centered, teacher out of sight S – S
5. Analyzing results	When the game is finished, ask students to comment on the results/compare the results/ discuss them in groups.	2 min.	Student-centered T – S
6. Follow-up	If any mistakes in the target language during the game were noticed, write them on the board and ask students to comment on them.	2 min.	Teacher-centered T – S

My big family

Brief description

Each student gets a card with a brief description of their character (Appendix E). The goal is to get the information about one of their relatives (question on the bottom of the card) by talking to other students.

Target language. (a) *У тебя/него/неё есть . . .* [You/he/she has . . .]; (b) *(Как) Его/её зовут?* [What is his/her name?]; (c) possessive pronouns.

Background knowledge. (a) family members, (b) jobs.

Introductory questions. (a) *У вас большая семья?* [Do you have a big family?]; (b) *Вы хорошо знаете, кто ваши родственники?* [Do you know well who your relatives are?]; (c) *У вас есть родственники, которых вы не знаете?* [Do you know relatives that you are not acquainted with?]; (d) *Как часто вы и ваша семья вместе вечером дома?* [How often do you and your family spend time together in the evening at home]?

Questions likely to be asked. (a) *Как вас зовут?* [What is your name?]; (b) *У вас есть . . . ?* [Do you have . . . ?]; (c) *Как его/её зовут?* [What is his/her name?]; (d) *У /него/неё есть. . . . ?* [Does he/she have . . . ?]; (e) *Кто вы/он/она по профессии?* [What is your/his/her profession?].

Differentiation and extension

After the mingling game, ask students to write a short story about all the relatives they talked to.

Language tandem partners

Brief description

Each student receives a card with a brief description of their character (Appendix F). The goal is to find a person who would be an ideal language exchange partner based on the languages their characters speak and want to learn, hobbies, and personal traits.

Target language. (a) hobbies; (b) *Мне/тебе/вам нравится/нравятся* . . . [I/you like . . .]; (c) the accusative case with non-animated nouns (*Я люблю* . . . [I like . . .]).

Background knowledge. (a) numbers 1–100; (b) countries and nationalities; (c) *изучать/знать . . . язык* [to study/know . . . language], *говорить по-* . . . . [speak . . .]; (d) jobs.

Introductory questions. (a) *Как вы обычно изучаете иностранные языки?* [How do you usually study foreign languages?]; (b) *Что лучше – изучать много грамматики или много говорить?* [What is better: to study a lot of grammar or to speak a lot?]; (c) *Вы часто говорите с друзьями по-русски?* [Do you often speak Russian with friends?]; (d) *Вы знаете, что такое языковой тандем?* [Do you know what language tandem is?]; (e) *Как вы думаете, почему это популярно?* [What do you think it's so popular?].

Questions likely to be asked. (a) *Как вас зовут?* [What is your name?]; (b) *Откуда вы?* [Where are you from?]; (c) *Сколько вам лет?* [How old are you?]; (d) *Кто вы по профессии?* [What is your profession?]; (e) *У вас есть хобби? Вы любите* . . . *?* [Do you have a hobby? Do you like . . . ?]; (f) *Вам нравится/нравятся. . . . ?* [Do you like . . . ?]; (g) Вы *говорите по-* . . . *?* [Do you speak . . . ?].

Differentiation and extension

Lower-language-proficiency students work in pairs and write a profile of a prospective language tandem partner similar in age, interests, etc. Higher-language-proficiency students write their profile and a profile of an ideal language tandem partner.

Have I met you before?

Brief description

This is a summary task appropriate for the end of the first semester of study. Each student receives a card with a brief description of their character (Appendix G). The game takes place at the imaginary party. The characters find each other looking familiar but cannot remember when and where they met before. They have to find it out by talking to each other and filling in the interview form.

Target language. (a) question words, (b) hobbies, (c) work, (d) studies, (e) traveling.

Background knowledge. (a) past tense; (b) reflexive verbs; (c) the accusative, prepositional, and instrumental cases; (d) talking about age.

Introductory questions. (a) *У вас много друзей?* [Do you have many friends?]; (b) *Вы помните, где и когда вы с ними познакомились?* [Do you remember when and where you met them?]; (c) *Вы часто ходите на вечеринки?* [Do you often go to parties?]; (d) *Что вы делаете, если на вечеринке видите знакомого человека, но не помните, как его/её зовут?* [What do you do if you see somebody who looks familiar but you don't remember them?].

Questions likely to be asked. (a) *Как вас зовут?* [What is your name?]; (b) *Кто вы по профессии?* [What is your profession?]; (c) *Вы были в/на. . . . ?* [Have you been at . . . ?]; (d) *Вы любите. . . . ?* [Do you like . . . ?]; (e) *Вы говорите по-. . . ?* [Do you speak . . . ?]; (f) *Где вы учились/ работали/ путешествовали . . . ?* [Where did you study/work/travel?]; (g) *У вас есть друг/ подруга/ девушка, которые/ которая/ которые . . .?* [Do you have a friend/girlfriend who . . .?].

Lessons learned

After using mingling games for several years in classes with adult and young learners, we observed a tendency for a positive response to such activities. Students generally commented positively, saying that "the game was fun," they "did not notice how fast time ran while playing these games," they "feel like [they] can actually speak in Russian," they "did not expect [they] can start speaking that fast." Nevertheless, there were several issues that we faced, especially in groups with adult learners.

Some students – in our estimate, less than 10% of all students with whom we tried mingling games – do not understand why they "waste time on games" when they need to study. That was mostly noted among more mature students, raised in a traditional educational system, who treated games as entertainment. Therefore, we find it important to communicate the learning objectives of the game to students clearly and explicitly. With mingling games, the most evident learning objective is to facilitate speaking skills; it might be presented as, "This game will prepare you for a situation where you order food in a café, get to know new people, etc." In some cases of severe resistance to playing games during class time, the authors had to replace the word "game" with "task" or "activity" to avoid further dissatisfaction and remove the competition element from the game.

At times, we encountered situations when adult students were not willing to move around the classroom. One of the explanations was the stress of being in a potentially awkward situation while participating in mingling games. When this happened, the authors started with a more "quiet" version of the game – when students stay at their desks and talk to as many neighbors as they can reach. On the second and third attempt to introduce such activities, it is recommended to ask students to connect to more peers, which will encourage the students to stand up and walk around the classroom.

With the forced switch to online learning during the pandemic, the authors tried to play mingling games online. It should be mentioned that it proved possible with platforms that have an option of breakout rooms (e.g., Zoom). Playing form-focused games like *Find the Partner Who* . . . and *Matching Pairs* was difficult, as it took too much time to solve organizational issues online. But meaning-focused or scenario mingling games run smoothly in an online setting, since they suggest longer communication in pairs and therefore less work for the teacher to change the partners in the breakout rooms.

Appendix A

Find the person who . . . sample worksheet

Тема "Ты говоришь по- . . .?"

Задание: Найди, кто в группе говорит . . .
[Task: Find someone who speaks . . .]

	Вопрос	Имя	Больше информации
по-английски	*Пример:* **Вы** *говорите* по-английски? **Ты** *говоришь* по-английски	*Пример:* Мария,	
по-немецки	. . . .	. . . .	
по-французски	. . . .	. . . .	
по-японски	. . . .	. . . .	
по-китайски	. . . .	. . . .	
по-испански	. . . .	. . . .	
по-итальянски	. . . .	. . . .	

Appendix B

Matching pairs sample worksheet – words

Тема "Национальности и страны"

Задание: Найдите в классе студента из такой же страны, как у вас на карточке.
[Task: Find a student who is from the country on your card.]
Например:

- Вы из Америки?
- Да, я из Америки./Нет, я не из Америки.

Америка	Англия	Франция	Германия
Италия	Австрия	Япония	Швейцария
Китай	Турция	Португалия	Бразилия

Appendix C

Matching pairs sample worksheet – sentences

Тема "Свободное время"

Задание: Найдите в классе студента, у которого на карточке такое же предложение, как и у вас.
[Task: Find a student whose sentence is identical to yours.]
Например:

- Ты любишь гулять в парке?
- Да, я люблю гулять в парке.
- Я тоже.
- Ты гуляешь в парке вечером?
- Нет.

1. В свободное время я люблю гулять в парке.
2. Я часто гуляю в парке вечером.
3. Я редко гуляю в парке, но часто гуляю в центре города.
4. В свободное время я люблю читать книги.
5. Иногда я читаю книги в парке.
6. Я никогда не читаю книги, потому что я много работаю.

Appendix D

"Live Domino" sample worksheet

Тема "Еда"

Задание: Найдите студентов, у которых на карточке есть такие же слова как и у вас (не показывайте карточку). Решите, кто будет справа, а кто слева. Соберите живую цепочку.

[Task: Find students who have the same words as yours (do not show them your card). Decide who should be on the right and on the left. Assemble a live chain.]

Например:

- У тебя есть . . . ?
- Нет, у меня нет./Да, у меня есть. . . .

пицца	кофе	хлеб	рыба
кофе	йогурт	рыба	мясо
йогурт	чай	мясо	рис
чай	яйцо	рис	картошка
яйцо	хлеб	картофель	пицца

Тема "Вопросительные слова"

Например:

- У тебя есть слово "Почему"?
- Да!
- Отлично. У меня вопрос "Почему ты здесь?"

КТО	. . . ТЫ ЗДЕСЬ?	КОГДА	. . . ТЫ? ТЫ ИЗ ИТАЛИИ?
ПОЧЕМУ	. . . У ТЕБЯ ДЕЛА?	ОТКУДА	. . . ЗДЕСЬ БАНК?
КАК	. . . ТЫ НЕ ПОНИМАЕШЬ?	ГДЕ	. . . ЯЗЫКИ ТЫ ЗНАЕШЬ?
ЧТО	. . . ТЫ РАБОТАЕШЬ? УТРОМ?	КАКИЕ	. . . ЭТО? ЭТО МАША?

Appendix E

My *big family* role cards

Instructions: Print out the cards depending on the number of students in class. If there are 6 students in the class, print out card 1–6; if 8 students, 1–8.

1
Имя: Константин
Профессия: инженер
Брат: Георгий. Он врач.
Сестра: Ксения. Она юрист.
Дети: сын и дочь
Жена: француженка. Она архитектор.
Мама: на пенсии.
Кто ваша жена? (Как её зовут?)

2
Имя: Бриджит (из Франции)
Профессия: архитектор
Муж: инженер.
Мама: преподаватель
Папа: журналист
Сын: школьник. Изучает английский язык.
Дочка: изучает экономику в университете.
Кто ваша дочь? (Как её зовут?)

3
Имя: Мария
Профессия: студентка. Изучает экономику.
Мама: француженка, архитектор
Брат: школьник. Изучает английский язык.
У вас есть папа. У него есть мама – ваша бабушка Она на пенсии.
Кто ваш папа? (Как его зовут?)

6
Имя: Георгий
Профессия: врач
Женат.
Дочь: Полина
У вас есть брат. Его жена француженка.
Ваша мама работает?

7
Имя: Ксения
Профессия: юрист
Мама: Нина Фёдоровна
Вы замужем.
У вас есть два брата. Один брат инженер.
Как его зовут?

8
Имя: Натали
Профессия: менеджер
Дочь: Марина
Мама: преподаватель
Вы не замужем. У вас есть сестра. У неё есть сын и дочь. Её сын школьник, а дочка – студентка.
Кто ваша сестра?

4
Имя: Максим
Профессия: Школьник. Изучает английский язык.
У вас есть папа. У него есть мама – ваша бабушка. Она на пенсии.
У вас есть мама. У неё есть папа. Он журналист.
Кто ваша сестра? (Как её зовут?)

5
Имя: Нина Фёдоровна
Профессия: На пенсии.
Дети: два сына и дочь.
Один сын – инженер. Его зовут Константин. Другой сын – врач.
Как его зовут?

9
Имя: Мари Дюпюи
Профессия: преподаватель
Муж: журналист
Дети: две дочки
Внуки: две внучки и внук.
Как их зовут?

10
Имя: Жак Дюпюи
Профессия: журналист
Дети: одна дочь – менеджер, другая архитектор.
Жена: преподаватель.
Как её зовут?

Appendix F

Language tandem partners role cards

Instructions

Print out the cards depending on the number of students in class. The matching pairs are on one line. If there are 6 students in the class, print out the first 3 lines; if 8 students, 4 lines.

имя: Алла
страна: Беларусь
возраст: 69
профéссия: пенсионéрка
хóбби: книги, óпера, балéт, фильмы
языки: французский

имя: Жаклин
страна: Франция
возраст: 74
профéссия: пенсионéрка
хóбби: опера, литература, искусство, история
языки: русский, испанский

имя: Кирилл
страна: Россия
возраст: 27
профéссия: дизáйнер
хóбби: кинó, дизáйн, мультфильмы, анимé
языки: японский, английский

имя: Кенжиро
страна: Япония
возраст: 20
профéссия: студент, изучает историю кино
хóбби: дайвинг, современное искусство
языки: русский, французский

имя: Марина
страна: Казахстан
возраст: 37
профéссия: преподавáтель музыки
хóбби: óпера, путешéствия, итальянская кухня
языки: немéцкий, английский

имя: Тобиас
страна: Австрия
возраст: 40
профéссия: музыкант
хóбби: джаз, путешéствия, альпинизм, вино
языки: русский, английский

имя: Алёна
страна: Россия
возраст: 32
профéссия: секретáрь
хóбби: танцы, книги, путешéствия, спорт
языки: испанский, итальянский

имя: Хосе
страна: Испания
возраст: 42
профéссия: менеджер в отеле
хóбби: сальса, вино, путешéствия, бегает марафоны
языки: русский, немéцкий

и́мя: Алексе́й **страна́**: Беларусь **во́зраст**: 42 **профе́ссия**: юри́ст **хо́бби**: да́йвинг, сёрфинг, спорт **языки́**: англи́йский, фи́нский	**и́мя**: Сальме **страна́**: Финля́ндия **во́зраст**: 35 **профе́ссия**: экономист **хо́бби**: виндсерфинг, танцы, трекинг, поёт в хоре **языки́**: русский, английский, шведский
и́мя: Диана **во́зраст**: 18 **страна́**: Армения **профе́ссия**: студе́нтка **хо́бби**: фотогра́фия, рисование, комиксы, корейское кино **языки́**: корейский, английский	**и́мя**: Соу **во́зраст**о́: 17 **страна́**: Корея **профе́ссия**: студентка **хо́бби**: музыка, рисование, оригами, скейтбординг **языки́**: русский, английский

Appendix G

Have I met you before? role cards

САША
Родился 31 год назад в Москве.
Учился в школе, где изучал физику и математику, а потом в университете изучал физику.
Саша программист. Год назад работал в Финляндии, в Хельсинки. Там у него есть друг и коллега. Он финн. Он тоже программист. У него есть девушка – англичанка. Саша видел её один раз год назад, когда она была в Хельсинки.
Сейчас Саша работает в Москве. Два раза в неделю Саша занимается капоэйрой. Саша не женат. Но два года назад он познакомился с девушкой в Турции на пляже. Она была русская. Отдыхала с друзьями. Саша её помнит, но не знает, как её зовут.
У него есть младшая сестра. Она живёт в Петербурге, потому что у неё там друг. Он бармен. Один раз, когда его сестра и её друг были в Москве, они вместе обедали в ресторане.

ЛЕНА
Родилась 31 год назад в Екатеринбурге.
Училась в Екатеринбурге в школе № 9. Потом три года в университете в Екатеринбурге и два года изучала архитектуру в магистратуре в университете в Москве.
Сейчас Лена архитектор в компании в Москве. Компания большая. Лена много путешествует по работе.
В этом году была в Англии в Манчестере и познакомилась там с англичанкой. В самолёте Лена говорила с молодым человеком из Петербурга.
В выходные она волонтёр в организации, работает с детьми.
Не замужем.
Два года назад Лена отдыхала в Турции с друзьями и на пляже познакомилась с мужчиной. Он русский. Она его помнит, но не знает, как его зовут.

МИЛА
Мила изучала английский язык в школе в Москве 10 лет. Потом она изучала английский язык и литературу в университете.
Девять лет назад изучала английский язык в Манчестере и жила в семье. Она и её английская сестра много говорили, гуляли вместе.
Мила живёт сейчас в Москве. Преподаёт английский язык на курсах и по скайпу.
Два раза в неделю у неё есть тренировки. Мила занимается капоэйрой.
В выходные она волонтёр, работает с детьми.

САРА

Родилась 23 года назад в Манчестере. Девять лет назад одна русская студентка жила в её семье. Они были подруги.

Сара архитектор в Манчестере. У неё есть коллеги в России. В этом году они неделю работали в Англии.

Год назад она была в Петербурге. В баре она познакомилась с архитектором из Москвы.

У неё есть бойфренд, финн. Он программист и работает в Финляндии уже два года. У него был там друг из России. Сара видела его один раз в баре год назад. Но сейчас этот друг работает в Москве.

Много путешествует. Последний раз в аэропорту в Берлине Сара познакомилась с мужчиной из России. Он немного говорил по-английски. Она знает, что он инженер.

ФЁДОР

Родился 31 год назад в Екатеринбурге. Учился в школе № 9 в Екатеринбурге. Изучал физику и математику в университете в Москве.

Фёдор — инженер.

Изучал три месяца английский язык на курсах. У него была преподаватель — девушка. В свободное время она занимается капоэйрой.

Фёдор много путешествует по работе. В этом году он познакомился в аэропорту в Берлине с девушкой из Англии и первый раз говорил по-английски не на уроке.

Последний раз он был на конференции в Петербурге и в поезде познакомился с молодым человеком и девушкой. Её семья живёт в Москве, но молодой человек никогда не был там.

СЕРГЕЙ

Сергей родился в Москве.

Он учился в школе, где изучал физику. Потом он учился в университете в магистратуре, где изучал архитектуру.

Сергей — архитектор в маленькой компании.

Год назад Сергей был в Петербурге и познакомился в баре с англичанкой. Сергей немного говорил по-английски. Потом он учился на курсах, изучал английский язык три месяца. У него был преподаватель — девушка.

В свободное время она занимается капоэйрой. Сергей ещё не был в Англии, но очень хочет.

МИХАИЛ

Михаил живёт в Петербурге.

Он бармен в баре. У него есть девушка. Она родилась в Москве, но сейчас она и Михаил живут вместе в Петербурге. Её родители и брат живут в Москве. Михаил видел их один раз в ресторане.

Когда Михаил был в поезде, он познакомился с мужчиной. Он инженер и был на конференции в Петербурге.

Год назад в баре, где Михаил работает, он познакомился с англичанкой и архитектором из Москвы. Он знает неплохо английский язык, и они говорили по-русски и по-английски.

Михаил хочет говорить ещё лучше, поэтому изучает английский язык по скайпу. Его преподаватель — русская молодая женщина, она живёт в Москве.

Михаил любит путешествовать и разговаривать с людьми. В этом году в самолёте он говорил с девушкой. Она архитектор и должна была работать в Англии неделю.

Interview Form

Ваше имя ....

Имя человека	Где и когда вы встречались?
....	
....	
....	
....	
....	
....	

Notes

1 Long (1988, 1991) observes that grammar instruction comes in two flavors: focus on form and focus on formS. The former refers to drawing "students' attention to linguistic elements as they arise incidentally in lessons whose overriding focus is on meaning or communication" (Long, 1991, pp. 45–46). The latter refers to the traditional teaching of discrete points of grammar as separate lessons.
2 See Bondarenko (2022) for the discussion on L1 use with beginners.

References

Ahmadian, M. J. (2012). Task repetition in ELT. *ELT Journal, 66*(3), 380–382.

Akishina, A. A., & Kagan, O. E. [Акишина, А. А., и Каган, О. Е.]. (2002). *Learning to teach* [Учимся учить]. Russkiy Yazyk, Kursy [Русский язык, Курсы].

Asonova, G. A. [Асонова, Г. А.] (2013). Grammar-communicative tasks with game elements as a way to activate Russian as a foreign language acquisition [Грамматико-коммуникативные упражнения с элементами игры как способ активизации владения русским языком как иностранным]. *Proceedings of Southern Federal University. Philology* [*Известия Южного федерального университета, Филологические науки*], *3*, 79–85.

Averi, M. [Авери, М.] (2017). *Soroka* [*Сорока*]. Averi, M.

Bondarenko, M. (2022). Rethinking authenticity in SLA from the perspective of L1 use: An emerging concept of cognitive authenticity. In L. Will, W. Stadler, & I. Eloff (Eds.), *Authenticity across languages and cultures: Themes of identity in foreign language teaching & learning* (pp. 97–115). Multilingual Matters.

Borzova, E. (2014). Mingles in the foreign language classroom. *English Teaching Forum, 2*, 20–27. https://files.eric.ed.gov/fulltext/EJ1035883.pdf

Chou, M. H. (2014). Assessing English vocabulary and enhancing young English as a Foreign Language (EFL) learners' motivation through games, songs, and stories. *Education 3–13, 42*(3), 284–297.

Dolmatova, O., & Novacac, E. [Долматова, О., и Новакак, Е.]. (2017). *Tochka Ru: Russian Course. Textbook A1* [*Точка Ру: Курс по русскому языку. Учебник A1*]. Pero. https://www.tochkaru-book.com/en/

Folse, K. S. (2006). *The art of teaching speaking*. University of Michigan.

Karsudianto, F. (2020). Improving students' motivation and self-confidence in speaking using mingling games. *Journal of Applied Studies in Language, 4*(1), 1–8.

Kaznishkina, I. [Казнишкина И.]. (2019). *Communicative games* [Коммуникативные игры]. Russkiy Yazyk, Kursy [Русский язык. Курсы].

Kitaygorodskaya, G. A. [Китайгородская, Г. А.]. (1986). *Methodological principles of intensive teaching of foreign languages* [Методические основы интенсивного обучения иностранным языкам]. Moscow University Press [Издательство Московского университета].

Kolesova, D., & Kharitonov, A. [Колесова, Д., и Харитонов, А.]. (2011). *Igra Slov* [*Игра слов*]. Zlatoust [Златоуст].

Kotelnikova, D., & Bogomolova, E. [Котельникова, Д., и Богомолова, Е.]. (2019). *"Klass! A1.1" Coursebook in Russian for non-native speakers* [*"Класс! A1.1" Учебный комплекс по русскому языку для иностранных учащихся*]. Derzhavin Institute [Державинский Институт].

Long, M. (1980). *Input, interaction, and second language acquisition* [Unpublished doctoral dissertation]. University of California at Los Angeles.

Long, M. (1988). Instructed interlanguage development. In L. Beebe (Ed.), *Issues in second language acquisition: Multiple perspectives* (pp. 115–141). Newbury House.

Long, M. (1991). Focus on form: A design feature in language teaching methodology. In K. de Bot, R. Ginsberg, & C. Kramsch (Eds.), *Foreign language research in cross-cultural perspective* (p. 39). John Benjamins.

Manchón, R. M., Vasylets, O., Schwieter, J. W., & Benati, A. (2019). Language learning through writing: Theoretical perspectives and empirical evidence. In J. W. Schwieter & A. Benati (Eds.), *The Cambridge handbook of language learning* (pp. 341–362). Cambridge University Press.

Mozelova, I. [Мозелова, И.]. (2019). *Russian Souvenir [Русский сувенир]*. Russkiy Yazyk, Kursy [Русский язык. Курсы].

Mufidah, U., & Fitriani, A. (2022). Mingle game for teaching speaking. *Journal of English as a Modern and International Language, 1*(1), 1–10.

Nakhabina, M. M., Stepanenko, V. A., Kolovska E. G., & Plotnikova O. V. [Нахабина, М. М., Степаненко, В. А., Кольовска, Е. Г., и Плотникова, О. В.]. (2020). *Hello Russia!* [Привет, Россия!]. Kuchkovo pole [Кучково поле].

Ponkratova, E. M., Kobernik, L. N., & Omelyanchuk, E. L. [Понкратова, Е. М., Коберник, Л. Н., & Омельянчук, Е. Л.] (2017). Communicative games in learning Russian as a foreign language [Коммуникативные игры при изучении русского языка как иностранного]. *Modern Problems of Science and Education* [*Современные проблемы науки и образования*], *4*, n.p.

Robinson, P. (2005). Cognitive complexity and task sequencing: Studies in a componential framework for second language task design. *International Review of Applied Linguistics, 43*, 1–33.

Swain, M., Brooks, L., & Tocalli-Beller, A. (2002). Peer-peer dialogue as a means of second language learning. *Annual Review of Applied Linguistics, 22*, 171.

Chapter 4

Trivia games for student-centered learning in the Russian-language classroom

Maria Khotimsky

CHAPTER SUMMARY

The chapter outlines the approaches of using trivia games in Russian as a second/foreign language classes within broader benefits of game-based learning in foreign languages. Trivia games engage individual learners or teams in answering questions on a given topic and offer many opportunities for creating interactive, student-centered activities in both face-to-face and online teaching. Thanks to flexibility in defining the game topic, trivia games may be form- or content-focused and can be used at different levels of language proficiency. The competitive aspect of the game allows to turn review and practice into student-centered lessons that foster classroom community and create opportunities for spontaneous communication and meaning negotiation. The chapter offers a sample lesson for an intermediate-level classroom that can be used for a unit or semester review class. The chapter concludes with a critical analysis of digital tools for creation of custom-made trivia games and offers suggestions for adapting the trivia games for different proficiency levels, as well as for project-based activities.

Краткое содержание главы

В статье рассматриваются подходы к использованию игры-викторины на уроках русского языка как иностранного в общем контексте игрового подхода к преподаванию иностранных языков. Игра-викторина, в ходе которой игроки или команды соревнуются в ответах на вопросы на заданную тему, может быть использована в организации интерактивных уроков как в классе, так и в занятиях онлайн. Выбор темы игры и типы вопросов позволяют широко варьировать тематику игры – вопросы могут быть посвящены как грамматике, так и историческим, географическим, культурологическим и пр. темам – и адаптировать уровень сложности вопросов в соответствии с педагогическими задачами курса. Момент игры и соревнования создает возможности для спонтанного общения между студентами во время обсуждения и выбора вариантов ответов. В статье предложен план подготовки и проведения урока-викторины, основанного на вопросах, созданных студентами, и посвященного повторению учебного раздела; аналогичный урок может стать завершающим занятием семестра. Помимо этого, в статье обсуждается использование компьютерных приложений для создания игры-викторины и предлагаются варианты адаптации игр-викторин для разных уровней владения языком, а также для проектных заданий.

Trivia games in L2 Russian classroom

Trivia – a popular fact quiz or game played in educational and entertainment contexts around the world – can be successfully adapted for teaching Russian as a second or foreign language (RSL; RFL) within a student-centered pedagogy approach (Nuss & Martin, 2022), as well as within the project-based learning framework. In this chapter, I offer examples from practice and critically examine the use of trivia game model for purposes of vocabulary and grammar review, as well as share suggestions on adapting this game for retrieval and practice purposes. The chapter conceives a trivia-based class model as a teaching model that not only allows students to practice the key language structures and vocabulary patterns but also fosters spontaneous communication and promotes classroom community building.

After a brief overview of existing literature on trivia and similar games in language education, I offer a detailed outline of a trivia-based L2 Russian lesson at the second year (intermediate–mid) level and then discuss some modifications of the game that employ digital tools to imitate traditional trivia games (such as *Jeopardy*) and can be used for shorter review sessions and classroom practice. Finally, I will share some examples of using trivia game creation as a student project.

Literature overview

Research into games in second language education has proliferated in the past years, although publications on using games for the instruction of RSL and RFL are fewer than in other languages. Whether scholars discuss online games or traditional board games, games developed specifically for language learning or adapted for classroom use, the advantages of game-based learning are manifold. Such seminal publications as Plass et al. (2020), Reinhardt (2018), and Reinders (2012) address a variety of pedagogical advantages of using games and game-enhanced activities that aid various aspects of learning, including motivational, cognitive, affective, and sociocultural. Hayo Reinders aptly summarizes the parallels between the world of games and foreign language instruction:

> Games can contribute to the implementation of pedagogic principles that are becoming increasingly mainstream, such as the use of tasks, authentic forms of interaction and collaboration, and community-based and situated learning. Most importantly, perhaps, games place learners at the heart of the learning and teaching process and in this way may have an impact on language education as a whole.
>
> (Reinders, 2012, p. 2)

Game-based activities create opportunities for authentic interactions and meaning construction through practicing the language of gaming and negotiating game strategy (Reinhardt, 2018, p. 106). The focus on the game takes away pressures and anxiety and leads to improved opportunities for practice and learning: "Learning in well-designed games is an epiphenomenon of play rather than a point of play" (Reinhardt & Thorne, 2020, p. 418). As a result, games in a classroom setting offer safe practice space, allowing for comfortable and fun opportunities to repeat, correct mistakes, and replay dialogue scenarios while practicing language patterns and engaging in communicative situations. In addition to creating an environment that promotes student engagement and authentic interactions, language instructors use a variety of games to model real-life situations and create an environment for collaboration, negotiation, and meaning exchange. In a recent literature review regarding the link between games and learning, Dubreil (2020) summarizes: "[A]n increasingly robust corpus of research in Second Language Acquisition (SLA) demonstrates the potential and effectiveness of games for LC2 [second language and culture] learning in the area of vocabulary, pragmatics, literacy, and multilingual engagement" (Dubreil, 2020, p. 251). This is particularly important within the contemporary transformative language pedagogy framework that emphasizes transactional tasks and collaborative learning (Leaver & Cassel, 2020, p. 254).

Several recent studies in the field of RFL pedagogy have addressed the use of games in the language classroom as an important element of task-based student-centered teaching (Nuss & Whitehead Martelle, 2022). Scholars have discussed using online games (Spasova, 2021), role-play games (Pastushenkov, 2022), and integrating online games and game-based activities into the classroom after the pandemic (Klimova, 2021). There are also several helpful anthologies of games designed or adapted for language learning purposes at different levels. For example, Anna Leontyeva (who is also a contributor to this volume) has published two editions of her book on games in RSL classes, offering examples of authentic and adapted games that help revise and practice grammar patterns, promote student interaction, and generate spontaneous communication (Leontyeva, 2018, 2020). Alexei Razin's language school in Tallin, Estonia, advocates for a game-based approach to teaching, and his book *Играют все!* [Everyone is Playing] describes many types of games, including energizer (or warm-up) games, games for introducing new vocabulary, and role-play games (Razin & Kingisepp, 2018). Another resource that includes many activities for beginner levels is *Русский язык, Игровое пособие для начинающих* [*Russian Language, a Game Manual for Beginners*] (Zakorchevnaia [Закорчевная], 2020). Capitalizing on the potential of games for classroom or program community building, they have been used to facilitate cultural events, such as the use of the modified version of the trivia game "*Что? Где? Когда?*" [What? When? Where?] for community building activities in the UWM Flagship program (Evans-Romaine et al., 2021).

Among the wide variety of language learning games and game-inspired activities, trivia games (a game or competition in which participants are asked questions about facts from different fields of knowledge) offer a great capacity for learning and community building. They are particularly suited for creating student-centered and discussion-based classes devoted to conversation practice or topic review. "Trivia" (typically referred to as *викторина* in Russian) involves a contest between individuals or teams, where participants compete in responding to questions on cultural, historical, geographical, or linguistic facts. The questions can be read out loud by the teacher or by the opposing teams, which offers an extra opportunity for listening practice (Crawford, 2001), or projected on the board, as in trivia-based game shows, such as *Jeopardy*, *Who Wants to Be a Millionaire*, and other popular games. As Michael Crawford explains, this format is excellent for "getting students to talk beyond themselves." Trivia-type games "can be adapted to learner's interests and make it a very useful source for content for teaching conversation" (Crawford, 2002, p. 23). Because the questions can be tailored to the class content and level, this activity is easily adaptable to the pedagogical needs and goals of different classes.

The format of the game lends itself nicely to creating an engaging, student-centered activity that, on the one hand, offers ample chances to review specific patterns or content areas but, on the other hand, avoids monotony thanks to the atmosphere of a game and the element of competition. As trivia-based activities gain popularity in classroom instruction, it is imperative that the field of RFL engages in the discussion of its affordances to L2 Russian pedagogy. Based on my literature review, recent publications in Russian language pedagogy do not include a critical discussion and evaluation of trivia games. In what follows, I will discuss approaches to structuring trivia-based language learning tasks that can either fill an entire classroom session or be used as a shorter review activity.

Trivia game as a student-centered review and practice lesson

The case study discussed here has been successfully implemented in second- and third-year RFL classes, but it can be adjusted to different levels and topics. Such sessions work well for review, summarizing a unit based on historical or cultural facts, as well as topics related to academic life, science, inventions, and discoveries. In other words, suitable for situations where students can use their active vocabulary to discuss various facts of history, culture, science, geography, etc. Grammar and vocabulary content in such units often include expressions of dates (year, decade, century), the use of participles, and gerunds (verbal adverbs), in connection with topics in history, geography, science, technology, and basic discoveries. These topics often focus on such verbs as *изобрести* [to invent], *открыть* [to discover], *создать* [to create], *доказать* [to prove], *построить* [to build], *основать* [to establish]. This activity typically concludes the unit, at which point students are expected to know the key vocabulary and be comfortable using it in conversation. The following sample lesson plan is followed by a more detailed description of key elements of the class, as well as modification of this lesson using online trivia game platforms for class activities and project-based tasks.

Lesson plan: science trivia game for second- or third-year RFL class

Lesson goal. Review key vocabulary and grammar elements of the unit (such as participles, gerunds, and date expressions); practice communicative skills (negotiation of responses, sharing opinions, negotiating meaning, supporting peers during discussion, and collaboration); review and learn new trivia facts about the history of science.

Preparation (assigned for homework). A short overview introducing the game format and showing sample questions.

Lesson plan:

1. Warm-up (3–5 minutes): as students arrive and settle for the class, the teacher can share sample questions and ask to rephrase them using a participle form, for example, *"В каком году открыли XX?"* – *"В каком году был открыт XX?" "Кто написал роман XXX?"* – *"Кем был написан роман XXX?"* Alternatively, the instructor can share the slide with phrases that help introduce opinion or assess the answer, such as *по-моему, я думаю, мне кажется; это верно, это неверно* [in my opinion, I think, it seems to me; this is correct, this is incorrect].
2. Introduction (3 minutes): the instructor gives a brief overview of the game logistics, divides the students into two teams, and asks the students to share the questions they had created as part of homework and select 10 (+2) questions for the game. Each group is asked to come up with a name for their team.
3. Small-group work (15 minutes): students work in small groups and take turns sharing their questions. Teammates practice answering the questions. Once all students have shared their questions, the team selects the questions to use in the game.
4. Team game (20–25 minutes): the instructor writes the team names on the board and invites the students to put away electronic devices. The game begins. Team members take turns posing the questions, deliberating about the answers, and sharing their responses. The opposing team confirms the correct answer.
5. Wrap-up discussion (5–7 minutes): winners are congratulated (optionally, the winning team or both teams receive small treats and prizes). Then, the instructor projects "questions about questions"; students share their impressions on the most fun, surprising, and interesting facts they learned (or forgot) during the game.
6. Concluding remarks and homework assignment.

Assessment and feedback. The instructor offers feedback on the student's homework (correcting formal elements of the questions). During the lesson, as students work in small groups, the teacher joins each group to check the questions again and, where needed, to offer small corrections or suggestions for rephrasing.

Sample questions and preparation for the game

The teacher explains that the following class will be in the form of a trivia game competition, and shows several sample questions. Students are tasked with writing the questions for the game using models that they have encountered in previous class materials and reading discussions. Sample questions here reflect some discussion topics in *Russian for STEM* class, where students practice and review active and passive participles while discussing significant contributions to science and technology.

- **Active participles**. What is the name of the scientist/author/explorer/writer who had written, created, proven (the expression which uses past active participle)?
  Sample questions: *Как зовут физиков, получивших Нобелевскую премию за открытие графена?* [What is the name of the physicists who received the Nobel Prize for their discovery of graphene?] *Как зовут инженера, руководившего полётом Юрия Гагарина?* [What is the name of the engineer who oversaw Yuri Gagarin's flight?]

- **Passive participle and review of dates**. What year, decade, or century something was discovered (built, created, proven, described, predicted)?
  Sample questions. *В каком году был основан Московский Государственный Университет?* [In what year was the Moscow State University founded?] *В каком веке было изобретено радио?* [In what century was the radio invented?]

- **Passive participle + instrumental case of the subject** (a construction that is often difficult to master). By whom was something discovered (built, created, proven, described, predicted)?
  Sample questions: *Кем был открыт периодический закон химических элементов?* [By whom was the periodic law of chemical elements discovered?] *Кем была создана известная компьютерная игра "Тетрис"?* [By whom was the famous computer game Tetris created?]

- **Gerunds (verbal adverbs)**. Describing a historical context or "accidental" discoveries.
  Sample question: *Как зовут учёного восемнадцатого века, который открыл атмосферу Венеры, наблюдая солнечное затмение?* [What is the name of the eighteenth-century scientist who discovered the atmosphere of Venus while observing the solar eclipse?]

In the case study of science trivia facts, students can include some questions about scientists and discoveries that were explored in the course curriculum or refer to texts discussed in class, as well as some questions about the general history of science facts. Students must provide a factually correct answer to their questions as part of their homework. The assignment and question topics can be modified depending on the course or unit topic and grammar content. Depending on the group size, students write 5–8 questions (more questions for a smaller group, and fewer questions for a larger group, to allow time for sharing).

Since the study of participles is often paired with historical content, this review activity can easily be tailored to a variety of topics. In addition to grammatical focus, this unit yields itself nicely for review and practice of vocabulary in different domains as well as creating a summative lesson to conclude the unit, such as the study of geography, historical periods, films, traditions, and other content-based topics.

Trivia questions may be submitted as part of homework, in which case the instructor can correct them ahead of time. Alternatively, students can bring their questions to class. Then, the teacher has the job of curating the questions during small-group work and making corrections as the teams prepare for the game. The case study in this chapter focuses on science trivia facts, but this format is well-suited for many other themes, such as history, cultural history, the study of traditions or holidays, geography, and many others.

Team discussion in class

To start the game, the class is divided into two teams. Each team is tasked with selecting a team name in connection with the game topic. The following 15–20 minutes, the two teams share and answer the questions each student wrote. Students must speak the target language when moderating the discussion; they take turns posing their questions to the teammates, asking them to respond, and providing correct answers. This is an excellent moment for spontaneous conversation practice, since the students are focused on recalling trivia facts and often produce spontaneous responses that come naturally in the context of game preparation, such as: "*Я не знал(а)! Хороший вопрос! Это очень трудно! Давайте выберем этот вопрос!*" [I didn't know! Great question! This is very hard! Let's pick this question]. In case when in the heat of the game everyone forgets some well-known basic facts, there is always a lot of laughter. The teammates listen to their group questions, answer them, and discuss if the question is too easy, too hard, or too specific and select their questions. Depending on the number of participants, the goal is to have each student on the team contribute a question and be ready to ask their question clearly during the game round.

Each team selects ten main and two extra questions, in case there is a question overlap or a tiebreaker situation. Depending on the size of the group, each student shares all the questions they brought or select a few to share with their teammates as they develop the question set for the opponent team.

During this part of the lesson, it is important the teams sit on opposite sides of the classroom, if space allows, so they don't hear each other. With online classes, this is easily arranged through breakout rooms. The instructor splits the time evenly between the two teams and listens to their discussions (if needed, helping to rephrase and make sure the general content of the question is within the target vocabulary).

Conducting the game in class

The teacher writes the team names on the board and acts as the game moderator, prompting the teams to ask their questions and monitoring the timing of responses. Students agree to set their phones aside and not to look up the answers during the game. Depending on the length of the class, the teacher can set the maximum time for the teams to confer and discuss their responses.

The teacher invites a student from team A to ask the question; students in team B deliberate and announce their answer. A countdown timer can be used here as well. If the answer is correct, team B gets a point. The teacher keeps track of correct responses on the board. If the question must use a word that requires clarification, the teacher may write that word on the board. Then, a student from team B asks their question, and team A deliberates and announces their response. The preparation steps and the shared context allows for consistent target language use – an important and challenging part of RFL instruction (Comer, 2013). Since the context of the game is clear, it is easy to keep it entirely in the target language, for example: *Команда А задаёт вопрос. Команда Б готова? Кто хочет задать следующий вопрос? Осталась одна минута!* [Team A asks the question. Is team B ready? Who would like to ask the next question? One minute left!]

After the questions have been exchanged by each team, the teacher tallies the responses. In case of a tiebreaker, students may ask an additional question. And if the answer is even, it's a draw, or *победила дружба* [friendship has the victory].

De-brief and reflections

If there is time at the end of the session, the teacher may project a slide with "*вопросы о вопросах*" ["questions about the questions"]:

- What was your favorite question? [*Какой вопрос вам понравился больше всего?*]
- What was the most difficult question? [*По-вашему, какой вопрос был самым трудным?*]
- What did you learn today? [*Что вы узнали сегодня?*]
- What did you know before but forgot? [*Какие факты вы знали раньше, но забыли во время игры?*]

At the end of such a trivia game class, students often remark how fun it was and feel accomplished as they realize that they were speaking in the target language for the entire hour. Moreover, during several semesters, students have requested to play a similar game again when reviewing a different unit or conducting end-of-semester review. This positive response by the students shows that even though the learners are repeating the key patterns (be it dates, unit vocabulary, or grammar constructions, such as participles that they learned during the unit), the focus on the competitive aspects of the game and sharing the knowledge of trivia facts creates an authentic communication situation. This game, inherently, has many features we strive to integrate into a language classroom: negotiation of meaning and strategy, team discussion, decision-making, competition, and applause for correctly answered questions. All this creates ample opportunities for authentic and spontaneous communication, making learning practice an epiphenomenon of play.

JeopardyLabs review trivia game

A different version of a trivia game can be played using the formats of popular game shows, such as *Jeopardy* or *Who Wants to Be a Millionaire?* These platforms are discussed briefly in Khotimsky and Leontyeva (2022), and I would like to offer further ideas here. Although there are many platforms for creating online quiz games, a reliable and free choice is *JeopardyLabs* (https://jeopardylabs.com/), where instructors can also find examples of existing games, many with cultural content. *Flippity* is another easy-to-use resource that allows to create trivia games (among other activities) using Google spreadsheets: https://flippity.net/ (for a more detailed overview, see Spasova, 2021).

Jeopardy games typically include several question categories in the ascending question difficulty (from 100 to 500 points). TV game questions are traditionally framed as statements (e.g., "The longest river in Siberia"), but the online game template is editable, so instructors may use trivia facts or trivia questions in the game. Depending on the content of the class and the pedagogical purpose of the game, it can be more form-focused (game categories recap the grammar of the unit, such as "cases," "time expressions," "pronouns," aspect pairs, etc.) or content-focused (using such categories as "holidays," "traditions," "film characters," and others in accordance with the class content). The *JeopardyLabs* platform is free, although its affordable paid version allows instructors to upload or embed images and videos in the questions.

During the game, the class is divided into several teams (the number of teams can be adjusted); in addition, the platform allows assigning short team names, which helps the game atmosphere and aids community building. The teams take turns selecting the category and strategizing the question choices and responding (the teacher or the game moderator reveals the correct answer, which is part of the template). The platform is very easy to use, and it also automatically tallies the score, so the instructor can focus on team interaction. Depending on the question number and difficulty, this game may take 20–25 minutes to play (time may vary depending on the number of categories and the speed of responses). It offers an engaging opportunity to review vocabulary or grammar topics or to create a summary of the unit and discuss key topics of the course. This game is also well-suited for conversation table or social hour activities.

A variation of the *Jeopardy* game includes soliciting questions from the students. As part of homework and review, students submit questions addressing several categories that will be featured in the game. The teacher reviews the assignment and incorporates several questions from each student into different categories. In addition to typical game strategy, there is also an element of anticipation, luck, and recognition, as the game is based on student-generated content. Similar to the game discussed in the previous section, playing *Jeopardy* enables the teacher to maximize comprehensible use of the target language: "*Какой вопрос?* [Which question?]/*Какая категория?* [Which category?] – "*Падежи 500*" [Cases 500]. There is usually a lot of excitement around question category and number negotiation, all of which take place in the target language.

Trivia game project

Jeopardy-style trivia can also serve as a project-based task for a unit of the entire course, in which students work individually, in pairs, or in small groups to develop the game and facilitate a game session in class. Ideally, students should create the questions in advance and have the instructor review them and suggest corrections. This game can be form- or content-focused. The main difference with this setup is that one student or a small group of students then serves as game hosts, and the teacher may opt to join one of the teams.

Students would need to notify the instructor ahead of time that they are working on such a project to make schedule adjustments. Coordinated in advance, such class creates an opportunity for maximizing the communicative aspect of language learning: the student(s) encourage their classmates to create team names, record them in the game, and prompt each team to take turns in responding to questions. With science or geography trivia, the teacher might join one of the teams; however, in the case of a grammar review, it may give an unfair advantage to one of the teams. This truly becomes a student-led class that includes peer-to-peer interaction and negotiation in the target language, allowing ample opportunities for spontaneous communication as the teams discuss their strategies for question choice and deliberate about the answers. Based on students' informal feedback, they enjoyed being "teacher for the day" and using target language when serving as game moderators.

Lessons learned

This game has been a popular activity in my second- and third-year Russian classrooms in MIT, successfully using both traditional team-based trivia and the *Jeopardy*-style trivia game. I have used it since 2015 in second-year RFL classes and in third-year RFL content courses. It is particularly effective as a summative activity for such topics as geography, history, culture, science, and technology – in other words, topics where students can share trivia facts. At the beginner and intermediate levels, trivia games serve well as a focus on grammar or vocabulary practice. Lastly, these games can be used for end-of-term celebration activities and extracurricular events.

One of the key lessons for team-based trivia is to balance the limited class time between preparation, team deliberation, and the actual game: oftentimes, discussions and deliberations last longer as students try to brainstorm the answers, which leaves little time for reflection.

I would also recommend that teachers take the time to model discursive exchanges for students at lower levels, such as the phrases needed for moderating the game, discussing the choices of questions, and reflecting on the question content. This can be facilitated by using a handout or a slide with key phrases that are helpful for sustaining the group conversation in Russian.

The third "lesson learned" is the emphasis on using familiar vocabulary in phrasing the question or adding an extra challenge of rephrasing the questions using grammatical forms that should be practiced more (e.g., encouraging the students to rephrase *Кто открыл . . . ?* [Who discovered . . .] through question models that include participles, such as *Кем были открыты . . . ?* [By whom were . . . discovered] or "*Как зовут исследователя, открывшего . . . ?*" [What is the name of the researcher who discovered . . .]).

Lastly, during the game preparation stage, it's helpful to have a time limit, and if one of the teams is ready sooner, the instructor may join them for practicing their questions.

In terms of the game dynamics, students in different groups have experimented with adding more negotiation into the game. For example, the teams can deliberate and decide whether they may allow "half point" scores for responses that have a small deviation from the correct answer (such as suggesting a date range in place of a specific year). Students also enjoy giving clues for responses, all of which increase the communicative aspect of the game. Common student responses at the end of such class sessions are "This was fun," "It was great to speak Russian the entire class," and "I learned a lot today."

The trivia game class session usually flies by, creating authentic communication and information exchange in the target language. The game setup enables the students to share information, make choices, exchange ideas, and create a team strategy, all while speaking the target language and learning (or recalling) a variety of facts on the class topic. In sum, within the broad benefits of the game-based approach, trivia games can be specifically used to expand the range of topics for discussion, create an environment for maximizing target language use, and promote social interaction while building classroom community.

References

Comer, W. (2013). Thinking through teacher talk: Increasing target language use in the beginning Russian classroom. *Russian Language Journal*, *63*(1), 89–110.

Crawford, M. (2002). Teaching conversation with trivia. *English Teaching Forum Magazine*, April 2002, 20–25.

Crawford, M., & Powell, T. (2001). Developing listening subskills with trivia. *The Language Teacher*, *25*(5), 10–13.

Dubreil, S. (2020). Using games for language learning in the age of social distancing. *Foreign Language Annals*, *53*(2), 250–259. https://doi.org/10.1111/flan.12465

Evans-Romaine, K., Murphy, D., Tumarkin, A., Marshall, L., & Almuratova, A. (2021). Connecting through language and culture learning during the COVID-19 pandemic: The University of Wisconsin – Madison Russian Flagship Program. *Russian Language Journal*, *71*(2), 23–38.

Khotimsky, M., & Leontyeva, A. (2022). Lessons of the Pandemic: A critical look at digital tools for online and face-to-face instruction of Russian as a foreign language. In S. Nuss & C. Martin (Eds.), *Student-centered approaches to teaching Russian: Insights, strategies, and adaptations*. Routledge.

Klimova, O. (2021). From blended learning to emergency remote and online teaching: Successes, challenges, and prospects of a Russian language program before and during the pandemic. *Russian Language Journal*, *71*(2), 73–86.

Leaver, B., & Cassel, C. (2020). The shifting paradigm in Russian language pedagogy: From communicative language teaching to transformative language learning and teaching. In E. Dengub, I. Dubinina, & J. Merrill (Eds.), *The art of teaching Russian* (pp. 147–162). Georgetown University Press.

Leontyeva, A. [Леонтьева, А]. (2018, 2020). *50 games for Russian language classes* [50 Игр на уроках русского языка]. Russkii Yazyk. Kursy [Русский язык. Курсы].

Nuss, S., & Whitehead Martelle, W. (Eds.). (2022). Task-based instruction for teaching Russian as a foreign language: Perspectives and practice. In S. Nuss & W. Whitehead Martelle (Eds.), *Task-based instruction for teaching Russian as a foreign language* (pp. 1–15). Routledge.

Nuss, S. V., & Martin, C. L. (Eds.). (2022). *Student-centered approaches to Russian language teaching: Insights, strategies, and adaptations.* Taylor & Francis.

Pastushenkov, D. (2022). Task-based peer interaction in Russian as a second/foreign language classes. In S. Nuss & W. Whitehead Martelle (Eds.), *Task-based instruction for teaching Russian as a foreign language* (pp. 152–170). Routledge.

Plass, J., Mayer, R., & Homer, B. (Eds.). (2020). *Handbook of game-based learning* (pp. 409–436). MIT Press.

Razin, A., & Kingisepp, L. [Разин, А., и Кингисепп, Л.] (2018). *"Everyone plays!" 101 communication games for teachers of Russian as a foreign language* [*"Играют все!" 101 коммуникативная игра для учителей русского языка как иностранного*]. Keelekeskus. https://gamekeskus.ee/ru/kursused/elektronnaja-kniga-igrajut-vse/

Reinders, H. (2012). Introduction. In H. Reinders (Ed.), *Digital games in language learning and teaching* (pp. 1–10). Palgrave Macmillan.

Reinhardt, J. (2018). *Gameful second and foreign language teaching and learning. Theory, research, and practice.* Palgrave McMillan.

Reinhardt, J., & Thorne, S. L. (2020). Digital games as language-learning environments. In J. Plass, R. Mayer, & B. Homer (Eds.), *Handbook of game-based learning* (pp. 409–436). MIT Press.

Spasova, S. (2021). Flippity for online games and tools. *FLTMAG*, March 4, 2021. https://fltmag.com/flippity-online-games-tools/

Zakorchevnaia, L. R. [Закорчевная, Л. Р.] (2020). *Russian language. A game book for beginners* [Русский язык. Игровое пособие для начинающих]. Flinta.

Part III

Building language structures through games

Chapter 5

The use of authentic games in teaching L2 Russian grammar

Anna Leontyeva and Ekaterina Schnittke

CHAPTER SUMMARY

Authentic games – games that are played by people for entertainment outside the educational environment – are most often used in language teaching for developing vocabulary and speaking skills, but rarely for teaching grammar. In this chapter, we argue for the potential of authentic games to develop grammatical accuracy by offering opportunities for multiple repetitions of linguistic patterns. We review the literature on the history of using authentic games in the instruction of Russian as a foreign language (RFL) and then demonstrate how authentic games and their adaptations can be integrated into the curriculum of university courses for students with different levels of proficiency. We will share concrete examples of games that address some of the grammar points that are particularly challenging to L2 Russian learners: expressions of similarity (тоже [also], такой же, как [the same as], etc.), modal constructions with нужен [needed], instrumental constructions with and without the preposition с [with], the noun–adjective agreement and genitive plurals of nouns (кот-ов [cat-GEN.PL] vs. лошад-ей [horse-GEN.PL]). We propose three strategies for using and adapting authentic games for teaching purposes: (1) with no modifications, (2) modifying some of the game elements and facilitating additional output, and (3) modifying an authentic game based on popular game mechanics. The paper provides a practical guide to implementing the proposed games in teaching L2 Russian.

КРАТКОЕ СОДЕРЖАНИЕ ГЛАВЫ

Аутентичные игры – игры, в которые мы играем без принуждения извне, для удовольствия, а не ради достижения каких-либо образовательных результатов, – в современной методике преподавания иностранных языков (в том числе русского языка как иностранного – РКИ) используются чаще всего при работе со словарем или для развития навыков устной речи, но достаточно редко используются для обучения грамматике. В данной главе мы предлагаем обзор истории использования аутентичных игр в преподавании РКИ в России и мире.

DOI: 10.4324/9781003369721-8

Мы демонстрируем грамматический потенциал аутентичных игр и доказываем, что такие игры могут стать отличной заменой стандартных подстановочных упражнений на повторение изучаемых грамматических конструкций. Данная возможность обусловлена тем, что, играя в аутентичную игру, мы, как правило, многократно повторяем во внешней или внутренней речи одну и ту же фразу. Если эта фраза интересна с точки зрения усвоения грамматических структур языка, игру можно смело использовать в качестве упражнения на повторение даже на начальных уровнях освоения языка. При подготовке аутентичной игры для урока РКИ, предлагается использовать одну из трех стратегий: (1) использовать игру без изменений, (2) изменить элементы игры, не соответствующие уровню учащихся, добавив правило экстернализации внутренней речи, или (3) использовать механику популярной аутентичной игры, полностью заменив ее сеттинг на более актуальный для студентов конкретной группы. В работе представлены конкретные примеры работы с аутентичной игрой на занятиях. Мы рассматриваем игры, актуальные при работе со следующими грамматическими темами: конструкции, выражающие сходство (*тоже, такой же, как*), конструкции со словом *нужен*, конструкции с творительным комитативным (*с чем-либо*) и инструментальным (*чем-либо*), согласование существительного и прилагательного в именительном падеже по роду и числу и образование форм родительного падежа множественного числа существительных (*кот-ов* vs. *лошад-ей*). Для каждой из рассматриваемых игр описаны варианты работы с ней.

Why authentic games?

Playing games is a long-standing tradition in a language learning classroom. The field of ludic *research* in language teaching has particularly flourished since the emergence of digital technologies and almost exclusively focuses on the integration of computer games (Reinhardt, 2018; Reinhardt & Sykes, 2012). On a *practical* level, authentic games, digital or analog, are predominantly used for raising students' motivation, developing their vocabulary (Boyle, 1993; Nurmukhamedov & Sadler, 2020; Tsai & Tsai, 2018), pragmatic competence (Ko & Eslami, 2021; Sykes, 2009; Shirazi et al., 2016), and conversational skills (Pastushenkov, 2022; York, 2020; York et al., 2019), but seldom for grammar acquisition (Leontyeva [Леонтьева], 2018). Activities that fall under the umbrella of "grammar games" are rarely authentic games, as they often do not meet some of the essential criteria to qualify as games (discussed in section "The principles of a game"). Rather, they may be game-informed (Reinhardt & Sykes, 2012) and include some game elements (scores, competition) but remain essentially non-game activities. In this chapter, *authentic games* refers to games that are played by people for entertainment outside the educational environment. Some examples include chess, poker, dominoes.

The need for ecological, real-life activities that aim at grammar acquisition is especially urgent in teaching morphologically rich languages, such as Russian (Comer, 2020; Nuss, 2022; Kogan & Bondarenko, 2022). We believe that authentic games or their adaptations can fill this need: they have proven to be replayable and liked by native and L2 Russian speakers.

Authentic games have a great potential for increasing grammatical accuracy of language learners because they imply multiple repetitions of the same language pattern. These repetitions often happen in the player's mind only and usually do not get verbalized in an authentic setting (see examples in section "The 'externalize!' technique"). To unlock this potential output, we propose to bring these internal language patterns to surface through a technique of inner speech externalization. Thus, even silent games could afford meaningful interaction that leads to output with a high density of target forms.

We open the conversation by reviewing the gaming landscape in L2 Russian pedagogy. Next, we identify the principles that govern our method of choosing and using games and analyze the theoretical underpinnings behind these principles. Finally, we describe five games that aim to help L2 learners of Russian achieve high accuracy in the use of five Russian language structures.

Games in the Russian-language classroom

Games as a pedagogical tool became popular in teaching RFL since the communicative approach (Canale & Swain, 1980; Littlewood et al., 1981) has become a widely accepted teaching model. Many RFL teachers have resorted to the wealth of literature on games in English as a foreign language (EFL) (Hadfield, 2003; Lee, 1965; Nurmukhamedov & Sadler, 2020; Rinvolucri & Davis, 1995; Ur & Wright, 1992; Wright et al., 2006) and adapt them for their own purposes. Many descriptions of games specific to teaching RFL have also appeared in and outside Russia (Akishina [Акишина] et al., 1990; Bitekhtina & Vaishnore [Битехтина и Вайшноре], 2009; Boyle, 1993; Kaznyshkina [Казнышкина], 2012; Kitaygorodskaya [Китайгородская] et al., 1993; Klementieva & Chubarova [Клементьева и Чубарова], 2007; Kogan & Kapustin, 2020; Leontyeva [Леонтьева], 2010, 2018; Razin & Kingisepp [Разин и Кингисепп], 2018; Slabuho [Слабухо], 2015; Stohler & Makarova, 2011; Esmantova [Эсмантова], 2008). Games in these collections use gamifying elements, such as dice, cards, and game boards, as accessories for performing linguistic or non-linguistic tasks. Even though these games make learning more engaging and interactive, most of them would not normally be played outside the classroom, and very few can qualify as *games* based on the criteria developed in ludology (detailed in the next section). Moreover, even when authentic or original author games are used, they usually target vocabulary: *Alias* (Nurmukhamedov & Sadler, 2020; Balakina [Балакина], 2020; Obukhova [Обухова], 2015; Skorik [Скорик], 2016), its Russian version *Шляпа* [hat] (Leontyeva [Леонтьева], 2018), *Code Names* or speaking skills (*Rory-story Cubes*), and *Экивоки* [equivocation] (Leontyeva [Леонтьева], 2018; Obukhova [Обухова], 2015; Smirnova [Смирнова], 2020).

The few examples of popular authentic games used for grammar practice include *tic-tac-toe*; *bingo* (lotto); *Simon Says* (Wright et al., 2006; Akishina & Kagan [Акишина и Каган], 2014); board games featuring verbs of motion, for example,

Такси [Taxi] (Obukhova [Обухова], 2015); dominoes for learning cases (Kitaygorodskaya [Китйагородская] et al., 1993; Leontyeva [Леонтьева], 2018); and some other board games described in Leontyeva [Леонтьева] (2018). However, there are very few, if any, reports of game implementation that could serve as practical guidance to teachers, even in the more prolific EFL literature. A notable exception to the digital and theoretical biases of game research is the work done within the multiliteracy approach (Cope & Kalantzis, 2013), which promotes the use of traditional and "low-tech" commercial tabletop games in the classrooms in addition to digital ones (deHaan, 2019; Jones, 2020; York, 2019, 2020; York et al., 2019; York et al., 2021, and other publications of *Ludic Language Pedagogy (LLP)*, n.d.). Although within this stream of research the emphasis is not *on* the playing but rather *around* it, the works of the LLP project provide much insight and guidance to game implementation in L2 instruction, most notably in the areas of teacher mediation and empirical accounts of actual game-based practice.

Leontyeva [Леонтьева] (2018) noted and demonstrated that tabletop games have an enormous potential for teaching grammar. We would like to elaborate on this statement, supporting it with a theoretical framework and providing specific examples from practice. We will begin with the major principles of selecting or developing a game for grammar.

Three principles of a game for grammar and their theoretical underpinnings

Principle 1: the game must be a game

Following Johan Huizinga, we believe games must be "accompanied by a feeling of tension, joy and the consciousness that it is different from ordinary life" (Huizinga, 1949, p. 28). Roger Caillois identifies core criteria that constitute a game activity based on Huizinga's work (Caillois, 1961, pp. 9–10):

- The game is *free*. It is played voluntarily for fun, and players are free to enter or quit it whenever they wish.
- The game is a *separate* occupation, isolated from ordinary life and limited to its own time and space.
- The game's results are *uncertain* and cannot be predetermined.
- The game is *unproductive*. It creates no wealth or goods. Prizes are not a product of the game in the economical sense. Even in games that involve money as their element, for example, gambling, money merely passes from one owner to another.
- The game is either governed by *rules* which model game reality and suspend ordinary laws and behaviors during playing or is a make-believe: players accept its alternative reality and act *as if* they were part of this reality.

The advantage of authentic games for teaching grammar is that we do not have to be concerned about the degree of their "gameness." They are games by definition, played and enjoyed by many. However, there is one criterion posited by Caillois that requires a special consideration. According to Caillois and Huizinga, a game is a voluntary activity. The player always has the option to stop or quit the game. In a classroom setting, we hardly give such freedom to our students. We solve this problem by bringing to class games of high appeal or by developing new games based on the game mechanics of other popular games. We also provide students with opportunities to freely choose a game to be replayed. Our main criterion for choosing a game is the game's reputation among peer native speakers: if they play the game for fun, our learners will most likely enjoy it too. When we play games with friends and family, we are constantly on guard for their teaching potential.

Principle 2: the game is a task

One of the major qualities of games is that they provide meaningful, interactive, goal-oriented activities with a non-linguistic outcome. With these properties, games can be paralleled to a task, defined in the task-based language teaching (TBLT) as a meaning-oriented activity that requires learners to use the target language in order to achieve a specified objective (Bygate et al., 2001) and provides a solid theoretical underpinning for our choice of focus on form. Theoretical and practical considerations for teaching RFL through task are most recently developed in Nuss and Whitehead Martelle (2022).

We focus on games that, in TBLT terms, yield "inherently repetitive tasks" (Gatbonton & Segalowitz, 2005, p. 332), in which the activity goal is attained through repeating the target form over and over. Attaining an increase in grammar accuracy through focus on form is thus a natural and welcome "side effect."

The uniqueness of game-based tasks is that they can be implemented at any level, including novice.[1] It was argued elsewhere that the best suited tasks for beginner learners are those that are input-based (Erlam & Ellis, 2019; Kogan & Bondarenko, 2022). Games afford output-oriented tasks at all proficiency levels, if one applies the technique of "inner speech externalization."

The "externalize!" technique

Sometimes, the opportunities of repeating the desired language patterns are embedded in the game, as, for example, in the *Noodles* game discussed in section "The games." Others require minor modifications to afford a repetitive task. Many games are played silently or with minimal language output, like "Yes!" or "Oh, no!" This does not necessarily mean that the game does not suit our purpose, as an internal monologue is constantly spinning in the player's head, even when the person is not required to say anything. For example, a chess player might be saying to herself something like, "I can't move here, so I'll go there." This pattern is repeated over and over, and that's what we want to bring out and verbalize. The technique for doing so is the "externalization of the inner speech." Taking advantage of the "magic circle" that delineates the game space and suspends real-world rules (Huizinga, 1949), we introduce a magic spell rule: "Externalize!" This technique is illustrated in section "The games" by the games of memory, dominoes, and grammar SET.

Pedagogical implications

The game being a task implies a specific procedure of three-stage progression of gaming implementation: pre-, during, and post-play (Gilabert & Malicka, 2021; Willis, 1996). One of the benefits of such an incremental approach is reduction of the cognitive load in the case of complex game rules by "distinct separation of gameplay and tutorial stages" (York, 2020, p. 7).

The benefits of task repetition translate into the recommendation of replaying the game (Ahmadian, 2013). Practitioners who use board games in their L2 teaching have repeatedly noted that the first playing attempts are usually less enjoyable due to an incomplete grasp of the rules and expected language requirements (York, 2019, 2020). It is usually in the subsequent gameplays that learners can perform more fluently, both as players and as language users, and genuinely enjoy playing. Replaying is also desirable from the ecological perspective: people do replay their favorite games. To this end, in our L2 classes we offer our students opportunities to choose a game from the ones previously played. Such practice provides a great tool for space repetition and formative assessment.

Within a setting that is bound to a prescribed curriculum with its own learning objectives, the game-based task can fit into a present-practice-produce (PPP) lesson design as a less-guided or independent practice at any level.

Principle 3: the game should be "cost-effective"

While acknowledging the diverse benefits of games in L2 pedagogy, teachers are often concerned about the activity being time-consuming. It takes teachers' time and effort to design and create a game. Then it takes class time to explain and learn the rules. The initial trial-and-error stages of gameplay are often slow. One commonly heard caveat of integrating games in L2 teaching is the heavy cognitive tax resulting from the necessity to simultaneously attend to the complex game rules and new language patterns (Reinhardt, 2018, p. 107; York, 2020). All these are reasonable concerns, and we suggest some "cost-effectiveness" criteria to consider when selecting or developing a game.

The game gains should outweigh its expenditures

The expenditures here are the time and effort spent on game development, explanation and learning the rules, and gameplay itself. The gains are commensurate with the density of target patterns the game affords and with student agency. The density is the number of target forms per unit of time and the share of target forms in the overall speech output during the game. Student agency is the involvement of any given student in producing target forms at any given point of time. How long does a student need to wait for her turn? How long is each student's move? How much is a student engaged during the silent phase while waiting for her turn?

Pedagogical implications

Using or adapting authentic games is the simplest way to save time and effort spent on the design, creation, and explanation of rules. The more familiar a game is or the simpler its rules are, the more cost-effective it is. The Noodles game [Лапша] (section "The games" later) is an example of an authentic game originally developed for purposes other than language teaching that can be brought to class unmodified.

Sometimes we need to make minor changes to an existing game, such as finding images to align with the vocabulary of the students or balancing grammatical forms across grammatical categories, for example, gender, number, etc. This strategy is illustrated by the memory [Мемори] and the dominoes [Домино] games (section "The games" later).

Sometimes we borrow well-known game mechanics and adapt them for our own game that we develop from scratch. This can be extremely time-consuming, and it is crucial to carefully weigh the gains against the expenditures in this case. Does the game address an important language challenge faced by the majority of learners? Will you be able to reuse this game? Will you be able to recycle the game by adjusting it to other grammar topics? For example, our game Baba Yaga's Zoo [Зоопарк Бабы-Яги] (section "The games") was developed for practicing genitive plurals of nouns but could be used with no changes whatsoever for practicing the declension of numerals or the conjugation patterns of the verbs *менять (что на что)* [change (something for something)], *нехватать (кому чего)* [be missing (something for someone)], etc.

The games

In this section, we will describe the games we use to teach grammar. First, we will show how we use an authentic game with no modification (the Noodles [*Лапша*]). Then we will present three games that require slight modifications along with the introduction of the "Externalize!" rule to achieve our teaching goals (memory [*Мемори*] and dominoes [*Домино*]). Finally, we will talk about the games we developed in our teaching practice based on popular game mechanics (grammar SET [*Сет: грамматика*] and Baba Yaga's Zoo [*Зоопарк Бабы-Яги*]).

This section illustrates that many authentic games feature a very distinct language pattern repeated by players multiple times. If this pattern aligns with our teaching objectives, we can bring the game to class and use it for practice that targets this pattern. The teacher's challenge here is to notice this pattern and introduce it into the players' required output.

A short remark on our teaching environment is due before we begin. We teach RFL in a tertiary setting to students with various L1s and at different Russian proficiency levels; most of these students participated in a one-semester exchange program. Our teaching is informed by the weak version of the communicative approach (Canale & Swain, 1980; Littlewood et al., 1981; Mitchell, 2002; Richards, 2006; Farrell & Jacobs, 2020) and some elements of TBLT with a focus on form (Long, 2016; Willis, 1996). We use games described in the following as a replacement for less-guided or independent practice. We strive to collect or create games for every grammar topic and thus minimize or eliminate the mechanical drill altogether.

The Noodles [Лапша], intermediate and advanced

We begin with a party game called the **Noodles** [Лапша], originally created by the V-Agon [В-Агон] laboratory of educational games (Novosibirsk; https://lab-igr.vsite.biz/#home) for developing lateral thinking and soft skills. In this game, the players are shown pairs of pictures with well-known cultural phenomena that seemingly have nothing in common, for example, Marilyn Monroe in one picture and the pyramid of Cheops in the other. The players have one minute to explain in writing why the two phenomena in the pictures are shown together. Then all the explanations are read aloud, and each player votes for the best one. The author of the best explanation gets a point, and the next pair of pictures is shown to the players. It is important to suggest explanations that are not only unique but also fit other players' tastes and are likely to score points. The object of the game is to score the highest points.

Target grammar

Note that all the explanations require one grammar pattern – constructions that express similarity. Therefore, depending on the level of proficiency of our students, the game is a perfect way to practice constructions with *тоже* [also] (*Мэрилин Монро очень красивая и пирамида Хеопса тоже (красивая)* [Marilyn Monroe is beautiful, and the pyramid of Cheops is also beautiful] (novice low–novice high); *как . . . так и . . .* [as . . . as]; *. . . такой же, как и . . .* [the same as]; *они оба/обе . . .* [both are]; *и тот и другой . . .* [both are] etc. (intermediate high and advanced).[2]

Materials

The pictures can be prepared in advance by the teacher. Alternatively, the pictures can be supplied by the students in a pre-game task (two or three words per student) and then be randomly paired. While this reduces the surprise effect, it is a useful time-saver for the teacher and a way for students to have a voice.

How to play

The game can be played in teams of four to six players. In larger groups, the best choices within each group can be voted on by the entire class. Whether teaching online or offline, we use Padlet, an interactive board that allows for sharing the explanations, voting, and quick corrective feedback if needed.

Time

Five rounds (approximately 15 minutes total time) are a good number to enjoy the process, but it can be changed according to your time limits.

Memory [Мемори], novice high and intermediate low

This popular game provides a good example of how externalized inner speech can help us achieve our teaching goals. The object of the game is to turn over as many pairs of matching cards as one can.

Target grammar

Our teaching objective is to provide a context for practicing constructions with a dative subject and the modal *нужен* [*needed*]: *X-у нужен Y* [*X needs Y, lit. Y is needed for X*]. The modal must agree in gender and number with the noun, which requires much practice, especially at the novice high and intermediate low levels.

Materials

You will need 8 or 12 picture cards with images that reflect the communicative topic that this construction is associated with. In our textbook, the topic is "health" [Здоровье]. We use eight words for different kinds of medications, counterbalanced across gender and number: *микстура* [medicine, mixture], *мазь* [ointment] (f); *сироп* [syrup], *спрей* [spray] (m); *обезболивающее* [painkiller], *жаропонижающее* [fever reducer] (n); *таблетки* [pills], *капли* [drops] (pl).

Modifications

The only modification to the original rules is the introduction of the "Externalize!" rule. The inner speech we want to verbalize runs like this: *О! Таблетки! Мне нужны еще таблетки. Хм, нет, это не таблетки, а сироп. Мне не нужен сироп* [Oh, pills! Now I need more pills. Mm, these are not pills; this is a syrup. I don't need syrup].

How to play

The game can be played in groups of two or three during less-guided practice, with all playing cards on the table, facedown. The object of the game is to collect a greater number of pairs of identical cards. The teacher monitors the students' activity and notes mistakes, if any, on the board to discuss later.

Time

When played with eight cards, as suggested here, the game takes approximately 10 minutes. The popularity of this game is an important advantage and time-saver, as there is no need to spend much time explaining game mechanics or rules.

Dominoes [Домино], intermediate

The traditional version of dominoes has been shown to help practice Russian cases (Kitaygorodskaya [Китайгородская] et al., 1993; Leontyeva [Леонтьева], 2018). In what follows we propose another way of using *dominoes* to teach grammar through adding the "Externalize!" rule along with changing game design, while keeping most of the well-known traditional rules and the mechanics of matching.

In the traditional version, the game contains 28 tiles, each divided into two halves, each half featuring a number of pips – from zero to six. The players match the number of pips on the tiles in their hands to the number of pips on the tiles laid out on the table). The objective is to empty one's own hand while blocking the opponent's. The score is determined at the end of the game by counting the pips on the tiles left in each player's hand. The player with the least number of pips is the winner.

Target grammar

We use *dominoes* to practice the instrumental case with or without the preposition *с* [with]: *коробка с . . .* [a box with . . .] vs. *делать что-то чем-то* [to do something with something (an instrument or material)] that in Russian uses a noun in the instrumental case: *рисовать кистью* [to paint with a brush, lit. to paint + brush.INSTR]. Instrumental constructions cause much trouble to L2 Russian learners, and even advanced students tend to use the preposition where it should not be.

We play this game at intermediate level, rather than at novice high, when the instrumental of instrument (писать ручкой [write with a pen]) is introduced, because we have observed that these competing constructions begin to get confused at intermediate level.

Modifications and materials

We keep the general mechanics of *dominoes*, but with the following modifications:

1. We replace playing *tiles* with playing *cards*.
2. We replace the pips with images: *actions*, ranked 1–6; matching *instruments*, also ranked 1–6 to correspond with action images; and a *box*, ranked 0.

   The **action images** stand for verbs *писать* [write], *убивать* [kill], *фотографировать* [take pictures], *вытираться* [dry oneself], *рисовать* [paint], and *резать* [cut].
   The nouns for the matching **instruments** must be counterbalanced across number and declension type. We have chosen:

   - Two nouns for *-а/-я* declension, one hard, one soft stem:

     ручка [pen] and
     магия [magic]

   - Two nouns for masculine/neuter non-*а/-я* declension, one hard stem, one stem ending in *-ц* that takes the "soft-series" endings:

     смартфон [smartphone] (masculine) and
     полотенце [towel], (neuter)

   - One feminine noun ending in soft sign:

     кисть [brush]

   - One plural noun:

     ножницы [scissors]

   The "**box**" image replaces 0 and represents a noun that requires the preposition *с* [with]: *коробка с . . .* [a box with something].

3. The next modification concerns the number of pieces. The traditional *domino* set contains 28 tiles. In our version, there are no repeating combinations, since the matching images are not identical (as they are in the traditional game). In our set, each of the seven "action" images and a "box" combines with each of the "instrument" images, yielding 7 × 7 = 49 pieces (see Figure 5.1).

   The "action" images are ranked from 1 to 6 with red digits, whereas their matching instruments have blue digits. The "box" image has no number.
   Tip: In an easier-to-make (and play!) version, the images could be replaced with words.

4. Finally, we introduce the "Externalize!" rule: the students are instructed to verbalize why they are combining these specific pieces: *Можно писать ручкой!* [One can write with a pen!] *Коробка с магией!* [A box with magic!]

How to play

The game can be played by 2–4 players like the original dominoes, but each player draws eight cards from the stock, not seven. The players take turns matching the

писать 1	писать 1	писать 1	писать 1	писать 1	писать 1	писать 1
ручка 1	магия 2	смартфон 3	полотенце 4	кисть 5	ноги 6	коробка 0

побеждать 2	побеждать 2	побеждать 2	побеждать 2	побеждать 2	побеждать 2	побеждать 2
ручка 1	магия 2	смартфон 3	полотенце 4	кисть 5	ноги 6	коробка 0

фотографировать 3	фотографировать 3	фотографировать 3	фотографировать 3	фотографировать 3	фотографировать 3	фотографировать 3
ручка 1	магия 2	смартфон 3	полотенце 4	кисть 5	глаза 6	коробка 0

вытираться 4	вытираться 4	вытираться 4	вытираться 4	вытираться 4	вытираться 4	вытираться 4
ручка 1	магия 2	смартфон 3	полотенце 4	кисть 5	глаза 6	коробка 0

рисовать 5	рисовать 5	рисовать 5	рисовать 5	рисовать 5	рисовать 5	рисовать 5
ручка 1	магия 2	смартфон 3	полотенце 4	кисть 5	глаза 6	коробка 0

смотреть 6	смотреть 6	смотреть 6	смотреть 6	смотреть 6	смотреть 6	смотреть 6
ручка 1	магия 2	смартфон 3	полотенце 4	кисть 5	глаза 6	коробка 0

коробка 0	коробка 0	коробка 0	коробка 0	коробка 0	коробка 0	коробка 0
ручка 1	магия 2	смартфон 3	полотенце 4	кисть 5	глаза 6	коробка 0

Figure 5.1 Sample domino tiles.

ends of the action cards with those of the instruments. Red numbers must match blue ones. In other words, an action cannot be matched to the same action card (say, "write" with "write"). Only an "action instrument" combination with the same number on it or a "box instrument" is acceptable. The "box" can also combine with itself: "a box with a box" is fine. At the end of the game, the score is determined by counting the sum of numbers on the cards left.

Grammar SET [Сет: грамматика], novice low

We use SET [Сет], a card game by Marsha Jean Falco, to show how an authentic game can be adapted by changing its content *and* rules while keeping its mechanics. The object of the original game is to identify a SET of 3 cards from 12 cards placed faceup on the table according to intricate rules that we leave out of the chapter.

Target grammar

We opt out of the original rules and only borrow the idea of searching for sets and the real-time game mechanics[3] to practice the formation of adjectives that follow complex combinatorial rules which, in our experience, are dreaded by novice and often neglected by more advanced Russian learners, especially in writing. Our grammar SET [Сет: грамматика] addresses this specific issue.

The new game objective

The objective of our game is to gather four sets of 3 out of 12 cards. A SET is **an adjective stem**, **an ending,** and **a noun** that would yield a grammatical phrase. The players do so based on the variables of (1) the adjectival stem type (hard, as in *красный* [red]; soft, as in *синий* [blue]; or mixed, as in *хороший* [good], *русский* [Russian], *горячий* [hot]) and (2) the **gender** and the **number** of the noun.

Materials

For this game you will need 96 cards:

- 32 for nouns (8 × 4 for three genders and plural)
- 32 for adjective stems (8 × 4 for hard stems; stems ending with *г, к, х*; stems ending with *ж, ч, ш, щ*; and soft stems)
- 32 for adjective endings (we made 3 cards of *-ой*, 2 of *-ый*, 4 of *-ий*, 5 of *-ая*, 3 of *-яя*, 4 of *-ое*, 3 of *-ее*, 2 of *-ые*, and 6 of *-ие*)

We reached this combination through several trials and believe it strikes a good balance for dynamic gameplay, but the number of cards, of course, can be changed.

The nouns can correspond to the content of the unit that introduces adjectives or teacher's discretion. We made our deck with "Food" [*Еда*] vocabulary; see examples by following this QR code:

How to play

Similar to the original *SET*, the game is played by 2–6 players. At the beginning of each round, 12 random cards are laid faceup on the table. The rest of the cards are in the deck. Players begin searching for sets of an adjective stem, an ending, and a noun to form a correct phrase, for example, *свеж- + -ий + хлеб* [fresh bread]. The first player to find a set has to say a sentence using their phrase as a subject and adding to it a possessive pronoun as a predicate: *Свежий хлеб – мой!* [The fresh bread is mine!]. If all the other players agree that the sentence and the adjective form are correct, the player keeps these three cards and puts the next three cards from the deck faceup on the table. If no sets could be assembled, three additional cards from the deck are drawn, and the searching process continues. One point is earned for each correct set. The player with the highest score wins.

Time

10–15 minutes

Baba Yaga's Zoo [*Зоопарк Бабы-Яги*], intermediate low

We conclude with a game that has no known prototype but is based on the mechanics used in many popular games: collecting sets of cards by trading with other players. We made this game for our *Russian through Drama* class, in which we staged a play that featured folklore characters, hence the specific vocabulary. In this game, the evil Baba Yaga [Баба-яга] will let you through the zoo gate only if you give her 300 animals of a kind she "likes." If she "likes" your offering, you win; if not, you can try again. The object of this game is to collect 300 of "something" to please Baba Yaga's whimsy.

Target grammar

We use **Baba Yaga's Zoo** to practice the genitive plural noun forms, another challenging point of Russian grammar.

Materials

There are 112 cards divided into two decks: the main deck for the players (100 cards) and the control deck for Baba Yaga (12 cards). Each card features a picture of an animal (or a bird), 12 kinds of them, with a number next to it (50, 100, 150, or 200).

- One of the following numbers:
  - 50 (three cards of each kind)
  - 100 (two cards of each kind)
  - 150 (one card of each kind)
  - 200 (one card of each kind)

- For example, *пятьдесят крокодилов* [50 crocodiles], *двести сов* [200 owls], *сто пятьдесят оленей* [150 deer] or *сто попугаев* [100 parrots].

The names of the animals are counterbalanced to include all four possible genitive plural endings: zero, *-ов, -ей, -ев*. Here is what the card looks like (see Figure 5.2):

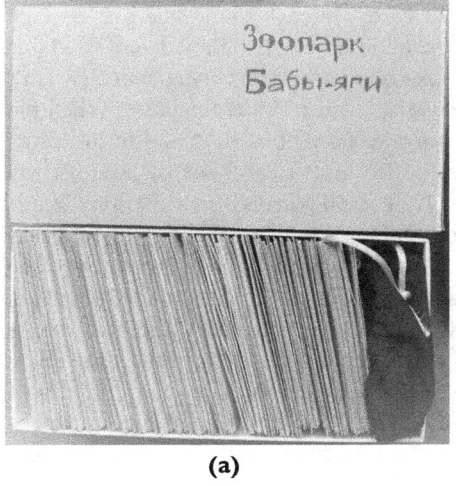 

(a) (b)

Figure 5.2a, b Baba Yaga's Zoo.

Yaga's cards are green, whereas players' cards are yellow and orange. A player collects *300 зайцев* [300 hares] for gifting (150 + 100 + 50) and wins this round: "300 hares" is the first card of the green deck. Baba Yaga "takes" the gift and gives the player a diamond as a point.

To make the game more dynamic, we add:

- 12 jokers: pictures of animals without numbers – can denote any number of these animals, one for each animal
- 7 cards with wings – *крылья* [wings]. Wings can only have number 50 on them, and the set of "wings" for Baba Yaga must total 600 rather than 300. Winged creatures (birds or flying insects) also count as *wings*: to get the number of wings, the number of creatures is multiplied by two.

In addition, there are:

- 2 cards with a magic wand, meaning "any creature in any number."

For groups of two or three players, we recommend adding:

- 7 cards with eyes, meaning "you may look at the cards drawn and trade one card from your hand for a card you need."

If you play in a large group (of four or more people), there is no need for eye cards.

How to play

To start, each player gets six cards from the main deck. To collect 300 animals (or 600 wings), the players have to trade their cards. In each round, the players take turns laying one card from their hand on the table, saying that they do not need this number of these animals. For example: *Мне не нужны 100 крокодилов* [I don't need 100 crocodiles]/*Отдаю 100 крокодилов* [I give 100 crocodiles]. When the cards from all the players are laid, players take turns to collect one of the cards offered by their partners. If a player decides to take a card, she or he must say something like *Мне нужны 50 попугаев* [I need 50 parrots]/*Беру 50 попугаев* [I take 50 parrots]. If there is nothing they need, he or she says "*Пас!*" [I'll pass], and the turn moves to the next player. When all the players have made their moves, the remaining cards are discarded and the players draw cards from the main deck to get six in hand. Then the next round begins. Once someone collects 300 animals of one kind, he or she may call Baba Yaga and check if she accepts the gift (game ends) or not (game continues). To check if Baba Yaga likes the gift, three cards are drawn from the top of the control deck and laid faceup. If at least one of them matches "the gift," the gift is accepted. A good strategy is to collect several sets and present them at once to increase the probability of acceptance; however, there is a chance that Baba Yaga accepts someone else's gift first.

Teacher mediation

In a pre-game activity, the teacher introduces the elements of the game. The best way to help students get the gist of the game is to begin playing it. The teacher's participation as a player in this kind of game is crucial. While playing, the teacher models the correct language, walks the students through the game, and provides corrective feedback.

Time

The game time varies. If the game continues too long, the teacher may suggest that the players cooperate to prepare collective presents for Baba Yaga. This improves the likelihood of winning and bringing the game to an end.

Authentic games replace traditional exercises

Authentic games can be used in language classrooms not only for raising students' motivation, developing their vocabulary, pragmatic competence, and conversational skills but also for grammar acquisition as well. This becomes possible if we accept that a typical authentic game is often based on multiple repetitions of one pattern. If a game affords patterns relevant to the grammar taught, we can bring the game to our class. Playing the game, our students repeat one target construction many times, just like they do during regular textbook-based practice.

Sometimes we are lucky and there is no need to change a game at all. Sometimes it is enough to modify or simply drop some elements that prove to be too difficult for students. Finally, we may adopt the mechanics of a game but rearrange the setting completely. What is important is that the game we bring to our class keeps its authenticity. The main advantage of using authentic games in the language classroom is that it provides opportunities for practice while actually playing rather than pretending to play. Authentic games are first and foremost seen as a fun, real-life activity, the linguistic outcome being the welcome benefit. We do this activity first of all for fun, without obligation, getting a non-linguistic outcome of playing a game. From the TBLT perspective, authentic games constitute an effective task that stimulates interaction and gives opportunities for engaging with meaning-focused language.

Lessons learned

In the process of integrating authentic games into our classes, we learned valuable lessons. Some are positive; others point to potential caveats.

Authentic games are useful not only for conversation and language clubs but also for teaching grammar. When playing, we tend to repeat one language pattern multiple times. If the pattern meets our teaching goals, the corresponding game can be successfully integrated into a lesson to replace that offered by the textbooks' practice exercises, which specifically involve the repetition of the construction studied in a focused context.

The best way to find a suitable authentic game is to play a lot yourself and watch for the speech patterns involved, or to brainstorm possible mechanics that would afford a repeated contextualized usage of a particular form or construction. If the desired language pattern is hidden in the inner speech of the players, the teacher needs to bring it out to the surface by the magic "Externalize!" rule, whereby the students are requested to verbalize their thought process.

The focused nature of the output facilitated during gameplay makes the use of games at the beginner level as feasible as at higher levels of language acquisition.

Any game that we, as teachers, want to bring to class, especially an original game with borrowed mechanics, should first be tested outside the classroom to ensure that everything goes exactly as planned. Such test-play helps fine-tune the process and detect superfluous details and non-working rules. It may be the case that some flaws will not be detected before the first play in class. One example is our game Baba Yaga's Zoo. In its initial version, the game included cards with an eye image that allowed players to trade any three cards from their hand for any three cards from the discarded pile. During the game play in class, we realized that these cards are unnecessary for groups of four or more players, because in each round, the open bank of cards for exchange is large enough to sustain the game's dynamics.

Since some games are complex and cognitively taxing, it is imperative to introduce such games incrementally through pre-play activities. In this, one should abide by the best practices of the TBLT approach. The frame and space of this chapter do not leave room for a discussion of pre- and post-play activities we offer in class. In our future projects, we plan to zoom in and provide a step-by-step walkthrough guide for pre- and post-play activities.

The students' reactions to the games we bring to the classroom are the best indicators of the games' quality. If the students seem too confused or bored and stop playing as soon as the teacher stops the game, it is a sign for us to rethink and improve the game's instructions, its design, or even its entire idea. This happened to us too. Fortunately, we also witnessed a different situation: students who played enthusiastically did not want to stop playing even when the lesson was over, and even asked to borrow the game to play it at home.

Notes

1 Hereinafter, we refer to the ACTFL Proficiency scale (ACTFL, 2012).
2 One of the reviewers noted the resemblance of the *Noodles* game to the popular *Apples to Apples* game. Indeed, the goal in both games is to find similarities between two concepts. However, in *Apples to Apples*, the focus is on adjectives, which makes it perfect for practicing adjective–noun agreement: яблоко зеленое, и крокодил тоже зеленый [an apple is green and a crocodile is also green]. In contrast, in the *Noodles*, the similarity between two pictures is not restricted to adjectives, and thus, it allows for a wider range of similarity expressions. For example, an apple and a crocodile may be similar because both of them are dangerous: Яблоко, упавшее на голову, может быть так же опасно, как и крокодил [An apple that fell on one's head can be as dangerous as a crocodile], or because both are disliked by the speaker: Я не люблю ни яблоки, ни крокодилов [I like neither apples nor crocodiles].
3 In a real-time game, all players act simultaneously rather than wait for their turn.

References

ACTFL. (2012). *ACTFL performance descriptors for language learners.* www.actfl.org/resources/actfl-proficiency-guidelines-2012

Ahmadian, M. J. (2013). Working memory and task repetition in second language oral production. *Asian Journal of English Language Teaching, 23*(1), 37–55.

Akishina, A. A., & Kagan, O. E. [Акишина, А. А., и Каган, О. Е.]. (2014). *Learning to teach: For the teacher of Russian as a foreign language* [Учимся учить: Для преподавателя русского языка как иностранного] (9th ed.). Russkij jazuk, Kursy [Русский язык, Курсы].

Akishina, A. A., Zharkova, T., & Akishina, T. [Акишина, А. А., Жаркова, Т., и Акишина, Т.]. (1990). *Games in Russian language lessons: Educational visual aids* [Игры на уроках русского языка: Учеб. нагляд. пособие] (2nd ed.). Russkij jazuk [Русский язык].

Balakina, K. D. [Балакина, К. Д.] (2020). Role-playing games as a key technology for developing students' speaking skills outside the language environment [Ролевые игры как ключевая технология развития навыков говорения у студентов вне языковой среды]. *Russian Studies* [Русистика]*, 18*(4), 439–453.

Bitekhtina, N. B., & Vaishnore, E. V. [Битехтина, Н. Б., и Вайшноре, Е. В.]. (2009). Game tasks in the classroom for Russian as a foreign language [Игровые задания на занятиях по русскому языку как иностранному]. In *Live method: For the teacher of Russian as a foreign language* [Живая методика: Для преподавателя русского языка как иностранного]. Russkij jazuk, Kursy [Русский язык, Курсы].

Boyle, E. M. (1993). Beyond memorization: Teaching Russian (and other languages') vocabulary. *Foreign Language Annals, 26*(2), 226–232. https://doi.org/10.1111/j.1944-9720.1993.tb01169.x

Bygate, M., Skehan, P., & Swain, M. (2001). *Researching pedagogic tasks, second language learning, teaching and testing.* Longman.

Caillois, R. (1961). *Man, play, and games.* University of Illinois Press.

Canale, M., & Swain, M. (1980). Theoretical bases of communicative approaches to second language teaching and testing. *Applied linguistics, 1*(1), 1–47. https://doi.org/10.1093/applin/I.1.1

Comer, W. (2020). Reconceptualizing grammar instruction: Making it meaningful and communicative. In E. Dengub, I. Dubinina, & J. Merrill (Eds.), *The art of teaching Russian* (pp. 163–186). Georgetown University Press. www.jstor.org/stable/j.ctv18sqxnd

Cope, B., & Kalantzis, M. (2013). "Multiliteracies": New literacies, new learning. In *Framing languages and literacies* (pp. 115–145). Routledge.

deHaan, J. (2019). Teaching language and literacy with games: What? How? Why? *Ludic Language Pedagogy, 1*, 1–57. https://doi.org/10.55853/llp_v1Art1

Erlam, R., & Ellis, R. (2019). Input-based tasks for beginner-level learners: An approximate replication and extension of Erlam & Ellis (2018). *Language Teaching, 52*(4), 490–511. http://doi.org/10.1017/S0261444818000216

Esmantova, T. L. [Эсмантова, Т. Л.]. (2008). *Russian language: 5 elements: Level A1 (elementary)* [Русский язык: 5 элементов: Уровень А1 (элементарный)]. Zlatoust [Златоуст].

Farrell, T. S. C., & Jacobs, G. M. (2020). *Essentials for successful English language teaching* (2nd ed.). Bloomsbury Publishing.

Gatbonton, E., & Segalowitz, N. (2005). Rethinking communicative language teaching: A focus on access to fluency. *Canadian Modern Language Review, 61*(3), 325–353. https://doi.org/10.3138/cmlr.61.3.325

Gilabert, R., & Malicka, A. (2021). From needs analysis to task-based design: Methodology, assessment and programme evaluation. In N. P. Sudharshana & L. Mukhopadhyay (Eds.), *Task-based language teaching and assessment* (pp. 93–118). Springer.

Hadfield, J. (2003). *Intermediate grammar games*. Longman.
Huizinga, J. (1949). *Homo ludens: A study of the play-element in culture*. Routledge.
Jones, D. M. (2020). Games in the language learning classroom: Is the juice worth the squeeze? *Ludic Language Pedagogy*, *2*, 1–36. https://doi.org/10.55853/llp_v2Art1
Kaznyshkina, I. V. [Казнышкина, И. В.]. (2012). *Communication games: In lessons of Russian as a foreign language* [Коммуникативные игры: На уроках русского языка как иностранного]. Russkij jazyk, Kursy [Русский язык, Курсы].
Kitaygorodskaya, G. A., Goldstein, Y. V., & Smorodinskaya, T. E. [Китайгородская, Г. А., Гольдштейн, Я. В., и Смородинская, Т. Э.] (1993). *Bridges of trust: Intensive Russian language course* [Мосты доверия: Интенсивный курс русского языка]. Russkij jazyk, Kursy [Русский язык, Курсы].
Klementieva, T. V., & Chubarova, O. K. [Клементьева, Т. Б., и Чубарова, О. К.] (2007). *Multi-colored cases: A game for children from 7 to 77* [Разноцветные падежи: Игра для детей от 7 до 77]. Russkij Jazyk, Kursy [Русский язык, Курсы].
Ko, S., & Eslami, Z. R. (2021). Developing pragmatic competence in digital game worlds: A aystematic review. *TESL -EJ*, *25*(1).
Kogan, V., & Bondarenko, M. (2022). Russian and Russia through tasks for beginners. In S. Nuss & W. Martelle (Eds.), *Task-based instruction for teaching Russian as a foreign language* (pp. 77–97). Routledge. https://doi.org/10.4324/9781003146346-6
Kogan, V., & Kapustin, S. (2020). Conquering speaking anxiety with LinguaPolis. In U. Nurmukhamedov & R. Sadler (Eds.), *New ways in teaching with games*. TESOL Press.
Lee, W. R. (1965). *Language-teaching games and contests*. Oxford University Press.
Leontyeva, A. L. [Леонтьева, А. Л.]. (2010). *Interactive game "Metro" for students of Russian as a foreign language* [Интерактивная игра "Метро" для изучающих РКИ]. Manuscript.
Leontyeva, A. L. [Леонтьева, А. Л.]. (2018). *50 games in Russian language lessons* [50 игр на уроках русского языка: Учебное пособие]. Russkij jazyk, Kursy [Русский язык, Курсы].
Littlewood, W., William, L., & Swan, M. (1981). *Communicative language teaching: An introduction*. Cambridge University Press.
Long, M. H. (2016). In defense of tasks and TBLT: Nonissues and real issues. *Annual Review of Applied Linguistics*, *36*, 5–33. https://doi.org/10.1017/S0267190515000057
Ludic Language Pedagogy. (n.d.). *About*. Retrieved August 13, 2022, from https://llpjournal.org/about.html
Mitchell, R. (2002). The communicative approach to language teaching: An introduction. In A. Swarbrick (Ed.), *Teaching modern languages* (pp. 41–50). Routledge.
Nurmukhamedov, U., & Sadler, R. (2020). *New ways in teaching with games*. TESOL Press.
Nuss, S. & Whitehead Martelle, W. (Eds.). (2022). *Task-Based Instruction for Teaching Russian as a Foreign Language* (1st ed.). Routledge. https://doi.org/10.4324/9781003146346
Obukhova, T. M. [Обухова, Т. М.]. (2015). To play or not to play: Table games in lessons of Russian as a foreign language (lexical and communicative aspect) [Играть или не играть: Обзор настольных игр для занятий по русскому языку как иностранному (лексико коммуникативный аспект)]. In *Translation as a means of enriching world culture: Proceedings of the international scientific conference* [Перевод Как Средство Обогащения Мировой Культуры: Материалы Международной Научной Конференции] (pp. 169–177). FORUM Publishing [Издательство ФОРУМ].

Pastushenkov, D. (2022). Task-based peer interaction in Russian as a second/foreign language classes. In S. Nuss & W. Whitehead Martelle (Eds.), *Task-based instruction for teaching Russian as a foreign language* (pp. 152–170). Routledge.

Razin, A., & Kingisepp, L. [Разин, А., и Кингисепп, Л.] (2018). *"Everyone plays!" 101 communicative games for teachers of Russian as a foreign language* [*"Играют все!" 101 коммуникативная игра для учителей русского языка как иностранного*]. Keelekeskus. https://gamekeskus.ee/ru/kursused/elektronnaja-kniga-igrajut-vse/

Reinhardt, J. (2018). *Gameful second and foreign language teaching and learning: Theory, research, and practice*. Springer.

Reinhardt, J., & Sykes, J. M. (2012). Conceptualizing digital game-mediated L2 learning and pedagogy: Game-enhanced and game-based research and practice. In H. Reinders (Ed.), *Digital games in language learning and teaching* (pp. 32–49). Springer. https://doi.org/10.1057/9781137005267_3

Richards, J. C. (2006). *Communicative language teaching today*. SEAMEO Regional Language Centre.

Rinvolucri, M., & Davis, P. (1995). *More grammar games: Cognitive, affective and movement activities for EFL students*. Cambridge University Press.

Shirazi, M., Ahmadi, S. D., & Mehrdad, A. G. (2016). The effect of using video games on EFL learners' acquisition of speech acts of apology and request. *Theory and Practice in Language Studies*, *6*(5), 1019–1026. http://doi.org/10.17507/tpls.0605.16

Skorik, E. A. [Скорик, Е. А.]. (2016). Adaptation of the board game "Alias" for classes in Russian as a foreign language [Адаптация настольной игры "Alias" для занятий по русскому языку как иностранному]. In *Russian scientific and practical conference: Issues of the implementation of educational programs at preparatory faculties for foreign citizens* [*Всероссийская научно-практическая конференция: Актуальные вопросы реализации образовательных программ на подготовительных факультетах для иностранных граждан*] (pp. 439–445). A.S. Pushkin State Institute of the Russian Language [Государственный институт русского языка им. А.С. Пушкина].

Slabuho, O. A. [Слабухо, О. А.] (2015). The use of board games in teaching foreign students the conjugation of Russian verbs [Использование настольных игр при обучении иностранных студентов спряжению русских глаголов]. *Young Scientist* [*Молодой Учёный*], *19*, 612–614.

Smirnova, E. [Смирнова, Е.] (2020, April 24). Three card board games: Adaptable for Russian as a foreign language [Три карточных настольных игры: Адаптируем для РКИ]. *EduNeo*. www.eduneo.ru/tri-kartochnyx-nastolnyx-igry-adaptiruem-dlya-rki/

Stohler, U., & Makarova, E. (2011). The use of games in teaching Russian as a foreign language. *Rusistika*, *36*, 9–13.

Sykes, J. (2009). Learner requests in Spanish: Examining the potential of multiuser virtual environments for L2 pragmatic acquisition. In L. Lomika & G. Lords (Eds.), *The second generation: Online collaboration and social networking in CALL* (pp. 199–234). CALICO Monograph.

Tsai, Y. L., & Tsai, C. C. (2018). Digital game-based second-language vocabulary learning and conditions of research designs: A meta-analysis study. *Computers & Education*, *125*, 345–357. https://doi.org/10.1016/j.compedu.2018.06.020

Ur, P., & Wright, A. (1992). *Five-minute activities: A resource book of short activities*. Cambridge University Press.

Willis, J. (1996). A flexible framework for task-based learning. *Challenge and Change in Language Teaching*, *52*, 62.

Wright, A., Betteridge, D., & Buckby, M. (2006). *Games for language learning*. Cambridge University Press.

York, J. (2019). "Kotoba Rollers" walkthrough: Board games, TBLT, and player progression in a university EFL classroom. *Ludic Language Pedagogy, 1*, 58–114. https://doi.org/10.55853/llp_v1Wt1

York, J. (2020). Promoting spoken interaction and student engagement with board games in a language teaching context. In *Global perspectives on gameful and playful teaching and learning* (pp. 1–26). IGI Global. http://doi.org/10.4018/978-1-7998-2015-4.ch001

York, J., deHaan, J., & Hourdequin, P. (2019). It's your turn: EFL teaching and learning with tabletop games. In H. Reinders, S. Ryan, & S. Nakamura (Eds.), *Innovation in language teaching and learning* (pp. 117–139). Palgrave Macmillan. https://doi.org/10.1007/978-3-030-12567-7_7

York, J., Poole, F. J., & deHaan, J. W. (2021). Playing a new game – An argument for a teacher-focused field around games and play in language education. *Foreign Language Annals, 54*(4), 1164–1188. https://doi.org/10.1111/flan.12585

Appendix

Table 5.1 The games described in the chapter

	The Noodles	Memory (matching pairs)	Dominos	Grammar SET	Baba Yaga
Target language	Constructions expressing similarity (тоже [also], такой же, как [the same as], etc.)	Gender and number agreement of the Russian нужно [needed] (мне нужно лекарство [I need medicine], мне нужен спрей [I need spray], мне нужна мазь [I need ointment], мне нужны таблетки [I need pills])	Instrumental with or without the preposition с [with] (Можно писать ручкой [One can write with a pen] or Коробка с магией [Box with magic]; please give an example of a complete phrase)	Adjectival endings across stem type (soft, hard, and mixed). Gender and number agreement	Genitive plural nouns formation
Level	Intermediate and advanced (using different set of constructions for each level)	Novice high or intermediate low	Intermediate	Novice	Intermediate
Possible communicative topics	Culture, people, and their characters, social relationships	Any topic that is used for the modeling of this grammar	Everyday life, hobbies, or any other topic associated with the instrumental of instrument	Any topic that is used for the modeling of this grammar	Food, education, business, and customs

(Continued)

Table 5.1 (Continued)

	The Noodles	Memory (matching pairs)	Dominos	Grammar SET	Baba Yaga
Communicative topic in the examples provided in this chapter	Culture	Health and medicine	Everyday life	Food	Animals (zoo)
Materials	Digital presentation or cards with 5 ± 2 pairs of illustrations that seemingly have nothing in common	8–12 pairs of card decks balanced across the gender and number of the nouns illustrated	49 domino-style cards, where one end illustrates an action and the other an instrument	A 96-card deck with adjectival stems, endings, and nouns: 32 cards with nouns denoting food, 32 with adjectival stems, and 32 with adjectival endings in nominative case	112 cards for collecting sets (animals or birds and additional special features)
Playing time	Approximately 10 minutes	Approximately 10 minutes	Approximately 15 minutes	10 minutes or less	10–15 minutes
Objective	To write the most original explanation that other players will like	To flip over and collect as many matching cards as possible	To empty one's hand while blocking the opponent's	To find and collect sets of three cards based on the model "adjectival stem + adjectival ending + noun"	To collect 300 animals/birds of the same kind or 600 wings that match the object on the card from Baba Yaga's deck

	The Noodles	Memory (matching pairs)	Dominos	Grammar SET	Baba Yaga
Rules	Unchanged; players have a minute to explain in writing what two objects in the pictures have in common; each player votes for the best one in the round; the winner gets one point, and the next round starts.	Unchanged; the cards are laid facedown on a surface, and two cards are flipped faceup for each turn; the object of the game is to turn over pairs of matching cards (Wiki). An additional rule for inner speech to be externalized is added.	Unchanged game play, with modifications to the dominoes and the additional rule for inner speech to be externalized. Instruments are to be matched with corresponding actions. A container can combine with any instrument and with another container. To avoid ambiguities, actions are marked with red numbers, whereas instruments with blue. The blue ends can combine only with equivalent red ones.	Easy to grasp, replicating the original mechanics of SET game; 12 cards from the deck are laid faceup; the players find sets of three cards: "adj stem + adj ending + noun"; if the set found is correct, the player gets it and new three cards are drawn from the deck. There are no turns in this game – the first one to find gets the set. If no one finds at least one set, additional three cards are drawn from the deck and the game continues.	Easy to grasp, replicating a popular game mechanic of collecting and trading cards. Each player gets 6 cards from the main deck. To collect 300 animals (or 600 wings), the players have to trade their cards. In each round, the players take turns laying one card from their hand they want to trade on the table. When the deal is made, the remaining cards are discarded and each player draws another card. Once someone collects 300 animals of one kind, he/she turns over three cards from the top of the control (Baba Yaga's) deck. If at least one of them is the same as "the gift," then the gift is accepted. If not, the game continues.

(Continued)

Table 5.1 (Continued)

	The Noodles	Memory (matching pairs)	Dominos	Grammar SET	Baba Yaga
Desired output	Phrases with constructions expressing similarity	Externalized inner speech: мне (не) нужен/нужна/ нужно/нужны ещё... [I (don't) need...]	Externalized inner speech: instrumental constructions with and without the preposition с "with" коробка с ручкой [a box with a pen] vs. ручкой можно писать [one can write with a pen, lit.... write a pen.INSTR].	Sentences with modified nouns ates: Красная рыба – моя [Salmon (lit. red fish) is mine], Утренний кофе – мой [Morning coffee is mine] or Мягкие булочки – мои [Soft buns are mine]	Sentences with numerals requiring genitive plural: Отдаю 50 собак – беру 200 гусей [I give 50 dogs and take 200 geese]
Preparation caveats	The pictures should be easy to recognize and interesting. The teacher should know the students' interests and their cultural backgrounds well.	The images should be easy to associate with the words they denote. The words must be counterbalanced across the relevant categories.	The images should be easy to associate with the words they denote. The words must be counterbalanced across the relevant categories.	The endings should be counterbalanced across gender/ number and stem type, the stem across stem type, the nouns across gender/number.	The nouns standing for the animals/ birds should be counterbalanced across gen pl endings. Also, the number of each card should be optimal for dynamic play.

Chapter 6

Learning motion verbs through a board game
Insights from a cognitive linguistics perspective

Maria Bondarenko

CHAPTER SUMMARY

Board games' affordances for simulating reality in the form of repetitive actions in an inherently authentic game environment make them very attractive for second and foreign language (L2) education. Roll-and-move games, a type of board games in which the players roll a die and move a token along a path with a start and finish, simulate actions of motion and thus stimulate narrating motion events. This chapter conceptualizes how the affordances of games can be translated into an educational roll-and-move game *Я гуляю по Москве* [*Walking the streets of Moscow*] to support a context-oriented, item-based, and experience-driven approach to teaching basic Russian verbs of motion (RVoM) at low and intermediate proficiency levels. The chapter offers a brief overview of problems related to traditional teaching and learning of RVoM, introduces an alternative approach based on the strategies of *semantic labeling* and *narrative-communicative frames*, and offers the rationale for it, which is driven by cognitive linguistics. It also presents *Я гуляю по Москве* board game, along with teaching/learning scenarios enabled by it, and, finally, reflects on lessons learned from the implementation of this activity in L2 Russian classrooms.

КРАТКОЕ СОДЕРЖАНИЕ ГЛАВЫ

Способность настольных игр моделировать реальность в форме повторяющихся действий в аутентичной игровой среде делает их очень привлекательными при обучении иностранному языку. "Ходилки" (они же "бродилки"), тип настольных игр, где игроки бросают кубик и перемещают жетон по определенному маршруту на выпавшее число клеток, имитируют физическое перемещение в пространстве и, как следствие, стимулируют повествование о перемещении в рамках аутентичной коммуникации. Цель данной главы – представить обучающую игру-ходилку *Я гуляю по Москве* и продемонстрировать, как её свойства (аффордансы) имитировать повторяющиеся действия по перемещению в пространстве поддерживают

DOI: 10.4324/9781003369721-9

инновационный подход к преподаванию базовых глаголов движения на начальном уровне обучения русскому языку. Подход опирается на принципы когнитивной лингвистики и заключается в пошаговом усвоении отдельных глагольных форм в определенных контекстных значениях с опорой на личный опыт перемещения в пространстве самого обучаемого. Глава включает обзор игровых афордансов и проблем, связанных с традиционным преподаванием русских глаголов движения, представляет альтернативный подход, совмещающий метод *семантических этикеток* и *повествовательно-коммуникативных рамок*, и разъясняет его теоретические основания. В главе даются примеры конкретных обучающих сценариев, которые поддерживает игра *Я гуляю по Москве*, и, наконец, обсуждаются уроки, вынесенные из многолетнего опыта использования предлагаемого метода на занятиях русского языка.

Affordances of board games relevant to L2 education

Board games have a number of affordances that make them an effective tool for second and foreign language (L2) education. In environmental psychology (Gibson, 1979) and sociocultural L2 pedagogy (van Lier, 2004), the term *affordances* refers to possibilities for actions offered by the environment, both natural and sociocultural. Artifacts, such as board games, belong to the sociocultural environment or the educational sociocultural environment, when used in the classroom.

The affordance for *simulating reality* is the first important for L2 learning affordance provided by board games. According to Hawkinson (2013), board games were an evolution in gaming that began to "tie elements of gameplay to a physical representation, which can be regarded as the beginnings of simulated gameplay" (p. 318). Board games (like all games) also offer an affordance for *repetitive actions in an inherently authentic environment*. Following the pioneering work by Johan Huizinga (1955), subsequent specialists in game studies (e.g., Callois, 2001; Salen & Zimmerman, 2003; Suits, 2005; Turner, 1982) define the game (or the play) as an alternative reality established through restrictions (rules) that regulate human behavior within the game environment and fence this environment off from the external world. Exploring the "game" from the perspective of concept studies, Wierzbicka (1996, p. 159) attributes to this concept the following semantic features: (1) human action (animals can play, but they do not play games); (2) duration (a game cannot be momentary); (3) aim: pleasure; (4) "suspension of reality" (the participants imagine that they are in a world apart from the real world); (5) well-defined goals (the participants know what they are trying to achieve); (6) well-defined rules (the participants know what they can do and what they cannot do); and (7) unpredictable course of events (nobody can know what exactly is going to happen).

Thus, the game rules limit behavior within the game to prescribed, mostly repetitive, actions. However, the imposed restrictions themselves are perceived as natural and authentic, since the game remains *per se* an authentic sociocultural activity. Following the rules is a natural prerequisite for a game. Once the individual ("gamebreaker" in terms of Huizinga) decides to ignore them, the game reality is ruined. Moreover, the restrictions and repetitive actions provide both a concrete achievable goal and the means for achieving it. Therefore, restrictions and repetitions become desirable, enjoyable, and motivating and provide a sense of competition with other players or oneself. It makes the players repeat the same actions again and again without getting bored.

Thanks to the unique combination of affordances for reality simulation and repetitive actions in an inherently authentic game environment, board games overcome eternal fight in L2 education between the claim for authenticity and "fun" on the one hand and the necessity of drill practice on the other. This fight is particularly acute in teaching languages with a rich morphological structure, such as Russian. From this perspective, the pedagogical benefits of board games in L2 classrooms can be compared with those of using songs with catchy refrains, or "inherently repetitive tasks," described by Gatbonton and Segalowitz (2005) as activities where "repetition is the means by which the activity goal is attained" (p. 332). Because of the "high consistency of situation-utterance correspondences across the repeated events," games and inherently repetitive tasks "lead to automaticity in both reception and production" (Gatbonton & Segalowitz, 2005, p. 333). Thus, from a cognitive perspective, game-assisted inherently repetitive tasks can be considered an alternative to the traditional way of teaching/learning linguistic structures through "grammar rules."

It is not surprising that the usage of board games, both authentic ones and tailor-made for pedagogical purposes, has been recognized in the literature as a promising pedagogical tool for L2 learning, irrespective of learners' age and L2 proficiency (Krupina [Крупина], 2014; Obuhova [Обухова], 2015; York & deHaan, 2017). Board games promote motivation (Garris et al., 2002; York, 2020), collaborative learning (Faya Cerqueiro & Chao Castro, 2015; Poole et al., 2019), and spoken interaction (York, 2020). They also help overcome speaking anxiety (Fung & Min, 2016; Kogan & Kapustin, 2020) and contribute to the acquisition of vocabulary (Sorayaie Azar, 2012; Obuhova [Обухова], 2015; Uberman, 1998) and grammar (Paris & Yussof, 2012, 2013; Phuong & Nguyen, 2017). York (2020) describes board games as a mediating tool for authentic communication in the L2 classroom.

Roll-and-move games (sometimes equated with race games or pursuit games) is a term referring to a type of board games in which the players roll a die and move the token along a path with a starting point and finish and in which landing on certain spaces may trigger specific actions (e.g., *Snakes and Ladders*, *Monopoly*, or *Traveller's Tour Through the United States*). This type of board games often identifies the moving token with the player and the track with real-world repetitive motion events (e.g., strolling around a city, traveling across a country, wandering around a building from one stop to another).[1]

This chapter conceptualizes how the previously described affordances of games can be translated into a roll-and-move board game *Я гуляю по Москве* [*Walking the Streets of Moscow*] to support a context-oriented, item-based, and experience-driven approach to teaching basic Russian verbs of motion (RVoM). This approach has been suggested as an alternative to traditional teaching of RVoM at low and intermediate proficiency levels (e.g., Bondarenko, 2019; Castellví & Markina, 2022; Markina, 2018; Six, 2018a, 2018b, 2019). The chapter starts with a brief overview of problems related to teaching and learning RVoM, introduces an alternative approach based on the strategies of *semantic labeling* and *narrative-communicative frames*, and clarifies the rationale for it based on the principles of cognitive linguistics. It also presents samples of specific teaching/learning scenarios, enabled by the board game *Я гуляю по Москве* and, finally, reflects on lessons learned from the experience of using this game in Russian L2 classrooms.

Problems related to teaching/learning RVoM

Russian verbs of motion (RVoM) have been commonly recognized as one of the most difficult topics in the instruction of L2 Russian for many reasons.

The first is the complexity of how motion events are encoded in Russian. Apart from the four universal characteristics of motion – the figure (moving object), ground (goal of motion), path (the followed course), and manner of motion (Slobin, 2004; Talmy, 2000) – RVoM are sensitive to the lexicosyntactic category of aspect, which includes the subcategory known as "directionality of motion" (Isačenko, 1960). Moreover, Russian requires differentiation between motion on foot and motion by means of transportation. However, even though there is no generic verb of motion in Russian, ХОДИТЬ/ИДТИ can be generalized for motion that does not take place on foot (Nesset, 2008; Rakhilina, 2004), and here, ИДТИ is used much more often in a metaphorical sense (Nesset & Janda, 2022). In practice, this means that contextual meanings of different RVoM are determined by a complex combination of grammatical, pragmatic, and situational variables difficult to encapsulate in an explicit grammatical "rule" (Bitehtina & Judina [Битехтина и Юдина], 1986; Six, 2019).

The second reason is the fuzziness of the category of "RVoM" itself (Bondarenko, n.d.; Paškina [Пашкина], 2007). For example, RVoM traditionally comprises two groups: unprefixed and prefixed RVoM. However, only unprefixed verbs have two distinct imperfective variations, each associated with one of two kinds of basic stems, called multidirectional or nondirectional (e.g., ХОДИ- ЕЗДИ- ЛЕТА- БЕГА- ПЛАВА- ВОЗИ- ВОДИ-) and unidirectional (e.g., ИД- ЕХА- ЛЕТЕ- БЕЖА- ПЛЫ- ВЕЗ- ВОД-).[2] Prefixed RVoM come in standard imperfective/perfective verbal pairs (e.g., ПРИХОДИТЬ-ПРИЙТИ, УХОДИТЬ-УЙТИ). Applying the same term "RVoM" to linguistic phenomena with different properties might confuse both teachers and learners regarding how to explain and process verbs considered RVoM.

Finally, besides the linguistic complexity and the issues of definition, researchers and practitioners (e.g., Gagarina, 2009; Gepner, 2016; Gor et al., 2009; Hasko, 2009; Israeli, 2017) have reported serious difficulties that L2 learners of Russian have encountered with acquiring RVoM through the traditional teaching approaches.

Traditional approaches to teaching prefixed and unprefixed RVoM

Any Russian L2 instructor knows that the major conceptual tool for explaining the semantics of unprefixed RVoM has traditionally been the "directionality" – more precisely, the number of directions, which support the opposition *multi- vs. unidirectional [многонарпавленные vs. однонапраленные]* verbs or stems. Unidirectional (ИДТИ-like) verbs refer to motion proceeding in/from a single direction, while multidirectional (ХОДИТЬ-like) verbs refer to motion in/from more than one direction, such as round trips, movement to a certain goal and then back to the course of motion, habitual or repeated motion, random (aimless) motion in different directions, and the ability to perform the movement in a certain manner. Castellví et al. (2022) and Gagarina (2009) observe that most traditional textbooks start the instruction of RVoM with unprefixed verbs in the present tense and put off introducing the past tense as well as prefixed RVoM. Usually, instruction focuses on contrasting paired unprefixed RVoM, based on multi-/unidirectionality (Я ХОЖУ-Я ИДУ, Я ЕЗЖУ-Я ЕДУ) or means of transportation (Я ИДУ-ЕДУ, Я ХОЖУ-ЕЗЖУ), without questioning the frequency of contextual co-occurrence of such contrasted pairs in real speech.

For prefixed RVoM, traditional instruction suggests introducing them through their derivational relationship with unprefixed RVoM having the same stems (e.g., ИДТИ → ПРИЙТИ-ПРИХОДИТЬ, УЙТИ-УХОДИТЬ). This is the reason that the introduction of prefixed RVoM is usually postponed "until two or even three years after the beginning of language learning" (Gagarina, 2009, p. 465). Correct use of prefixed RVoM is viewed as "depending largely on the speaker's correct understanding of the principal meanings of prefixes, on the one hand, and on his ability to grasp correctly the implications of the context and choose the required prefix, on the other" (Muravyova, 1975, p. 267). Therefore, instruction usually focuses on training learners to contrast the meanings of prefixes by studying a list of prefixes with decontextualized examples and doing grammar-oriented exercises where different prefixed RVoM occur in minimal contexts, often little related to each other (e.g., Bitehtina & Judina [Битехтина & Юдина], 1986, pp. 46–51; Ivanova [Иванова], 2010; Mahota, 1996, part II; Muravyova, 1975, pp. 259–264; Nagajceva [Нагайцева], 2019, pp. 11–13; Bogomolova & Petanova, 2008 [Богомолова и Петанова]; Skvorcova & Poljakov [Скворцова и Поляков], 2021).

Searching for theoretical and empirical foundations of alternative approaches

In recent years, numerous publications have shown an emerging interest in alternative approaches to RVoM in the field of theoretical linguistics, empirical research on RVoM acquisition, and classroom-oriented reflections (for an in-depth review, see Bondarenko, n.d.).

A careful review of multiple attempts to conceptualize the difference between ИДТИ-like and ХОДИТЬ-like verbs demonstrates that "directionality" is not the only way to explain the semantics of paired unprefixed RVoM (e.g., Bernickaja, 2017, 2019; Gagarina, 2009; Nesset, 2000; Kagan, 2007; Paškina [Пашкина], 2007).

Analyzing the traditional opposition of multi-/unidirectional verbs, Bondarenko (2019; n.d.) demonstrates that it is deeply rooted in structural linguistics, which imposes a universal meaning (invariant) for all contextual realizations (variants) of the same stem (e.g., Padučeva, 2004). In so-called "strong" speech positions, a variant fully represents the invariant's features. While in "weak" positions, a variant is distanced from its invariant to the extent that it can be confused with the realizations of different invariants in speech. For example, the utterance *Я сейчас еду в офис* [I am on my way to the office] fully demonstrates the idea of unidirectional motion associated with the verb ЕХАТЬ. However, the utterances *Я еду в Берлин и Штудгарт на два дня. Вернусь в субботу, и мы сразу встретимся* [I am going to Berlin and Stuttgart for two days. I will be back on Saturday, and we will meet right away] or *Каждое утро я еду в офис* [Every morning I go to the office] can cause confusion about the number of directions these motions involve. Bondarenko (2019; n.d.) suggests that because of the "gray zones" where semantic confusion is possible, the traditional structural linguistics-based approach fails to provide tools for successful instruction and acquisition of RVoM. She presumes that cognitive linguistics, which has been recently used for exploring the phenomenon of RVoM (e.g., Gor et al., 2010; Nesset & Janda, 2022), can supply pedagogical ideas for an alternative approach to teaching/learning RVoM.

Cognitive linguistics view language as "usage-based," that is, as the product of physical interaction with the world (Littlemore, 2009, p. 1; Wulff & Ellis, 2018). It also means that "a language is learned 'bottom-up' through exposure to usage events" (Taylor, 2006, p. 574). Cognitive linguistics conceptualizes verbs of motion through the notions of the *motion event* and *construction*. A *motion event* is a mental representation of a situation containing motion (Talmy, 2000). On the one hand, it is a cross-national element of human cognition that is related to a type of physical experience common to all human beings. On the other hand, different languages express motions in different ways through constructions actualized within a *narrative style* (Slobin, 2004, pp. 2, 10). A *construction* is a lexicogrammatical pattern in which words are organized and is capable of conveying meaning (Littlemore, 2009, p. 156). Unlike "grammar rules," constructions often take the form of "image schemata" (embodied prelinguistic structures of experience). Littlemore (2009) finds the construction grammar view of language potentially useful for L2 teachers because it better reflects how linguistic knowledge is processed in the brain.

Cognitive linguistics thus suggests the following principles for alternative instruction in RVoM:

1. Learners of Russian have experience of motion embodied in their physical memory mediated by other languages they speak.
2. Every motion event can be identified through a specific pragmatic context in which it occurs. Therefore, there is no need to search for an abstract universal

rule (e.g., directionality) to explain the specific contextual meaning of an RVoM. Every speech situation requiring a specific RVoM used in a specific form can be taught independently of others, that is, through item-based learning.
3. Encoding (= learning), viewed as the process of developing constructions, can rely directly on the association between a specific form of an RVoM, the description of its contextual meaning, and the learner's empirical experience of motion.
4. In language, a motion event is always represented in a specific speech context where individuals report (narrate) motion events related to real-world situations.
5. The order of introducing different motion events and related RVoM in the L2 classroom should be context-dependent, that is, depending on their linguistic frequency, salience, and communicative value, and on the communicative needs of learners, rather than on the logic of formal grammar.
6. Russian L2 teachers should carefully select teaching/learning activities aimed at the acquisition of RVoM according to the principles described. We should prioritize activities that are based on and profit from learners' individual experiences of motion.

Situational item-based and experience-driven approaches to teaching RVoM at low proficiency levels

Even though many Russian L2 teachers and textbooks have been using separate elements of context-, item-, and experience-based approaches to teaching RVoM (e.g., Arhipova [Архипова], 2006; Bitextina & Judina [Битехтина и Юдина], 1986; Kagan et al., 2006; Karavanov [Караванов], 2010; Mahota, 1996; Muravyova, 1975; Ruiz-Zorrilla et al., 2006), including the usage of roll-and-move board games (e.g., Akišina et al. [Акишина et al.], 1990; Kostomarov, 1988, p. 151; Kogan & Kapustin, 2020; Obuhova [Обухова], 2015),[3] to my knowledge, there have been only a few consistent attempts to substantiate this approach.[4] Thus, Six (2018a, 2018b, 2019) suggests a contextualized storytelling-based method of teaching RVoM. She prioritizes for initial input storytelling of a narrative about a completed round trip within the sequence of events (ХОДИЛ[5] = ПОШЁЛ-ШЁЛ-ПРИШЁЛ and ЕЗДИЛ = ПОЕХАЛ-ЕХАЛ-ПРИЕХАЛ) with a parallel drawing of pictograms. Approaching RVoM instruction from the lexical (Lewis, 1993) and task-based pedagogy's perspective, Castellví and colleagues (Castellví et al., 2022; Castellví & Markina, 2022; Markina, 2018) suggest the first systematic instruction on RVoM within a real-world related task of requesting/providing street directions (e.g., НАДО ИДТИ/ПОЙТИ/ПЕРЕЙТИ) with using a map as visual support. After that, learners move to narration about the route taken, which requires the usage of the same RVoM in the past tense. Finally, directly inspired by cognitive linguistics' approach to motion events, Bondarenko (2019) suggests an RVoM teaching model based on two complementary strategies: *semantic labeling* (rephrasing contextual meanings of motion situations in Russian), integrated into *narrative-communicative frames* (contextual speech situations in which specific meanings of RVoM occur).

All alternative approaches demonstrate common features. They (1) prioritize a situational, item-based, and experience-driven way to teach RVoM; (2) are based on inductive instructional logic and avoid abstract invariants; (3) prioritize a lexical approach (Lewis, 1993) and a usage-based approach to L2 instruction (Wulff & Ellis, 2018), which moves away from the grammar/vocabulary dichotomy and instead presents linguistic items as lexicogrammatical patterns integrating features of grammar and lexis (Halliday & Matthiessen, 2013); (4) introduce contextual situations related to the past tense at an early stage of instruction; and finally, (5) rely on learners' personal experience of motion. These features assert that storytelling, pictographic visualization, and motion simulation through doing a map- or board game–assisted tasks are the best learning activities to support the acquisition of RVoM.

Since the *semantic labeling* approach pays more detailed attention to board games[6] and considers more varieties of contextualized situations (including telling a story of a completed round trip), I will elaborate further on this method here.

Semantic labeling and the narrative-communicative frame

S*emantic labeling* means rephrasing in a target language the contextual meaning of a RVoM encoding a specific motion event. The rephrasing considers the essential contextual features (descriptors) of the motion event which make it possible to distinguish it from others. Visualized as "verbal labels" with pictographic support, the descriptors fall into two categories (Figure 6.1). The descriptors in the first category refer to the manner of motion: (1) ПЕШКОМ или НЕВАЖНО КАК, ПОТОМУ ЧТО МЫ В ГОРОДЕ [On foot or no matter how because we are within a city], (2) НА ТРАНСПОРТЕ или В ДРУГОЙ ГОРОД, В ДРУГУЮ СТРАНУ [By means of transportation or toward other country or city]. The second category includes descriptors combining temporal, aspectual, pragmatic, and real-world features: (1) Я БЫЛ там/(Я ПОСЕТИЛ это место) один или много раз [I was/have been there/I visited this place one or several times]; (2) Я БЫВАЮ/БЫВАЛ/БУДУ БЫВАТЬ там периодически [I used to visit/I visit/I will frequently visit this place]; (3) Я ПЛАНИРУЮ ПОСЕТИТЬ это место (Я СОБИРАЮСЬ туда) [I am planning to visit this place]; (4) Я В ПУТИ (Я ДЕЛАЮ ЭТО ПРЯМО СЕЙЧАС, В МОМЕНТ, КОГДА Я ГОВОРЮ) [I am on my way, I am doing that just right now, at the moment I am speaking].[7]

Combinations of labels from both categories provide instructional tools that connect a specific form of a RVoM and the context in which the form occurs, thereby suggesting paths for developing constructions (Figure 6.2).[8]

I take *narrative* to mean any utterance aiming to convey motion-related events in the present, past, or future tense. A *narrative-communicative frame* is a combination of thematic and situational features, communicative functions, and pragmatic intentions in which a narration occurs. Each narrative frame involves using one or

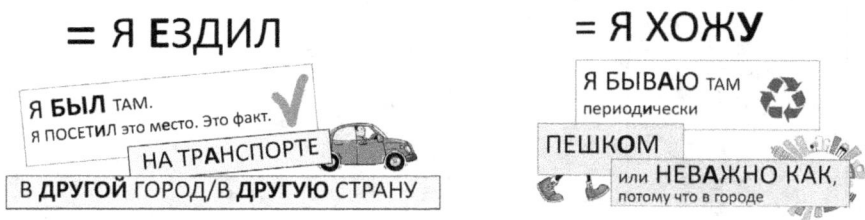

Figure 6.1 Two categories of descriptors used in the *semantic labeling* approach.

Figure 6.2 Examples of combining semantic labels to define contextual meanings of unprefixed RVoM.

many specific RVoM in a specific form. The combination of a narrative-communicative frame, one or many specific forms of RVoM, and related semantic labels collectively constitutes a learning/teaching scenario. Table 6.1 presents 12 scenarios for teaching basic RVoM as part of the first four semesters of standard Russian L2 instruction.

Table 6.1 Learning/teaching scenarios based on semantic labeling and communicative-narrative frames approaches

Learning/teaching scenarios[9]

#	COMMUNICATIVE-NARRATIVE FRAME ↔ SUGGESTION FOR CONTRAST	RVoM(s) (in infinitive and its formal characteristics: tense, aspect (type of RVoM in traditional terms) *optional/more advanced	SPECIFIC FORM(S) OF VERBS OF MOTIONS encoding the motion event related to the frame *optional/more advanced ↔ SUGGESTION FOR CONTRAST	SEMANTIC LABELS (paraphrasing) *optional/more advanced ↔ SUGGESTION FOR CONTRAST	Samples of questions guiding input/output	Semester, proficiency level
1	ПОВСЕДНЕВНЫЕ/ РЕГУЛЯРНЫЕ ЗАНЯТИЯ В ГОРОДЕ	ХОДИТЬ (unprefixed: multidirectional) **Present tense** *Past tense *Imperfective (analytic) future tense	Я ХОЖУ *я ходил *я буду ходить	Я БЫВАЮ *я бывал *я буду бывать ПЕШКОМ или НЕВАЖНО КАК, потому что мы В ГОРОДЕ	Что вы делаете/ чем вы занимаетесь? Когда вы ходите в университет? Вы любите бары? Вы часто ходите в бары и рестораны? Вы ходите в спортзал? Кто ходит в спортзал регулярно?	1st or 2nd semester Novice low/ mid/high A.1.1/A.1.2

Learning motion verbs through a board game   117

Learning/teaching scenarios[9]

2	🎲 **СПИСОК** (been there, done that): **МЕСТА, ГДЕ Я БЫЛ В ГОРОДЕ ОДИН ИЛИ МНОГО РАЗ** КОНСТАТАЦИЯ ФАКТА **В ПРОШЛОМ** ↔ ПОВСЕДНЕВНЫЕ/ РЕГУЛЯРНЫЕ ЗАНЯТИЯ В ГОРОДЕ	**ХОДИТЬ** (unprefixed: multidirectional) Past tense	Я ХОДИЛ ↔ Я ХОЖУ	**Я БЫЛ/ Я ПОСЕТИЛ + ПЕШКОМ или НЕВАЖНО КАК, потому что мы В ГОРОДЕ** ↔ Я БЫВАЮ	Кто уже ходил в русский ресторан? Когда ты ходил в кино последний раз? Что ты делал, куда ты ходил во время пандемии! **Игра "Я гуляю по Москве"**	1st or 2nd semester Novice low/ mid/high A.1.1/A.1.2
3	**МОИ ПОЕЗДКИ** в контексте **РЕГУЛЯРНЫЕ ЗАНЯТИЯ** a. **СТРАНЫ И ГОРОДА** *b. ПОЕЗДКИ В ГОРОДЕ (если транспорт важен для разговора)	**ЕЗДИТЬ** (unprefixed: multidirectional) Present tense *Past tense *Imperfective (analytic) future tense	Я ЕЗЖУ *(Раньше) я регулярно ездил *Я буду регулярно ездить	**= Я БЫВАЮ** *Я бывал *Я буду бывать **+ В ДРУГОЙ ГОРОД, ДРУГУЮ СТРАНУ** *НА ТРАНСПОРТЕ В ГОРОДЕ (если транспорт важен для разговора)	Ты много путешествуешь (путешествовал раньше)? Где ты бываешь регулярно? Куда ты ездишь регулярно?	2nd semester Novice mid/ high A.1.2

(Continued)

Table 6.1 (Continued)

Learning/teaching scenarios[9]

4	🌀 СПИСОК (been there, done that): КОНСТАТАЦИЯ ФАКТА/ОВ В ПРОШЛОМ, в контексте МОИ ПОЕЗДКИ↔ МОИ РЕГУЛЯРНЫЕ ПОЕЗДКИ	а. СТРАНЫ И ГОРОДА, ГДЕ Я БЫЛ 🌀*b. ПОЕЗДКИ В ГОРОДЕ (если транспорт важен для разговора)	Я ЕЗДИЛ ↔ Я ЕЗЖУ ЕЗДИТЬ (unprefixed: multidirectional) Past tense	Я БЫЛ Я ПОСЕТИЛ + ПОЕЗДКА В ДРУГОЙ ГОРОД, ДРУГУЮ СТРАНУ *В ГОРОДЕ НА ТРАНСПОРТЕ (если транспорт важен для разговора) ↔ Я БЫВАЮ	Куда ты уже ездил? Где ты уже был? Ты уже был в России или в другой стране, где говорят по-русски. Куда ты ездил во время пандемии? Куда ты ездил последний раз?	2nd semester Novice mid/high A.1.2
5	🌀 Я ОПИСЫВАЮ, ГДЕ НАХОЖУСЬ И ЧТО ДЕЛАЮ ПРЯМО СЕЙЧАС↔ МОЯ ЛОКАЛИЗАЦИЯ	а. ПЕШКОМ b. НА ТРАНСПОРТЕ	Я ИДУ (из/в/по) ↔ Я НАХОЖУСЬ Я ЕДУ (из/поиз/в/по) ↔ Я НАХОЖУСЬ ИДТИ ЕХАТЬ Present tense (unprefixed: unidirectional)	Я В ПУТИ Я НА ПУТИ в/из + ПЕШКОМ Я В ПУТИ/ Я НА ПУТИ в/из + НА ТРАНСПОРТЕ ↔ Я НАХОЖУСЬ	Алло? Где ты сейчас? Что ты делаешь прямо сейчас? Игра "Я гуляю по Москве"	2nd semester Novice mid/high A.1.2

Learning motion verbs through a board game 119

Learning/teaching scenarios[9]

6	🌀 **КОНКРЕТНЫЙ ПЛАН в ГОРОДЕ**		**ИДТИ/ПОЙТИ** (unprefixed: unidirectional/ prefixed ПО-) Present tense encoding the future/perfective future tense	Я ИДУ/Я ПОЙДУ ↔ Я ХОЖУ ↔ Я (УЖЕ) ХОДИЛ	Я ПЛАНИРУЮ (ПОЙТИ) Я СОБИРАЮСЬ **ПЕШКОМ или НЕВАЖНО КАК**, потому что мы **В ГОРОДЕ** ↔ Я БЫВАЮ ↔ Я БЫЛ	*Что ты планируешь/ собираешься посетить в городе? Что ты будешь делать завтра? Куда ты собираешься?* **Игра "Я гуляю по Москве"**	2nd semester Novice mid/ high A.1.2
7	🌀 **КОНКРЕТНЫЙ ПЛАН в контексте ПОЕЗДКИ**	a. **В ДРУГОЙ ГОРОД, ДРУГУЮ СТРАНУ** 🌀*b. ПОЕЗДКИ В ГОРОДЕ НА ТРАНСПОРТЕ (если транспорт важен для разговора)	**ЕХАТЬ/ ПОЕХАТЬ** (unprefixed: unidirectional/ prefixed ПО-) Present tense encoding the future/ perfective future tense	Я ЕДУ/Я ПОЕДУ ↔ Я ЕЗЖУ ↔ Я (УЖЕ) ЕЗДИЛ	Я ПЛАНИРУЮ (ПОЕХАТЬ)/*Я СОБИРАЮСЬ + **В ДРУГОЙ ГОРОД, ДРУГУЮ СТРАНУ** *В ГОРОДЕ НА ТРАНСПОРТЕ (если транспорт важен для разговора)		2nd semester Novice mid/ high A.1.2

(Continued)

Table 6.1 (Continued)

Learning/teaching scenarios[9]

8	🍥 **МЕЧТА**	**a. В ГОРОДЕ**	**ПОЙТИ/*СХОДИТЬ ПОЕХАТЬ/*СЪЕЗДИТЬ** + ПО-unidirectional stem (infinitive) или С-multidirectional stem (infinitive)	Я мечтаю, хочу/ хотел бы пойти = *сходить	**Я хочу/хотел бы ПОСЕТИТЬ**	Какое место в городе ты мечтаешь/ хочешь/хотел бы посетить? Куда ты мечтаешь/ хочешь/ хотел бы пойти/ сходить (в этом городе)?	2nd semester Novice mid/ high A.1.2
		b. В контексте ПОЕЗДКИ		Я мечтаю/ хочу/хотел бы ПОЕХАТЬ = СЪЕЗДИТЬ	**Я хочу/хотел бы ПОСЕТИТЬ**	О чём ты мечтаешь? Какие страны, какие города ты мечтаешь/ хочешь/хотел бы посетить? Куда (в какие страны, какие города) ты мечтаешь/ хочешь/хотел бы поехать/ съездить?	2nd semester Novice mid/ high A.1.2.

Learning/teaching scenarios[9]

9	🌀 БАЗОВЫЙ НАРРАТИВ в контексте ПЕШКОМ: ИСТОРИЯ В ОБЩИХ ЧЕРТАХ (basic narrative frame)	ХОДИТЬ, ВЫЙТИ, ПОЙТИ, ИДТИ, ПРИЙТИ unprefixed: multidirectional) (prefixed: perfective) (unprefixed: unidirectional) Past tense	КАК Я ХОДИЛ = а именно Я ВЫШЕЛ из … и ПОШЁЛ в … – ШЁЛ и ПРИШЁЛ в	Я ПОСЕТИЛ, Я БЫЛ ПЕШКОМ ИЛИ НЕВАЖНО КАК, потому что мы в городе = Я ОТПРАВИЛСЯ + ПЕШКОМ Я БЫЛ В ПУТИ + ПЕШКОМ Я ПРИБЫЛ ПЕШКОМ	*Расскажи в общих чертах, как ты ходил в … ?* *Что вы видели, кого вы встретили, что вы делали, что купили …* Игра "Я гуляю по Москве"	3rd semester novice high/ intermediate Low/mid A.2.1
10	🌀 БАЗОВЫЙ НАРРАТИВ в контексте ПОЕЗДКИ (рассказ о поездке): ИСТОРИЯ В ОБЩИХ ЧЕРТАХ (basic narrative frame)	🌀 a. В ГОРОДЕ НА ТРАНСПОРТЕ b. МОИ ПОЕЗДКИ В ДРУГОЙ ГОРОД, ДРУГУЮ СТРАНУ	ЕЗДИТЬ (unprefixed: multidirectional) ЕХАТЬ (unprefixed: unidirectional) ВЫЕХАТЬ ПОЕХАТЬ ПРИЕХАТЬ (prefixed: perfective) Past tense	КАК Я ЕЗДИЛ = а именно: Я ВЫЕХАЛ из И ПОЕХАЛ в – Я ЕХАЛ и ПРИЕХАЛ	Я ПОСЕТИЛ, Я БЫЛ + НА ТРАНСПОРТЕ = Я ОТПРАВИЛСЯ + НА ТРАНСПОРТЕ Я БЫЛ В ПУТИ + НА ТРАНСПОРТЕ + Я ПРИБЫЛ НА ТРАНСПОРТЕ	*Расскажи в общих чертах о поездке … .* *Расскажи в общих черта, как ты ездил в … ?* *Что вы видели, кого вы встретили, что вы делали, что купили …* Игра "Я гуляю по Москве"	3rd semester Novice high/ intermediate Low/mid A.2.1

(Continued)

Table 6.1 (Continued)

Learning/teaching scenarios[9]

11 ✻ **ДЕТАЛЬНЫЙ НАРРАТИВ в контексте ПЕШКОМ: ИСТОРИЯ В ДЕТАЛЯХ (С ПОДРОБНОСТЯМИ)** (detailed narrative frame)	**ХОДИТЬ** (unprefixed: multidirectional) **ИДТИ** (unprefixed: unidirectional) **ВЫЙТИ и ПОЙТИ, ОТОЙТИ, УЙТИ, ЗАЙТИ, ПЕРЕЙТИ, ПРОЙТИ, ПРИЙТИ ПОДОЙТИ, ВОЙТИ/ ЗАЙТИ/ *ПРОЙТИ в** (prefixed: perfective) Past tense	КАК Я ХОДИЛ = – Как Я ПОШЁЛ? ВЫШЕЛ из, ОТОШЁЛ от и в результате Я УШЁЛ из – Как Я ШЁЛ? На пути я ЗАШЁЛ в, ПЕРЕШЁЛ через, ПРОШЁЛ мимо – Как Я ПРИШЁЛ: Я ПОДОШЁЛ к и ВОШЁЛ/ ЗАШЁЛ в/*ПРОШЁЛ в	*Расскажите подробно, как ты (с)ходил в . . . *Что ты видел, кого ты встретили, что ты делали, что ты купил . . .* **Игра "Я гуляю по Москве"**	3rd or 4th semester Novice high/ intermediate Low/mid A.2.1/A2.2

Learning/teaching scenarios[9]

12	✱ ДЕТАЛЬНЫЙ НАРРАТИВ в контексте ПОЕЗДКИ: Я РАССКАЗЫВАЮ О ПОЕЗДКЕ В ДЕТАЛЯХ (С ПОДРОБНОСТЯМИ) (detailed narrative frame)	✱a. ПОЕЗДКИ В ГОРОДЕ b. ПОЕЗДКИ В ДРУГОЙ ГОРОД, ДРУГУЮ СТРАНУ	ЕЗДИТЬ (unprefixed: multidirectional) ЕХАТЬ (unprefixed: unidirectional) ВЫЕХАТЬ и ПОЕХАТЬ ОТЪЕХАТЬ УЕХАТЬ, ЗАЕХАТЬ, ПЕРЕЕХАТЬ, ПРОЕХАТЬ мимо ПРИЕХАТЬ ПОДЪЕХАТЬ, ВЪЕХАТЬ/ ЗАЕХАТЬ/ *ПРОЕХАТЬ в= (prefixed: perfective)	КАК Я ЕЗДИЛ = – Как я ПОЕХАЛ? Я ВЫЕХАЛ из, ОТЪЕХАЛ от, в результате Я УЕХАЛ из – Как Я ЕХАЛ? На пути я ЗАЕХАЛ в, ПЕРЕЕХАЛ через, ПРОЕХАЛ мимо – Как я ПРИЕХАЛ? Я ПОДЪЕХАЛ к, ВЪЕХАЛ/ ЗАЕХАЛ в/* ПРОЕХАЛ в	*Расскажите подробно о поездке....* *Расскажите подробно, как вы (съ)ездили в...?* *Что вы видели, кого вы встретили, что вы делали, что купили...* Игра "Я гуляю по Москве"	3nd or 4th semester Novice high/ intermediate Low/mid A.2.1A2.2

The order of the scenarios presented in Table 6.1 does not reflect the order in which they should be taught in the Russian L2 classroom. Furthermore, the scenarios should not all be introduced at once but, rather, gradually integrated into the communicative and thematic structure of the curriculum based on the principles of spiral-like design (cf. Bondarenko, in press). For example, the contextual meanings *я хожу* [I walk/I go on regularly] (=*я бываю* + *пешком или неважно как*, потому что *в городе* [I visit + on foot or no matter how because we are within a city]) combined with *последний раз я ходил* [Last time I went there] (=*я был* + *пешком* или неважно как, потому что *в городе* [I was there + on foot or no matter how because we are within the city]) can be introduced as part of the larger topic *повседневные/ регулярные занятия в городе* (что мы делаем/чем мы занимаемся регулярно в городе [Regular activities/my routine in the city (what we do on a regular basis in the city)]. While the verbal forms *я поеду/я еду* [I am taking a trip/I'll take a trip] (=*я планирую, я собираюсь*+*на транспорте*, в другой город или в другую страну [I am planning + transportation]) should be introduce within a distinct communicative-narrative frame: *мои поездки: конкретные планы* [My trips: concrete plans]. For these contextual meanings to be successfully acquired, they do not have to be contrasted with others, such as *я езжу/я ездил* [I go (transportation)/I went there], *я иду/еду* [I walk/I went there], or *как я ходил = вышел и пошёл-шёл и пришёл* [How I did it, my path: I left and headed to – I was walking and finally arrived], which belong to different communicative-narrative frames and rarely occur together in the same context. The level of complexity (e.g., number of new items) within each scenario should be adjusted according to learners' needs and proficiency levels.

In the table 6.1, the symbol ✿ marks scenarios that can be supported by the educational roll-and-move board game *Я гуляю по Москве* presented in the next section.

The roll-and-move board game *Я гуляю по Москве* for alternative teaching/learning of RVoM

The educational game *Я гуляю по Москве* (Figure 6.3) demonstrates how roll-and-move board games facilitate the acquisition of RVoM. The game board (template) was inspired by that of traditional roll-and-move boards. As mentioned earlier, roll-and-move games have the affordances for simulating repetitive actions of motion. Profiting from these affordances, *Я гуляю по Москве* simulates step-by-step motion through the city of Moscow and thus stimulates the narration about motion events in authentic communication. The board represents the landmarks of Moscow with respect to their geographic location on a map. In addition to learning RVoM, the game helps learners get to know the landmarks of Moscow.

Figure 6.3 Board game *Я гуляю по Москве* (available for free download at www.teacherspayteachers.com).

Rules and scenarios

1. Learners play in pairs or groups of three.
2. The starting point is Moscow City [*Район Москва-Сити*], and the endpoint is the Kremlin [*Кремль*].
3. The black-colored path means movement "on foot"; the red path means movement "via transport." The means of transportation are suggested by pictures.
4. In turns, the learners roll the dice and make a move according to the number of steps indicated.
5. In making the move, learners describe their motion or their location by using appropriate linguistic structures in a "phone call" role-play with partners: *Allo! Где ты сейчас? Что ты делаешь?* [Hello? Where are you? What are you doing?]. See scenario #5ab in Table 6.1: "*Я описываю, где нахожусь и что делаю прямо сейчас*" [I am describing where I am located and what I am doing right now].
6. If needed, the partners provide corrective feedback.
7. The complexity of the learners' verbal output within a given scenario depends on their level of proficiency, previous knowledge, the stage of RVoM acquisition at which the game is used (input, first practice, reviewing, deepening), and the learning objectives of the lesson. Thus, any scenario can be modified to increase its complexity. For example, the pattern *Я иду в* . . . [I am walking to . . .] can be replaced by *Я иду из . . . в* . . . [I am working from . . . to . . .] or, with more advanced learners, by *Я только что вышел из . . . . и иду в . . . ./Я иду из . . . . в . . . . Я уже недалеко от . . . . Я уже подхожу к . . .*" [I just got out of . . . I am walking to . . . /I am walking from . . . toward . . . I am already close to . . . . I am approaching . . . .].
8. Besides the basic scenario #5ab *Я описываю, где нахожусь и что делаю прямо сейчас* [I am describing where I am located and what I am doing just right now], the game supports other scenarios related to the usage of RVoM in the past tense, to name one or many (a list of) visited places (scenarios ##2, *3b), plans (scenarios ##6, *7b), wishes and dreams (scenarios ##8a), and general and detailed narratives (scenarios ##9, 10b, 11, 12b).
9. The scenarios can be combined in different ways within the same game. Here are some examples of combinations of scenarios for low-proficiency Russian L2 classes. In the middle of the game, the teacher suggests interrupting the "stroll across Moscow" and writing down a report about the places the students have already visited (scenario #6 *Список: места в городе, которые я посетил*" [A list of places I visited in the city]) and the places they will visit (scenario # 7 *Конкретные планы в городе* [Concrete plans in the city]) or they would like to visit (scenario # 8a *Мечты в городе* [Dreams in the city]*)*. After that, students resume the game. An alternative manner of combining the same scenarios is that upon "arriving" at specific landmarks, the learners receive a task (contextualized as questions from a person met at the landmarks or as a "phone call" or "text" from a friend) to report – orally or in writing – about the places they have visited and express their plans or wishes to visit other places on the board.

10. For more advanced learners, scenario #5ab: *Я описываю, где нахожусь и что делаю прямо сейчас* [I am describing where I am located and what I am doing just right now] may be made more challenging, as suggested in point 7, while scenario #6 *Список: места в городе, которые я посетил* [A list of places I visited in the city] should be replaced by scenario #10: *Базовый нарратив: история в общих чертах* [A basic narrative: a story in a few words] or scenario #12: *Детальный нарратив: история с подробностями* [Detailed narrative: a story with details]. The students can be asked to report in detail on their experience of visiting landmarks: *Я вышел из . . . и пошёл в . . . я шёл 10 минут . . . . я пришёл в . . . я был там 30 минут . . . после я вышел из . . . и пошёл в . . .* [I left and headed to . . . , I was walking for 10 minutes . . . I arrived . . . I spent 30 minutes there . . . then, I left and headed to . . .]. The repertoire of prefixed RVoM used within scenarios #10 and #12 may vary according to students' level of proficiency.

Integration of authentic virtual environments for additional tasks

If using a printed version of the game, the teacher can provide a list of additional tasks related to locations (landmarks) on the board. The learners can accomplish these tasks by using relevant websites. Here are some examples of such tasks:

- Цирк на "Воробьёвых горах" [Circus]. Сайт [Website]: https://greatcircus.ru. *Какой спектакль можно посмотреть сегодня в цирке? Сколько стоит билет?* [What show can you see today at the circus? How much is the ticket?]
- Пушкинский музей [Pushkin Museum]. Сайт музея [Website]: www.pushkinmuseum.art. *Узнайте часы работы музея (когда музей открывается и когда закрывается)? Сколько стоит билет? Какой это музей: это музей-квартира поэта Александра Пушкина? Что можно увидеть/посмотреть в музее? Музей находится близко от метро? Какая ближайшая (closest) станция метро* (используйте электронную карту: https://yandex.ru/maps)? [Find out the museum's opening and closing hours? How much does a ticket cost? What kind of museum is it: is it the museum-apartment of the poet Alexander Pushkin? What can we see in the museum? Is the museum close to the metro? What is the nearest metro station (use the digital map: https://yandex.ru/maps)?]
- Кремль [Kremlin]: Сайт музея [Website]: www.kreml.ru. *Узнайте часы работы (когда музеи Кремля открыты для туристов)? Есть ли виртуальные туры? Сколько стоит билет, если вы хотите посетить Оружейную Палату (это музей на территории Кремля)* [Find out the opening hours (when are the Kremlin museums open for tourists)? Are there virtual tours? How much does a ticket cost if you want to visit the Armory (it's a museum on the territory of the Kremlin)?].
- Большой театр [Bolshoi Theater]. Сайт театра [Website]: https://bolshoi.ru. *Какой спектакль идёт сегодня и завтра в театре? Сколько стоит билет? Это дорого для вас? Большой театр находится близко от метро? Какая*

ближайшая (closest) станция метро (используйте электронную карту: https://yandex.ru/maps)? [What show is playing today and tomorrow at the theater? How much is the ticket? Is it expensive for you? Is the Bolshoi Theater close to the subway? What is the closest subway station (use the digital map: https://yandex.ru/maps)?]

If a digital version of the board is used, the suggested tasks and related links may be integrated into the game board design.

Adapting the game to other geographical locations and teaching/learning scenarios

Using the same template, the teacher can modify the content of the game to explore different Russian and world cities or different countries. Adapted to a "cross-country travel mode," the game provides opportunities to practice other teaching/learning scenarios related to movement by different means of transportation (*ездить/ехать, летать/лететь* or *плавать/плыть*): scenario #7 *Список: страны, города и регионы, которые я посетил* [A list of countries, cities, regions I have visited]), scenario #8b *Мечты о поездках: страны, города и регионы, которые я хочу/хотел бы посетить* [Dreams trips: countries, cities, regions I want/would like to visit], and scenarios #10b and 12b *Поездки. Базовый или детальный нарратив: Как я ездил в. . . .* [Trips. Basic or detailed narrative: How I did my trip to . . .].

From playing a game to creating a game

In the classroom oriented toward task- and project-based pedagogy, within a telecollaborative project or an intensive Russian program, learners could be given the chance to develop their own games of discovery involving walking or traveling across different Russian or world cities and countries. Student-produced roll-and-move board games can be played in the classroom or may address a problem relevant to an authentic target-language community. For example, Canadian students can develop a board game as a final project that aims to enable Russian K–12 students or Russian-speaking Canadian émigrés to discover the landmarks of a Canadian city or the whole of Canada.

Lessons learned

The method of teaching RVoM with assistance of the board game *Я гуляю по Москве* has been developed in response to students' need to acquire RVoM within the traditional teaching of RVoM that is based on directionality. The game-based approach proposed here has been tested with French, English, and French/English bilingual learners of Russian in different classroom settings. It has also been integrated into the textbook *Tandem* (Bondarenko, 2014, 2015), which has been used, since 2014, at the University of Montreal (Canada), and into a set of instructional materials developed for the intensive Russian summer course at Middlebury College (USA) (Bondarenko, 2017), as well as at Middlebury Institute for International Studies in Monterey (USA). The most important practical lessons I learned from my experience of using this method are the following.

First, using the game *Я гуляю по Москве* is easy and intuitive for both learners and teachers. Any Russian L2 teacher, even a novice, can integrate it into their classroom with no specific preparation. The teacher is not expected to be a follower of the *semantic labeling* approach. *Я гуляю по Москве* can help conduct practice sessions within the traditional teaching of RVoM through the concept of directionality. Yet I am convinced that the explanation of the usage of RVoM through rephrasing their contextual meaning in the target language is much more intuitive and cognitively cost-effective for learners compared to the abstract concept of "direction of motion."

Second, the advantage of educational board games such as *Я гуляю по Москве* is that once they have been purchased or created by the teacher, they can be used many times for different purposes with different groups of students of different proficiency levels. Based on my experience, for beginner classrooms of first or second semesters of Russian, I would recommend focusing on the learning cycle comprising three basic scenarios (communicative-narrative frames) ##5ab, 6, and 7: Прямо сейчас Я ИДУ/ЕДУ(на) в/из (=Я НА ПУТИ в) – Я ХОДИЛ в (=Я БЫЛ/ПОСЕТИЛ) – Завтра Я ИДУ/ПОЙДУ (Я ПЛАНИРУЮ). Other basic scenarios, also important for beginners, must be introduced within distinct instructional activities addressing different thematic contexts (communicative-narrative frames), such as "Everyday activities in the city" combined with "The last time I visited this place" and "My travel experience: my traveling habits, visited places, plans, dreams."

Fourth, to fully benefit from the method, the teacher should ensure full immersion of learners into the game process that guarantees, in turn, their immersion in a specific motion event. For this reason, a game session should last at least 25–40 minutes. I would not recommend using the game as an additional 5-minute "fun" bonus at the end of the lesson that focused on "serious" grammar-oriented fill-in-the-blank-like exercises. If time is limited, I would recommend building a lesson around the game by using a backward task-based lesson design. Within this design, introducing new linguistic patterns (presentation) occurs just in time, and when needed, and is integrated into production, which is based on inherently repetitive tasks ensuring practice. Such a game-based lesson starts with the presentation of the task – game playing and strolling through the streets of Moscow – and then learners gradually discover or review how to speak about their motion actions in specific contexts. The first action *I am walking to* is contrasted with *I am located at . . .* The next action *I am moving by bus . . .* Then *I have already visited several places and I want to list them*, or *I am planning to visit some places*.

Finally, the inherently repetitive tasks-based immersion is useful for supporting deep cognitive encoding which underlays the acquisition of new linguistic patterns. Any teacher knows that this process often passes through a stage of deviation from the suggested acquisition strategy, including the rule explained. Even though learners understand the abstract grammatical rule (declarative knowledge), developing the procedural knowledge and a self-control mechanism to be able to reproduce new patterns in speaking require not only time but also specific strategies (paths of encoding). The role of the teacher is to help the learners identify and adjust erroneous strategies.

My experience shows that game-assisted teaching of RVoM can help facilitate and support this process. For example, on many occasions, I observed that after using a correct RVoM in a specific context several times, learners suddenly switch to a different (incorrect) verb or verbal form. It is especially relevant for scenario #6 that usually has the form of written practice in my Russian classes, in which learners are asked to report about the places they have "visited" in the city. The correct verb form for this context is Я ХОДИЛ В, supported by semantic labels Я БЫЛ В/Я ПОСЕТИЛ: *Я ходил на Арбат. Также я ходил в Музей Пушкина и в Ленинскую библиотеку. А ещё я ходил в цирк и в парк Горького*. However, it is very likely that incorrect forms, such as **Также я ШЁЛ в парк* or **А ещё я ПОШЁЛ в музей*, may appear in learners' speech. When asked to explain the logic behind these decisions, my students often said that they simply found it unusual to always use the same construction and decided to change it "just in case" or to use the verb suggested by an online translator. This deviation provides a golden opportunity for a "learning moment" (intake), which concerns the strategy of encoding, that is, the strategy of applying a rule.

The lack of training in rules application strategies during a real-life-like narration on real-life motion events is, in my opinion, the major reason (besides the abstract and confusing nature of suggested rules) that learners cannot correctly use the RVoM after years of instruction. The learning moment consists in realizing that the reference to a specific context is crucial for using RVoM correctly. The solution for this deviation is *Check the context!* (cf. Six, 2019) by using contextual rephrasing (*semantic labels*). *If the context does not change, there is no reason to change the verb.* The same motion event (even if it is repeated many times) must be expressed by the same verb or corresponding paraphrase (*semantic label*), even if it is very tempting to try something different instead. The verb forms Я ШЁЛ or Я ПОШЁЛ cannot be used in the context (or communicative-narrative frame) of "listing visited places" just because they refer to a different context, such as "basic narration" (КАК Я ХОДИЛ: Я ВЫШЕЛ И ПОШЁЛ – ШЁЛ И ПРИШЁЛ). The same strategy is recommended to verify suggestions provided by Google Translate.

Final remarks and call for empirical research

My experience of designing and using the game *Я гуляю по Москве*, supported by theoretical reflection, has led me to the following conclusions. Roll-and-move board games are a promising classroom activity for teaching and learning RVoM as part of an alternative approach, based on insights from cognitive linguistics. This approach prioritizes context-oriented, item-based strategies and is driven by the personal experience of motion. I also strongly support the general claim that the use of board games in L2 classrooms should not be restricted to "marginal moments" of optional fun but can in itself constitute a session for introducing, revising, or deepening content seen in class (e.g., Faya Cerqueiro & Chao Castro, 2015; Kogan & Kapustin, 2020; Uberman, 1998). It can be effectively integrated into task- and project-based learning scenarios.

For teaching/learning RVoM as part of a context-oriented, item-based, and experience-driven methodology, roll-and-move board games offer the following pedagogical affordances:

1. They ensure a personal experience of motion through simulation and offer a reasonable compromise between total physical body response (TPR) activities (Asher, 1966; Elliott & Yountchi, 2009) and the limitations of the L2 classroom.
2. They visualize the path and manner (on foot/transport) of motion.
3. By involving multiple repetitions of limited numbers of motion events and the verbalization of the same patterns, they support encoding through active retrieval from memory. Therefore, they can be considered "inherently repetitive tasks" (in terms of Gatbonton & Segalowitz, 2005).
4. They provide an opportunity for both oral and written output as a part of different teaching/learning scenarios.
5. As inherently collaborative activities, they capitalize on the advantages of collaborative L2 learning, including corrective feedback from peers.
6. They can be considered as a variety of task-based or project-based pedagogy and integrated with additional task-based and project-based activities, including ones in which learners design their own roll-and-move board game.
7. They can refer to both imaginary and real geographical and urban locations, with the latter providing opportunities to also deepen knowledge of the target culture.
8. When referring to real locations, they allow for the integration of additional task-based activities assisted by the Internet (e.g., exploring related websites to get additional information about landmarks).
9. Both paper and digital versions of board games can be used in face-to-face and distance learning.

I also realize the limitations of the game-based method supporting semantic-labeling approach to teaching RVoM I suggested in the chapter. Even though it is grounded in solid theoretical insights, there is a lack of classroom-based evidence proving its advantages over the traditional directionality-based methodology. There is a need for more classroom-based empirical comparative research aimed at testing the efficiency of roll-and-move games in the acquisition of RVoM. We can find inspiration for such study in similar research on task-based instruction of RVoM in Castellví and Markina (2022) and TPR-based instruction of RVoM in Elliott and Yountchi (2009). Another weak point of the suggested method, which it shares with other alternative approaches mentioned earlier in the chapter, is that the decision about the order in which contextual meanings of RVoM are introduced to learners is based on teachers' intuition about students' needs. Obviously, we need serious corpus-based studies to identify real frequency of different contextual forms of RVoM and their co-occurrence in the same contexts (e.g., Nesset & Janda, 2022). The result of such studies can validate teachers' intuition.

Notes

1 It is noteworthy that one of the first two known games designed and published in the United States was the 1822 roll-and-move game *Traveller's Tour Through the United States*, which combined elements of entertainment and education integrated into a simulation of the experience of exploratory cross-country travel. The board portrayed a map of the United States, with a connecting line drawn between numbered cities. Upon "arriving" at a city, the player must correctly name it and, if playing the advanced version, its population, or else lose a turn (Edwards, 2018; Hofer, 2003; Parlett, 1999).
2 There is no consensus with regard to both the terminology and the characteristics that different scholars use to explain the difference between ХОДИТЬ-like and ИДТИ-like verbs. See the discussion in Nesset (2000) and Bernickaja (2019).
3 The investigation of methodology explicitly or implicitly underpinning Russian-language textbooks and classroom practice with regard to introducing and practicing RVoM deserves a study of its own, which goes beyond the scope of this chapter.
4 See a detailed review of these approaches in Bondarenko (n.d.).
5 All Russian past-tense and subjunctive verb forms are quoted only in the masculine in order to simplify the presentation.
6 Although Six (2018a, 2018b) states the importance of playing board games in her webinar and conference talks, in her latest article, she emphasizes the importance of visualization through, for example, drawing pictograms and the use of authentic materials, such as city plans (Six, 2019).
7 The number of descriptors may vary according to contextual meanings that the teacher deems important for the curriculum. For example, the meaning of unprefixed multidirectional RVoM referring to the ability to perform a movement in a certain manner could be introduced with the semantic label "СПОСОБНОСТЬ. Я УМЕЮ."
8 Unprefixed RVoM can be also introduced through semantic labeling (when possible) or rephrasing/translation in students' L1. For example: Я ПРИЕХАЛ = Я ПРИБЫЛ НА ТРАНСПОРТЕ [I arrived by using a transportation]; Я ПРИШЁЛ = Я ПРИБЫЛ ПЕШКОМ или НЕВАЖНО КАК (потому что мы в городе) [I arrived (on foot)]; Я ПОШЁЛ = Я ОТПРАВИЛСЯ ПЕШКОМ [I headed to/set off to].
9 **BOLD CAPITAL LETTERS** are used in the table to emphasize semantic labels (paraphrasing) and additional descriptors characterizing the main motion event(s) within each scenario. These expressions should be introduced in Russian and regularly used by the teacher and learners to identify motion events. The text under * (asterisk) refers to optional suggestions for more advanced students. The symbol ♛ marks scenarios that can be supported by the educational roll-and-move board game *Я гуляю по Москве*.

References

Akišina, A., Žarkova, T., & Akišina, T. [Акишина, А., Жаркова, Т., и Акишина, Т.]. (1990). *Igry na urokah russkogo jazyka: učebnoje nagljadnoje posobije* [Игры на уроках русского языка: учебное наглядное пособие]. Russkij jazyk [Русский язык].

Arhipova, L. V. [Архипова, Л. В.]. (2006). *Izučaem glagoly dviženija* [Изучаем глаголы движения]. Tambovskij gosudarstvennyj tehničeskij universitet [Тамбовский государственный технический университет].

Asher, J. J. (1966). The learning strategy of the total physical response: A review. *The Modern Language Journal, 50*(2), 79–84.

Bernickaja, N. [Берницкая, Н.] (2017). Vinni Puh hodil v gosti k Piatočku. Vernulsja li on domoj? [Винни Пух ходил в гости к Пятачку. Вернулся ли он домой?] Problème de l'aller-retour. In V. Beliakov et Ch. Bracquenier (Dir.), *Contribution aux études morphologiques, syntaxiques et sémantiques en russe* (pp. 43–56). Presses Universitaires du Midi.

Bernickaja, N. [Берницкая, Н.] (2019). O grammatičeskoj oppositsii glagolov dviženija tipa IDTI/HODIT' v russkom jazyke [О грамматической оппозиции глаголов движения типа ИДТИ/ХОДИТЬ в русской языке]. *Voprosy jazykoznanija [Вопросы языкознания], 1*, 75–93.

Bitehtina, G. A., & Judina, L. P. [Битехтина, Г. А., и Юдина, Л. П.]. (1986). *Sistema raboty po teme "Glagoly dviženija"* [Система работы по теме "Глаголы движения"]. Russkij jazyk [Русский язык].

Bogomolova, A. N., & Petanova, A. J. [Богомолова, А. Н., и Петанова, Л. П.]. (2008). *Prihodite! Prijezžajte!... Priletajte!* [Приходите! Приезжайте!... Прилетайте!]. Zlatoust [Златоуст].

Bondarenko, M. (2014). *Tandem. Manuel de langue russe. Partie 3 (A.2.1). S prazdnikom!* [С праздником!]. ÉPublisher.

Bondarenko, M. (2015). *Tandem. Manuel de langue russe. Partie 2 (A.1.2). Iz Rossii s Liubovju.* [Из России с любовью]. ÉPublisher.

Bondarenko, M. (2017). Set of instructional materials. Level 2. *The 2017 summer immersion program of the Davis School of Russian*. Middlebury College [Unpublished manuscript], Middlebery, VE.

Bondarenko, M. (2019, February). 'Semantic labeling': An alternative strategy for teaching/learning basic verbs of motion at low-proficiency levels of Russian L2 instruction [Conference paper]. *The 2019 AATSEEL conference*. New Orleans, USA.

Bondarenko, M. (in press). Spiral-like design for teaching inflectional languages at elementary levels. In C. Corin, C. Campbell, & B. L. Leaver (Eds.), *Open architecture curricula design: Courses and concepts*. Georgetown University Press.

Bondarenko, M. (n.d.). *Approaches to teaching Russian verbs of motion under an epistemological loop: Structural linguistics vs. cognitive linguistics* [unpublished manuscript]. University of Montreal.

Callois, R. (2001). *Man, play and games*. University of Illinois Press.

Castellví, J., & Markina, E. (2022, August 30). The efficiency of task-supported and task-based approaches in teaching the verbs of motion in Russia [Conference talk]. *9th international conference on task-based language teaching*. Innsbruck, Austria.

Castellví, J., Markina, E., & Gamirova, D. (2022, June 1). Obučenije glagolam dviženija v praktičeskom kurse RKI na osnove celevyh zadanij (TBLT) [Обучение глаголам движения в практическом курсе РКИ на основе целевых заданий (TBLT)]. [Conference talk] *II Meždunarodnaja naučnaja konferencija "Russkij jazyk v novejših lingvističeskih, mežkulturnyh I glottodidaktičskih issledovanijah* [II Международная научная конференция "Русский язык в новейших лингвистических, межкультурных и глоттодидактических исследованиях"]. University of Bialystok, Bialystok, Poland.

Edwards, J. R. (2018). *Saving families, one game at a time.* https://vdocuments.mx

Elliott, E., & Yountchi, L. (2009). Total physical response and Russian multi-and-unidirectional verbs of motion: A case study in acquisition. *The Slavic and East European Journal, 53*(3), 428–450.

Faya Cerqueiro, F., & Chao Castro, M. (2015). Board-games as review lessons in English language teaching: Useful resources for any level. Los juegos de mesa como clase de revisión en el aula de lengua inglesa: recursos útiles para cualquier nivel. *Docencia e Investigación, 25*(2), 67–82.

Fung, Y. M., & Min, Y. L. (2016). Effects of board game on speaking ability of low-proficiency ESL learners. *International Journal of Applied Linguistics & English Literature, 5*(3), 261–271.

Gagarina, N. (2009). Verbs of motion in Russian: An acquisitional perspective. *The Slavic and East European Journal, 53*(3), 451–470

Garris, R., Ahlers, R., & Driskell, J. E. (2002). Games, motivation, and learning: A research and practice model. *Simulation and Gaming, 33*(4), 441–467.

Gatbonton, E., & Segalowitz, N. (2005). Rethinking communicative language teaching: A focus on access to fluency. *The Canadian Modern Language Review/La Revue canadienne des langues vivantes, 61*(3), 325–353.

Gepner, M. (2016). The semantics of motion verbs in Russian. *Baltic International Yearbook of Cognition, Logic and Communication, 11*(3). http://doi.org/10.4148/1944-3676.1105

Gibson, J. J. (1979). *The ecological approach to visual perception.* Houghton Mifflin Harcourt.

Gor, K., Cook, S., Malyushenkova, V., & Vdovina, T. (2009). Verbs of motion in higher proficient learners and heritage speakers of Russian. *The Slavic and East European Journal, 53*(3), 386–408.

Gor, K., Cook, S., Malyushenkova, V., & Vdovina, T. (2010). Russian verbs of motion: Second language acquisition and cognitive linguistics perspectives. In V. Hasko & R. Perelmutter (Eds.), *New approaches to Slavic verbs of motion* (pp. 361–381). John Benjamins.

Halliday, M. A. K., & Matthiessen, C. M. (2013). *Halliday's introduction to functional grammar.* Routledge.

Hasko, V. (2009). The locus of difficulties in the acquisition of Russian verbs of motion by highly proficient learners. *The Slavic and Eastern European Journal, 53*(3), 360–385. www.jstor.org/stable/40651162.

Hawkinson, E. (2013). Board game design and implementation for specific language learning goals. In *The 2013 Asian conference on language learning. Globalization, culture and society: What role does language play? Official conference proceedings* (pp. 317–327). International Academic Forum. ACLL2013_0169.pdf (iafor.org). Video recording of the talk: (23) Board Game Design for Learning Goals – YouTube.

Hofer, M. (2003). *The games we played: The golden age of board & table games.* Princeton Architectural Press.

Huizinga, J. (1955). *Homo Ludens; a study of the play-element in culture.* Beacon Press.

Israeli, A. (2017, February). Why can't we teach verbs of motion? [Conference talk]. *The 2017 AATSEEL conference*, San Francisco, USA. www.aatseel.org/100111/pdf/abstracts/1327/Israeli.pdf

Isačenko, A. V. [Исаченко, А. В.] (1960). *Grammatičeskij stroj russkogo jazyka v sopostavleniji s slovackim [Грамматический строй русского языка в сопоставлении с словацким].* II. Bratislava. Vid. Slovenskey Akadémie Vied.

Ivanova, V. Ja. [Иванова, В. Я.] (2010). *Sistema povtorenija i dalnejšego izučenija galgolov dviženija* [Система повторения и дальнейшего изучения глаголов движения]. SPbGASU [СПбГАСУ].

Kagan, O. (2007). On the semantics of verbs of motion in Russian. In Y. Falk (Ed.), *Proceedings of the 23 annual conference of the Israel Association for Theoretical Linguists* (pp. 1–15). www.iatl.org.il/?page_id=125

Kagan, O., Miller, F., & Kudyma, G. (2006). *В пути [V puti]. Russian grammar in context.* Pearson/Prentice Hall.

Karavanov, A. [Караванов, А.]. (2010). *Russkije glagoly dviženija: sistema, pravila, upražnenija* [Русские глаголы движения: система, правила, упражнения]. Drofa.

Kogan, V. V., & Kapustin, S. (2020). Conquering speaking anxiety with *LinguaPolis*. In U. Nurmukhamedov & R. Sadler (Eds.), *New ways in teaching with games* (pp. 77–79). TESOL Press.

Kostomarov, V. G. [Костомаров, В. Г.] (Ed.). (1988). *Russkij jazyk dlja vseh. Davajte pogovorim i počitajem* [Русский язык для всех. Давайте поговорим и почитаем]. Russkij jazyk [Русский язык].

Krupina, E. S. [Крупина E. С.] (2014). Iz opyta ispolsovanija nastol'nyh igr v obučeniji inostrannym jazykam v Sankt-Peterburgskom universitete MVD Rossiji [Из опыта использования настольных игр в обучении иностранным языкам в Санкт-Петербургском университете МВД России]. *Trudy Sankt-Peterburgskogo gosudarstvennogo universiteta kultury i isskustv [Труды Санкт-Петербургского государственного университета культуры и искусств], 202*, 127–131.

Lewis, M. (1993). *The lexical approach: The state of ELT and a way rorward.* Language Teaching Publication.

Littlemore, J. (2009). *Applying cognitive linguistics to second language learning and teaching.* Palgrave Mcmillan.

Mahota, W. J. (1996). *Russian motion verbs for intermediate students.* Yale University Press.

Markina, E. (2018). *Comparing focus on forms and task-based language teaching in the acquisition of Russian as a foreign language* [PhD Thesis]. University of Barcelona.

Muravyova, L. (1975). *Verbs of motion in Russian.* Russian Language Publishers.

Nagajceva, N. I. [Нагайцева, Н. И.]. (2019). *Vido-vremennyje značenija i slovoizmenenije glagolov. Sposoby glagolnogo dejstvija. Učebno-metodičeskoje posobije po russkomu jazyku dla inostrannyh studentov* [Видо-временные значения и словоизменение глаголов. Способы глагольного действия. Учебно-методическое пособие по русскому языку для иностранных студентов]. Har'kovskij nacionalnyj tehničeskij universitet [Харьковский национальный технический университет].

Nesset, T. (2000). Iconicity and prototype: A new perspective on Russian verbs of motion. *Scando-Slavica, 46*, 105–119.

Nesset, T. (2008). Path and Manner: An image-schematic approach to Russian verbs of motion. *Scando-Slavica, 54*(1), 135–158.

Nesset, T., & Janda, L. A. (2022). Securing strategic input for L2 learners: Constructions with Russian motion verbs. In H. C. Boas (Ed.), *Directions for pedagogical construction grammar. Learning and teaching (with) constructions* (pp. 161–178). De Gruyer Mouton.

Obuhova, T. M. [Обухова, Т. М.] (2015). *Igrat' ili ne igrat': obzor nastolnyh igr dlia zaniatij po russkomu jazyku (leksiko-kommunikativnyj aspect)* [Играть или не играть: обзор настольных игр для занятий по русскому как иностранному (лексико-коммуникативный аспект)]. In *Perevod kak sredstvo obogaščenija mirovoj kultury. Materialy naučnoj konferenciji. November 21–41 2015* [Перевод как средство обогащения мировой культуры. Материалы международной научной конференции 21–24 ноября 2015 г.] Online [Электронное издание] (pp. 170–178). Izdatelstvo FORUM ["Издательство ФОРУМ"]

Padučeva, E. [Падучева, Е.] (2004). O semantičeskom invariante vidovogo značenija glagola v russkom jazyke [О семантическом инварианте видового значения глагола в русском языке]. *Russkij jazyk v paučnom osveščeniji [Русский язык в научном освещении]*, *2*(8), 5–16.

Paris, T. N., & Yussof, R. L. (2012). Enhancing grammar using board game. *Procedia – Social and Behavioral Sciences*, *68*, 213–221.

Paris, T. N., & Yussof, R. L. (2013). Use of "time trap board game" to teach grammar. *Procedia – Social and Behavioral Sciences*, *105*, 398–409.

Parlett, D. (1999). *The Oxford history of board games.* Oxford University Press.

Paškina, E. S. [Пашкина, Е. С.] (2007). Glagoly dviženija russkogo jazyka: konceptualjno-terminologičeskij apparat [Глаголы движения русского языка: концептуально-терминологический аппарат]. *Vestnik Pravoslavnogo Svjato-Tihonovskogo gumanitarnogo universiteta. Serija 3: Filologija [Вестник Православного Свято-Тихоновского гуманитарного университета. Серия 3: Филология]*, *9*, 33–42.

Phuong, H. Y., & Nguyen, T. N. P. (2017). The impact of board games on EFL learners' grammar retention. *IOSR Journal of Research & Method in Education*, *7*(3), 61–66.

Poole, F., Clarke-Midura, J., Sun, Ch., & Lam, K. (2019). Exploring the pedagogical affordances of a collaborative board game in a dual language immersion classroom. *Foreign Language Annals*, *52*(4), 753–775.

Rakhilina, E. (2004). There and back: The case of Russian "go". *Glossos*, *5*, 1–34.

Ruiz-Zorrilla, M., Kornakov, P., & Castellví, J. (2006). *Kurs russkogo jazyka. Načal'nyj uroven'* [Курс русского языка. Начальный уровень]. PPU.

Salen, K., & Zimmerman, E. (2003). *Rules of play*. MIT Press.

Six, I. (2018a, February). Why can't we teach verbs of motion? [Conference talk]. *The 2018 AATSEEL conference*. Washington DC.

Six, I. (2018b, December). Verbs of Motion. Keep it simple yet meaningful [Webinaire talk]. *Aire LACTR*. https://actr.wildapricot.org/resources/Documents/VoM_Simple.pdf

Six, I. (2019). "V kakom kontekste?" ["В каком контексте?"]. *Russian Language Journal/ Russkij jazyk [Русский язык]*, *69* (Special Issue: In Honor of Olga Kagan), 213–234.

Skvorcova, G. N., & Poljakov, V. N. [Скворцова, Г. Н., и Поляков, В. Н.]. (2021). *Glagoly dviženija bez ošibok* [Глаголы движения без ошибок]. Russkij jazyk [Русский язык]: Kursy [Курсы].

Slobin, D. (2004). The many ways to search for a frog: Linguistic typology and the expression of motion events. In S. Strömqvist & L. Verhoeven (Eds.), *Relating events in narrative: Vol. 2. Typological and contextual perspectives* (pp. 219–257). Lawrence Erlbaum.

Sorayaie Azar, A. (2012). The effect of games on EFL learners' vocabulary learning strategies. *International Journal of Applied and Basic Sciences*, *1*(2), 252–256.

Stilman, L. (1951). *Russian verbs of motion*. King's Crown Press.

Suits, B. (2005). *The grasshopper: Games, life and utopia* (2nd ed.). Broadview Press.

Talmy, L. (2000). *Toward a cognitive semantics: Vol. II: Typology and process in concept structuring*. MIT Press.

Taylor, J. (2006). Cognitive semantics. In K. Brown (Ed.), *Encyclopedia of language & linguistics* (2nd ed., pp. 542–546). Elsevier.

Turner, V. (1982). *From ritual to theatre: The human seriousness of play*. PAJ Publications.

Uberman, A. (1998). The use of games for vocabulary presentation and revision. *Forum, 36*(1), 20–27.

van Lier, L. (2004). *The ecology and semiotics of language learning: A sociocultural perspective*. Springer.

Wierzbicka, A. (1996). *Semantics: Primes and universals*. Oxford University Press.

Wulff, S., & Ellis, N. C. (2018). *Usage-based approaches to second language acquisition* (Vol. 54, pp. 37–56). John Benjamins.

York, J. (2020). Promoting spoken interaction and student engagement with board games in a language teaching context. In M. Farber (Eds.), *Global perspectives on gameful and playful teaching and learning* (pp. 1–26). IGI Global. https://doi.org/10.4018/978-1-7998-2015-4.ch001

York, J., & deHaan, J. (2017). Board games and foreign language learning: Rationale and framework development. In G. Brooks (Ed.), *The 2016 Pan SIG Journal* (pp. 379–390). JALT.

Chapter 7

Game-based learning in L2 Russian classrooms

Interaction, multimodality, and practical suggestions

Olesia Pavlenko and Dmitrii Pastushenkov

CHAPTER SUMMARY

In this chapter, we discuss game-based learning (GBL) as a methodology for second language (L2) teaching and how teachers of L2 Russian can use these games in their classes. The chapter develops a discussion of theoretical considerations regarding GBL, including such fundamental concepts in second language acquisition (SLA) as interaction and multimodality. In addition to theory, we give specific examples of and talk about a variety of different games: from traditional games to next-generation "AAA games"[1] releases and online video games. We provide recommendations about how these games can be implemented in L2 Russian classes, talk about linguistic skills that GBL can help develop, and give examples of grammatical features that these games can focus on. Finally, we talk about some of the lesser-known features of the GBL platform Kahoot and provide links for the Kahoot mini-course that we developed for teachers of L2 Russian.

Краткое содержание главы

Данная глава посвящена обучению иностранным языкам на основе игр и тому, как преподаватели русского как иностранного могут использовать игры на своих занятиях. Глава начинается с обсуждения теорий, касающихся данного подхода. Мы анализируем такие фундаментальные понятия прикладной лингвистики как взаимодействие и мультимодальность. Глава также включает описание различных игр, от традиционных игр до релизов "ААА Игр" нового поколения и онлайн-видеоигр, и рекомендации относительно того, как эти игры могут быть реализованы на уроках русского языка. Мы поясняем, как данные игры могут помочь развить у студентов лингвистические, речевые и другие навыки и приводим примеры грамматических конструкций, которые эти игры помогают освоить. В заключительной части главы мы рассказываем о некоторых менее известных функциях платформы Kahoot и предоставляем ссылки на мини курс Kahoot, который мы разработали для преподавания русского языка как иностранного.

DOI: 10.4324/9781003369721-10

Game-based learning in the context of L2 Russian

Game-based learning (GBL) has been considered an effective and engaging methodology for second language (L2) education at different ages and proficiency levels (Al-Azawi et al., 2016; Karagiorgas & Niemann, 2017; Kaya & Sagnak, 2022). Research has shown that GBL can facilitate L2 vocabulary learning (Zou et al., 2021) and is often positively viewed by students (Fithriani, 2019). With few notable exceptions in the field of Russian language teaching (Tsabei, 2020), and despite the ongoing trend toward gamification of L2 education (adding game-like elements to learning activities) and adoption of game-based practices (use of games as learning activities), the majority of previous work in the area of GBL has been done with more commonly taught languages such as English. For example, the recent edited volume of *New Ways in Teaching with Games* edited by Nurmukhamedov and Sadler (2020) includes a large collection of games for ESL teachers. As the editors and authors of the present volume pointed out, when integrating games in L2 classes, it is important to consider a variety of different linguistic and cultural factors. In the present chapter, we discuss how L2 Russian teachers can use different types of games, from traditional activities to video games and GBL platforms, while taking into consideration the needs, motivations, and struggles of L2 Russian learners.

The chapter starts with a brief overview of second language acquisition (SLA) literature and GBL. In line with interactionist perspectives (for review, see Loewen & Sato, 2018), we argue that because gaming involves an active dialogue between teachers and students (including in peer interaction), it can positively impact L2 development. Interaction in GBL implies that learners receive linguistic input, which can also be multimodal and thus can help accommodate L2 learners' needs and strengths (Mayer, 2014; Paivio, 1991; Peters & Muñoz, 2020). In addition to the input, L2 learners can receive feedback and produce modified output (output in response to corrective feedback) while interacting with their teachers or peers during games. Input, output, and interaction have been viewed as key predictors of successful L2 development (Gass & Mackey, 2006; Long, 1996). Considering that the amounts of input, output, and interaction that students receive vary, we, as teachers, should try to provide more opportunities for interaction for them, including in the form of games.

In this chapter, we offer a description of various traditional games from Nurmukhamedov and Sadler's (2020) volume and how these games can be adapted for L2 Russian classes. The next section of the chapter focuses on lesser-known features of Kahoot, a game-based learning and testing platform that has become an integral component of many modern classrooms (Bratel et al., 2021; Wang & Tahir, 2020). In this section, we also discuss a mini-course in Kahoot for L2 Russian classes that we developed, tested in our practice, and offer here as an additional resource that accompanies this chapter. The chapter also includes descriptions of popular video games that have Russian localizations and ideas on how these games can be integrated into Russian-language classrooms in semester-long projects. For example, we talk about the "Metro" series developed by the

Ukrainian studio *4A Games* that was localized into several languages, including Russian. The chapter concludes with a "Lessons learned" section, in which we analyze our experiences using GBL in Russian language classes. In this chapter, we argue that GBL, in its many forms, benefits L2 Russian learning by making classes more interactive and engaging.

SLA perspectives on GBL: interaction and multimodality

GBL and SLA

Since childhood, games have become an integral part of our lives. As children, we learn by playing the same games repeatedly and by discovering new things through interacting with our parents, siblings, friends, and teachers. In the world of adult gaming, sales numbers have significantly grown since the early years of tabletop role-playing games and video games. For example, the video game *The Witcher 3: Wild Hunt*, which was fully localized into Russian, was developed by the Polish studio *CD Project Red* and has sold over 40 million copies. More and more adults enjoy gaming in its many forms, from mobile 1980s-like games to next-generation AAA releases with budgets comparable to those of modern blockbusters. According to Karagiorgas and Niemann (2017), gaming may soon become the most popular form of entertainment in the United States, with 183 million players overall and 5 million active gamers who play for more than 40 hours per week. Considering the recent technological advances (e.g., cloud gaming services such as Nvidia GeForce Now and PlayStation Plus Premium) and the ubiquity of games for different ages, GBL as a methodology has become more and more commonly used in education, including L2 classrooms. In their review of the literature focusing on ESL classes with learners from 11 to 18 years old and published between 2013 to 2020, Kaya and Sagnak (2022) pointed out that games can make learning an L2 more engaging, linking it to students' increased motivation and participation. Such active participation can subsequently lead to more autonomous learning. Different learning platforms that can be used for language learning, such as Kahoot and Quizlet, have thousands of active users (Bratel et al., 2021; Wang & Tahir, 2020). Al-Azawi et al. (2016) emphasized a very important idea: "the next generation of jobs will be characterized by increased technology use, extensive problem solving, and complex communication" (p. 135). These necessary skills can be trained in a GBL classroom.

In terms of individual linguistic skills, Fithriani (2019) suggested that games can help make grammar learning more engaging, which is particularly essential for L2 Russian classrooms because of the inflectional complexity of the language. Another skill that has been investigated in SLA literature on the topic of GBL is L2 vocabulary learning. In a recent review article, Zou et al. (2021) focused on such digital vocabulary learning gaming tools as simulation, role-playing, card, board, and gamified digital books. The authors concluded that digital GBL facilitated L2 vocabulary learning in both the short- and long-term. As it will be mentioned in the description of various games later in this chapter, the review article by Zou et al. (2021) has also shown that GBL can help improve L2 learners' reading and listening comprehension, as well as their pronunciation. Most of the games that we discuss in this chapter involve multiple skills and, in some cases, all four skills (reading, listening, writing, and speaking).

Interactionist perspectives on GBL

In one of the chapters from the first volume in the *Routledge Russian Language Pedagogy and Research* series, Pastushenkov (2022) discussed the popular role-playing game titled *Mafia* and how it can be used in L2 Russian classrooms. Role-playing games such as *Mafia* and *Werewolf* include active player interaction and thus can be implemented in L2 classrooms to facilitate learning in the form of teacher–student and peer dialogue. Similar to *Mafia* or *Werewolf* that can be played in face-to-face classrooms, many online video games, such as *Among Us*, also include deductive elements and interaction. In line with the interaction hypothesis (Long, 1996), a cognitive-interactionist framework considers the following constructs as the key elements of interaction: input, negotiation, output, and noticing (Gass & Mackey, 2006; Loewen & Sato, 2018). In role-playing games, students receive input from their peers and teachers, they negotiate meaning and provide feedback to each other, and finally, learners have the valuable opportunity to produce modified output, which indicates that learners incorporated the feedback that they received during interactions. As Loewen and Sato pointed out, "interaction plays a crucial role in SLA theory and pedagogy, and there appears to be no slowdown in this regard" (2018, p. 317).

L2 learners' interaction may also include elements of translanguaging, or switching between learners' linguistic repertoires (Wei, 2018). Some L2 teachers may try to avoid translanguaging practices, even though students' first language (L1) use can also help them learn the L2 (Bondarenko, 2022). For example, communicative tasks and GBL can create a platform where L2 learners can talk about the language that they are producing (e.g., in the form of vocabulary deliberations). This form of metalanguage has often been referred to as language-related episodes (LREs) in SLA literature, including papers on the topic of translanguaging (Pastushenkov et al., 2021). If learners discuss the language that they are producing, they can learn new vocabulary or grammar not just from their teacher and homework but also from their peers.

GBL and multimodality

When we talk about video games in L2 classes, we should mention the concept of multimodality. In line with previous theories, Peters and Muñoz (2020) argued that information (e.g., L2 input) is processed more efficiently when provided in spoken and written modes. More and more video games have been localized into multiple languages, such as Russian. For example, the best-selling *Metro* series developed by the Ukrainian studio *4A Games* and based on the novels by Dmitry Glukhovsky or the *Witcher* series and *Cyberpunk 2077* developed by the Polish studio *CD Projekt Red* have full Russian localizations. These video games involve both reading Russian subtitles and listening to Russian speech recorded by professional voice actors. In the role-playing games developed by *CD Projekt Red*, players can also choose between different dialogue options and thus change in-game interaction between the characters.

Traditional games in L2 Russian classes

"Pick the lie"

In this section of the chapter, we would like to describe different traditional games from Nurmukhamedov and Sadler's (2020) volume and how these games can be adapted for L2 Russian classes. We would like to start with Pick the Lie from the chapter by Paul McAleese; it is a variation of Two Truths and a Lie that requires writing and speaking. Students need to come up with three sentences about themselves. One of these sentences should be a lie. The game Pick the Lie can be adapted for different proficiency levels, lesson topics, or grammatical forms. For example, in beginner Russian classes, when students learn about locations and topics of conversations using the prepositional case, the teacher may ask them to write two truths and one lie about places that they have visited: *Я был на Аляске* [I was in Alaska] or *Я был в Мичигане* [I was in Michigan]. At higher Russian proficiency levels, teachers can ask their students to write three short paragraphs about themselves (e.g., such as tell us about a time when you solved a problem, or discuss your favorite or least favorite subjects at school). Teachers can guide their students and ask them to focus on different topics that they also discuss in class, such as their interests, future plans, favorite food, family, or traveling.

Teachers can place their students into groups or ask them to work individually. When one student says three sentences about themselves, their classmates should guess which one is a lie. Students are encouraged to be creative and innovative in their responses. The main advantage of this game is that students will compose full sentences and practice both writing and speaking. In addition to the prepositional case, teachers can ask their students to create sentences using *я буду* [I will] or perfective verbs (e.g., *я сделаю* [I will do it]) to practice the future tense in Russian. Verbs of motion can also be used in this activity (e.g., *Летом я поеду в Кострому* [In the summer, I will go to Kostroma]). This activity can also help students practice agreement in different cases (e.g., *Я раньше жил в маленьком городе* [I used to live in a small town.]).

"Two halves make a whole"

Another game that can include the four skills (listening, reading, speaking, and writing) is called Two Halves Make a Whole from the chapter by Jesse Conway. This game is similar to Apples to Apples or Cards Against Humanity. In L2 Russian classes, this game gives students the opportunity to practice complex syntactic constructions. Teachers can give students different incomplete sentences (e.g., one clause out of two) or ask their students to come up with their own sentences. An example would be sentences with *чтобы* [in order to] that are often taught at the end of the first year of Russian or at the end of the first semester of an intensive Russian course: *Чтобы хорошо учиться в Гарварде, я* . . . [To study well at Harvard, I . . .]. The challenge is to complete sentences using Russian. Students can work in groups of three to five students, and at the end of each round, after they hear everyone's complete sentences, they can vote and choose the response that they liked the most. In this activity, teachers can also ask their students to focus on certain grammatical forms or syntactic constructions. For example, this game can help students practice conditionals: *Если бы у меня был/была/было/были* . . ., *я бы* . . . [If I had . . . , I would . . .].

"List game"

The List Game from the chapter by Sara Peterson and Aaron Shayne promotes peer interaction in small groups. This game can be used at different proficiency levels but may be more appropriate for beginner Russian classes in discussions on familiar topics. In L2 Russian classes, teachers can give their students a prompt (e.g., *кислые фрукты* [sour fruit]) and 2–3 minutes to brainstorm their ideas in groups. After that, teachers can randomly ask one group of students to read their list, while the other group should check these words in their list. For example, if the first group reads *лимон* [lemon] and the second group also says *лимон* [lemon] if they have this fruit in their list, in this case, the second group would not get any points. If the words in the lists of two of these groups are different, the second group would get one point for each unique word in their list based on the teacher's prompt.

This game can also focus on Russian-language cases. Teachers can encourage students not only to write and say these words but also to practice genitive, accusative, or prepositional cases (both singular and plural forms): *У меня нет лимона* [I do not have a lemon], *Я люблю лимоны* [I love lemons], or *У меня нет лимонов в списке* [I do not have lemons on my list]. This activity can also be complemented by elements of task-based language teaching. For example, teachers can ask their students to work in pairs and pretend to be roommates. Each "roommate" needs to come up with a shopping list. After the students complete their lists, they need to compare them and figure out what things they have in common and what things are different and, afterward, come up with the final shopping list for the week. This activity would then resemble a consensus task like the one described in the next section of the chapter.

"Lost on a Deserted Island" or "Trip to Russia"

The game Lost on a Deserted Island from the chapter by Margherita Berti requires work in groups of 3–4. For this game, L2 Russian learners need to imagine that they are lost on a deserted island. Their teacher will then prepare a list with 15 items (e.g., a bottle of water, a small torch, a tent for two people, sunscreen, a soap bar, a 10 m rope, a pot, a box with matches, a penknife, a compass, a tin of salmon, a can of corn, a small blanket, five aspirins) and students will need to decide what items they would like to take, but based on the rules, they can choose only three items and explain the reasons they would like to take them. Students may be familiar with this consensus game/task as it is often used as an "icebreaker" at American universities. In Russian language classes, this game can be used to practice quantification, which may be introduced in the first or the second semester of Russian, depending on when the genitive case is taught: *одна коробка спичек* [one box of matches] or *двадцать две упаковки лапши* [twenty- two packs of noodles]). Teachers will need to model different sentence structures (e.g., *Мне нужен компас* [I need a compass]) depending on the lesson's goal. It may also be helpful to practice the construction *потому что* [because]: *Мне нужны двадцать две упаковки лапши, потому что лапшу легко готовить* [I need twenty-two packs of noodles because noodles are easy to cook.]

In this game, students will be able to develop three sentences providing arguments to support the reasons they choose these three specific items. Working on a more realistic scenario may also be helpful, even though you may add humor and encourage your students to be creative. A possible real-world task would be to pick up things for a "Trip to Russia" that students need or do not need: *Мне будет нужен рюкзак, потому что я буду много путешествовать.* [I will need a backpack because I will travel a lot.]. This activity may be used at different Russian proficiency levels, but it is probably more appropriate for high beginner or low intermediate learners of Russian.

"The Perfect Fortune Teller"

In the game titled The Perfect Fortune Teller from the chapter by Alex Blumenstock and Cameron Hill, students need to "predict" events that will happen to them or their peers using the future tense. Russian-language learners will be able to practice speaking in small groups. Developing familiarity with peers is significant because students will need to learn some background information about their partner in order to make "accurate predictions." This activity can be used at different proficiency levels and can help practice different grammatical constructions, such as the future tense with the auxiliary verb *буду/будешь/будете* [I will/you will] and the prepositional case – *Где я буду жить? – Ты будешь жить в большом доме в Сочи.* [– Where will I live? – You will live in a large house in Sochi.]

This game is similar to more realistic scenarios, such as a customer service experience or an interview, in a sense that the "fortune teller" needs to "predict" desirable answers and results for their partners. Teachers can facilitate this game by giving their students different sample questions (e.g., *Когда я найду работу своей мечты?* [When will I find a job of my dream?] or *Что я буду делать в 2077?* [What will I do in 2077?]). This activity will help learners practice the Russian grammatical aspect: "– *А я найду серёжки Екатерины II? – Да, конечно, ты найдёшь. – А сколько времени мне надо будет искать? – Чтобы найти серёжки Екатерины II, тебе потребуется всего 10 лет.* The Perfect Fortune

Teller can be used at different proficiency levels but may be more appropriate for intermediate and advanced Russian-language learners who can already make complex "predictions" and participate in longer dialogues.

"Have you ever . . . ?"

The game "Have you ever . . . ?" from the chapter by Jacqueline Foster can help Russian learners practice speaking, as well as help master some of the most difficult grammatical patterns in Russian, such as the aspect and verbs of motion, and use them in a meaningful context. Teachers can prepare a list of verbs in advance (e.g., in Quizlet), ask their students to focus on a specific topic (e.g., tourist destinations), or improvise. There is also a pre-made version of the game by Irina Parfenova. Traditionally, this game starts with a statement from one of the students in a small group, such as *Я никогда не был на Аляске* [I have never been to Alaska]. If one of the students in the group has actually been to Alaska, they will win a point (or lose a point, depending on how teachers and students want to play this game). Students may also work in pairs or small groups and practice the indefinite particle *нибудь* (e.g., in *когда-нибудь* [ever]): *Ты когда-нибудь ездила на поезде из Москвы во Владивосток?* [Have you ever taken a train from Moscow to Vladivostok?].

"Bring Home the Beaver"

The game Bring Home the Beaver from the chapter by Rebecca Shaw Sullivan is a unique practice for studying idioms. For example, teachers can prepare a list of idioms and remove some words (e.g., nouns) from a phrase: *. . . на двое сказала* (from *бабушка надвое сказала* [it remains to be seen] or *клевать . . .* (from *клевать носом* [nod off]). Teachers can create a word bank for their students. For example, to learn more about family members, teachers can add such words as *племянник* [nephew] or *прадедушка* [great-grandfather]. Students will need to investigate the missing words and try to explain what these idioms mean (the meanings or translations can also be given in a word bank). Teachers can also prepare pieces of paper with the words from the idioms and ask students to solve this puzzle. This activity will help practice Russian cases/conjugation/aspect/agreement because of the matching aspect of this game. A possible title for the game in Russian is *Бабушка Сказала* [*Babushka Said*]. Idioms can be introduced at different proficiency levels but may be more appropriate for high beginner students. For example, *клевать носом* [nod off] can be introduced with the instrumental case, and the word bank can include such nouns as *головой* [with one's head] or *ушами* [with one's ears).

"Space Crew"

The game Space Crew (or Saving Lives Using Commands and Transition Devices) from the chapter by Adriana D'Adamo Guillén encourages students to use imperatives and temporal adverbs in order "to save" their fellow astronaut (or *космонавт*). The entire class will need to participate in this activity. Students need to imagine that they are in space on a special mission. One of the crew members finds a hole in their space suit mask and loses their oxygen. The other members of the crew need to help their colleague and explain how to fix the hole in their mask and survive in space. Students need to use imperatives such as *возьми* . . . [take . . .] or *отрежь* . . . [cut . . .] and temporal adverbs such as *потом* [then] to explain the steps that can help overcome this problem. Complementary materials for this activity include a rubber band, a pencil, a plastic container, a paper clip, and a cup. Teachers can come up with different scenarios for this game (e.g., *на корабле стало слишком холодно* [it is too cold on the ship] or *у нас заканчивается еда* [we are running out of food]). This activity can be introduced with imperatives (typically in the first semester of Russian). However, the game may be more appropriate for higher proficiency levels since it can be challenging to give instructions in Russian.

Using Kahoot in creative ways

In this part of the chapter, we would like to talk about lesser-known features of Kahoot, one of the most popular GBL learning and testing platforms. Originated in Norway, Kahoot has become one of the most popular free resources to engage in classroom activities. Approximately 50% of K–12 students in the United States use Kahoot. Registration on the Kahoot platform is free.

The "Discover" page helps users filter information. Teachers can find a variety of different Kahoots using unique hashtags. For this chapter, we developed a mini-course for learning Russian as an L2 with nine Kahoot quizzes. You can find these Kahoots using the following hashtags:

#russian   #russianlanguage   #russiangrammar   #grammarinrussian   #langrus
#ruslang   #gamerussian   #russiangame

The "Library" page displays instructors' own Kahoots. This page shows information about drafts, favorites, and the files that were shared with the account. The "Reports" page shows students' progress. Before testing students using the Kahoot platform, teachers need to make sure to sign in; otherwise, the results will not be saved. On the "Groups" page, instructors can create a group, which can be helpful when Russian classes include additional conversation practice outside the main section. On the "Marketplace" page, Kahoot users can buy different courses. Teachers can also make their own course and add it to the "Marketplace."

We encourage the reader to try out the Kahoots we developed for this chapter. This course is a work in progress. The current version includes Kahoots on the three cases (prepositional, accusative, and genitive) that are commonly taught in beginner Russian courses. These quizzes can serve as a more engaging alternative to traditional fill-in-the-blank and multiple-choice quizzes. The tests are also competitive, which can help motivate Russian-language learners.

Kahoot! name	Link	QR	Q
Prepositional case Предложный падеж [test1]	https://bit.ly/3OWQPRg		10
Prepositional case Предложный падеж [test2]	https://bit.ly/43JL2CI		10
Prepositional case Предложный падеж [test3]	https://bit.ly/3WXnwQs		10
Accusative case Винительный падеж [test1]	https://bit.ly/42xjPIK		10
Accusative case Винительный падеж [test2]	https://bit.ly/3WONOnM		10
Accusative case Винительный падеж [test3]	https://bit.ly/43oJC0C		10
Genitive case Родительный падеж [test1]	https://bit.ly/43HWILz		10
Genitive case Родительный падеж [test2]	https://bit.ly/43pzO6p		10

Using video games in L2 Russian classes

As we pointed out earlier in this chapter, we, as L2 Russian teachers, should not underestimate the role of video games in the daily routines of our students (and the life of our society in general). Based on our observations, the Russian localization version of *Minecraft*, the most popular game ever made, uses the terms that can be employed in different L2 Russian learning activities: *ящики шалкера, лук ап, эндер сундук; черепа мобов: голова крипера, голова зомби, череп визер скелета . . . незеритовый скрап, незер-кварц, осколок призмарина, раковина наутилуса, мембрана фантома, сгусток магмы, панцирь шалкера, слеза гаста, звезда незера, стержень энда*, or *кристалл энда*. These "Minecraft terms" are part of the Russian language and, as such, internalize cases, agreement, and other inherent features of the Russian language. A student who learns Russian will understand many words in the game, because while they are often transliterated from English, they still follow the rules of Russian grammar. If students play *Minecraft* or other games, teachers can ask their students to talk about what they did in the game, what items they used, or what structures they built.

Roblox, another online game, has recently joined the list of the most popular games of all time. One of the distinct features of this game is that players can invite up to 200 friends from around the world to join them. Users can also see their friends online and chat with them in Russian. The chat feature is free and is included in many online games. In addition to speaking with other players, games like *Minecraft* and *Roblox* can help L2 Russian learners practice writing in Russian using the chat feature. These online games and the single-player games that we talked about earlier in this chapter (e.g., the *Witcher* series and *Cyberpunk 2077*) can also provide our students with opportunities for receiving multimodal input that can benefit their L2 learning experience.

In this part of this chapter, we would like to refer to our experience using an actual video game in L2 Russian classes. When one of the co-authors of this chapter taught Russian at a Midwestern university in the United States, one of his students asked if he could play the game *Metro: Exodus* in Russian to satisfy the requirement of a portion of their "choice assignment" in Russian. The "choice assignment" included different co-curricular language and cultural activities. For example, students could create a list of their favorite Russian songs on Spotify, YouTube Music, or other digital music services. The primary goal was to help students practice Russian outside their classes and help them immerse themselves within the culture. This type of activity could also be implemented in semester-long projects. The teacher/co-author of this chapter supported his student's decision, which was partially made possible by the "Photo Mode" option used in the game. "Photo Mode" allows players to take and edit pictures while playing the game. *Metro: Exodus* is set in a post-apocalyptic world and takes players to different Russian-speaking places: Moscow, the Volga, Yamantau, the Caspian Sea, the Taiga, and Siberia. In their final report, the student was asked to add pictures and describe his experiences playing the game in different regions. The *Metro* video game series is based on the novels of the contemporary Russian writer Dmitry Glukhovsky and can also complement courses in Russian contemporary culture and literature. These are just a few examples of how video games can be integrated in Russian language classes. We acknowledge that this topic is relatively new, and that more research needs to be done to learn more about how video games can be effectively used in Russian language classes.

Lessons learned

In this section, we would like to talk about some of the potential issues that we have encountered while implementing GBL in our Russian language classes. With regards to video games, a potential concern is that the input that L2 Russian learners receive from these games may not be comprehensible to them. We acknowledge that some narrative-driven role-playing games, such as *Cyberpunk 2077*, may be more appropriate for advanced learners of Russian. To support their students' learning, teachers can provide vocabulary and grammar aid, such as handouts containing useful vocabulary or grammar, beforehand. This is particularly beneficial because Russian is a morphologically rich language and can be challenging for L1 speakers of English and other languages that are not as inflectionally complex (Nuss, 2022).

It is also important to note that online games such as *Minecraft, Roblox, World of Warcraft, Call of Duty: Modern Warfare,* or *Counter-Strike: Global Offensive* have often been associated with emotional and even disrespectful dialogues between players. Having a classroom where students disrespect each other is a concern for any teacher. A potential solution is to have teachers serve as moderators (or hosts). Together with our students, we can help create a respectful environment where learners can receive valuable feedback and engage in a meaningful dialogue to maximize the benefits of game-based interaction. One of the highlights of our teaching experiences was when our students told us that they started playing games that we showed them in class (e.g., *Mafia* or Дурак [The Fool]) during their free time, as these games can help them use Russian and interact with their friends. Students also asked us to provide Quizlet and Kahoot links since these GBL platforms help them learn new vocabulary and grammar in a more engaging manner.

Based on our experience playing games for the first time in our Russian language classes, it is always helpful to have practice rounds or to try activities several times, as this helps students familiarize themselves with the procedures. Giving peer feedback may also require training. We found it beneficial to show students what to focus on in peer feedback, for example, do not correct every grammatical error of your classmate; ask clarification questions in Russian, if necessary; etc.

Finally, it is crucial to mention that GBL platforms such as Kahoot encourage teachers to create their own content. When users view their Kahoot profiles, they can see how many people took their tests. We would like to use this opportunity to encourage our colleagues to create their own content on platforms like Kahoot. We all have our unique experiences and teaching philosophies; by sharing our materials, we can learn so much from each other.

Impact of GBL on teaching and research directions

Overall, GBL goes in line with necessary considerations from previous SLA literature with regards to interaction (e.g., Loewen & Sato, 2018; Pastushenkov et al., 2021) and multimodal input (Peters & Muñoz, 2020). We strongly support the idea that the four skills are interconnected and that GBL can help L2 teachers connect them in their classes. GBL as an L2 teaching/learning methodology has been considered to be promising in previous research (e.g., Al-Azawi et al., 2016; Karagiorgas & Niemann, 2017; Kaya & Sagnak, 2022) and is viewed as an important future direction for Russian language classes in this chapter. As L2 Russian teachers ourselves, we wanted to share games and our theoretical considerations regarding GBL. Considering that Russian is underrepresented in SLA literature and that this volume is unique in this regard, we strongly encourage research on the SLA of less commonly taught languages and GBL.

Note

1 "AAA games" is a term used in the gaming industry to describe high-budget video games produced by large companies.

References

Al-Azawi, R., Al-Faliti, F., & Al-Blushi, M. (2016). Educational gamification vs. game based learning: Comparative study. *International Journal of Innovation, Management and Technology*, 7(4), 132–136. https://doi.org/10.18178/ijimt.2016.7.4.659

Bondarenko, M. (2022). Rethinking authenticity in SLA from the perspective of L1 use: An emerging concept of cognitive authenticity. In L. Will, W. Stadler, & I. Eloff (Eds.), *Authenticity across languages and cultures – Themes of identity in foreign language teaching & learning* (pp. 97–115). Multilingual Matters. https://doi.org/10.21832/9781800411050-010

Bratel, O., Kostiuk, M., Bratel, S., Okhrimenko, I., & Rudenko, L. (2021). Student motivation improvement in a foreign language acquisition via the use of distance learning technologies. *Applied Linguistics Research Journal*, 5(6), 121–134.

Fithriani, R. (2019). Communicative game-based learning in EFL grammar class: Suggested activities and students' perception. *JEELS (Journal of English Education and Linguistics Studies)*, 5(2), 171–188. https://doi.org/10.30762/jeels.v5i2.77

Gass, S. M., & Mackey, A. (2006). Input, interaction and output: An overview. *AILA Review*, 19(1), 3–17. https://doi.org/10.1075/aila.19.03gas

Karagiorgas, D. N., & Niemann, S. (2017). Gamification and game-based learning. *Journal of Educational Technology Systems*, 45(4), 499–519. https://doi.org/10.1177/0047239516665105

Kaya, G., & Sagnak, H. C. (2022). Gamification in English as second language learning in secondary education aged between 11–18: A systematic review between 2013–2020. *International Journal of Game-Based Learning (IJGBL)*, 12(1), 1–14. https://doi.org/10.4018/ijgbl.294010

Loewen, S., & Sato, M. (2018). Interaction and instructed second language acquisition. *Language Teaching*, 51(3), 285–329. https://doi.org/10.4324/9781315676968-1

Long, M. H. (1996). The role of linguistic environment in second language acquisition. In W. C. Ritchie & T. K. Bhatia (Eds.), *Handbook of second language acquisition* (pp. 413–468). Academic Press. https://doi.org/10.1016/b978-012589042-7/50015-3

Mayer, R. E. (Ed.). (2014). *The Cambridge handbook of multimedia learning*. Cambridge University Press.

Nurmukhamedov, U., & Sadler, R. W. (Eds.). (2020). *New ways in teaching with games*. TESOL Press.

Nuss, S. V. (2022). Morphology acquisition research meets instruction of L2 Russian: A contextualized literature review. In S. Nuss & W. Whitehead Martelle (Eds.), *Task-based instruction for teaching Russian as a foreign language* (pp. 15–35). Routledge. https://doi.org/10.4324/9781003146346-2

Paivio, A. (1991). Dual coding theory: Retrospect and current status. *Canadian Journal of Psychology/Revue Canadienne de Psychologie*, 45(3), 255–287. https://doi.org/10.1037/h0084295

Pastushenkov, D. (2022). Task-based peer interaction in Russian as a foreign language classes. In S. Nuss & W. Martel (Eds.), *Task-based instruction for teaching Russian as a foreign language* (pp. 152–170). Routledge. https://doi.org/10.4324/9781003146346-10

Pastushenkov, D., Green-Eneix, C., & Pavlenko, O. (2021). L1 use and translanguaging in ELL peer interaction: A problem or a useful tool? In C. Palmer & M. Devereaux (Eds.), *Teaching English language variation in the global classroom* (pp. 52–60). Routledge. https://doi.org/10.4324/9781003124665-7

Peters, E., & Muñoz, C. (2020). Introduction to special issue language learning from multimodal input. *Studies in Second Language Acquisition*, 42(3), 489–497. https://doi.org/10.1017/s0272263120000212

Tsabei, L. (2020). *The application of the game-based learning platform Kahoot! For teaching listening and speaking skills in the Russian language classroom* [Doctoral dissertation]. University of Colorado at Boulder.

Wang, A. I., & Tahir, R. (2020). The effect of using Kahoot! For learning – A literature review. *Computers & Education, 149*, 103818. https://doi.org/10.1016/j.compedu.2020.103818

Wei, L. (2018). Translanguaging as a practical theory of language. *Applied Linguistics, 39*(1), 9–30. https://doi.org/10.1093/applin/amx044

Zou, D., Huang, Y., & Xie, H. (2021). Digital game-based vocabulary learning: Where are we and where are we going? *Computer Assisted Language Learning, 34*(5–6), 751–777. https://doi.org/10.1080/09588221.2019.1640745

Part IV
Winning creative language at creative play

Chapter 8

Ludic acts of language acquisition

Role, dialogue, and stage for L2 Russian oral proficiency

E. Susanna Weygandt

CHAPTER SUMMARY

Communicative methods of second language pedagogy stress the importance of interactive dialogue in language learning. Drama is built out of dialogue. This chapter focuses on experiential/experimental approaches to language pedagogy that build speaking, reading, and grammar lessons out of dialogue of plays published in Russian and culminate in dramatic performances. The lessons detailed in this chapter grew out of my experience of guiding student groups during four performances. They were played by students of Russian in the liberal arts setting and summer intensive language studies university setting in the United States. When dramatic text is incorporated into language class, the process can be just as important as the result, so I give specific advice on working with multilevel cohorts of students, on connecting grammar instruction to the rehearsals, as well as on improving pronunciation and confidence in speaking Russian. These theater-inspired sessions can be conducted in between textbook units or as supplementary instruction. As a direct result of a theatrical performance, students demonstrated more resourcefulness with vocabulary and more control of various grammatical constructions. The most significant improvement was in pronunciation, in speaking with more ease and confidence, with frequently correct emphasis on stressed syllables in words, and with a wider range of vocabulary use.

Краткое содержание главы

Коммуникативные методы в преподавании языка делают акцент на значении интерактивного диалога в процессе обучения. Драма возникает из диалога. В структуре любой пьесы диалог имеет большое значение. Наше общение в жизни также строится на диалоге. В данной главе рассматриваются эмпирические и экспериментальные подходы к языковой педагогике на примере уроков разговорной речи, чтения и грамматики. Уроки созданы на основе диалогов из оригинальных русских пьес в сочетании с театрализованными представлениями. Занятия, о которых пойдет речь

DOI: 10.4324/9781003369721-12

в этой главе, возникли из моего опыта постановки четырех спектаклей, разыгранных студентами, изучающими русский язык в университете в Канаде, на гуманитарном факультете в университете США, и во время летнего интенсивного курса в США. Когда драматический текст используется на уроке иностранного языка, процесс может быть не менее важен, чем результат. Представленные здесь занятия вместе с примерами театральных постановок могут быть использованы в перерывах между изучением разных тем по основному учебному пособию или в качестве дополнительного материала к учебнику. Во время проверки владения студентами устной речью, проведенной до театрального представления, хотя уровень грамотности студентов был высоким, им требовалось больше времени для подготовки ответа, чем при проверке навыков устной речи после выступления. Студенты демонстрировали большую изобретательность в обращении с лексикой и более уверенно владели необходимыми грамматическими конструкциями. Наиболее значительное изменение в лучшую сторону наблюдалось в произношении: студенты говорили свободнее и увереннее, с корректным ударением и с расширенным словарным запасом.

Deep play and Russian language instruction

Several preeminent liberal arts colleges, universities, and immersive language programs have found the combination of theater and language study to help students improve their pronunciation of a foreign language, gain confidence in speaking, and build comradery in the classroom.[1] Communicative methods of language pedagogy stress the importance of interactive dialogue in language pedagogy (e.g., Swain, 2005). Drama is built out of dialogue. This article focuses on experiential/experimental approaches to language pedagogy (Kohonen et al., 2014; Kolb, 1984) by building speaking, reading, and grammar lessons out of dialogue of published Russian plays and in conjunction with dramatic performances. The lessons detailed in this article grew out of four performances played by students of Russian in the liberal arts setting, in summer intensive language studies program, and at a university in the United States. Language students at the novice level of learning Russian as a foreign language (RFL) performed scenes from *Дальше . . . Дальше . . . Дальше . . .* [*Further . . . Further . . . Further . . .*] by Shatrov [Шатров] (1988), and intermediate-/advanced-level students performed *Синий Слесарь* [*Blue Machinist*] by Durnenkov (2019), which takes place in a modern-day factory, where machine workers pass the time by composing haiku. Advanced-level students performed *Проект Сван* [*Project SWAN*] (2013), a contemporary drama by Andrei Rodionov and Katerina Troepolskaya about a hypothetical process of passing a poetry test in order to receive Russian citizenship, taking place sometime in the future. An additional performance, accomplished by students of novice-level Russian, was based on Bulgakov's *Мастер и Маргарита* [*Master and Margarita*]. This chapter puts forth an understanding of theater as deep play that absorbs students in the task at hand: engaging in interactive dialogue in the target language through role-playing.

Dramatic acting and games are forms of play. For instance, *играть роль* is often used to convey the meaning "to perform a role." Theater can be a type of deep play. Here it is apt to draw from some concepts about acting developed by the contemporary director Anatoly Vasiliev [Анатолий Васильев]. Anatoly Vasiliev (born 1942), one of Russia's most influential theater directors of the late twentieth/early twenty-first century, has defined his directing career by his approach to theatrical adaptations of Russian novels. Vasiliev's speech technique [*вербальная техника*] is the mechanism that undergirds the unique experiments with dialogue in his adaptations of novels.[2] The premise of Vasiliev's verbal technique is contextualized in a broader theory of acting coined by him as *theater of play* [*игровой театр*]. Vasiliev's co-collaborator, Mikhail Butkevich [Михаил Буткевич], wrote the book *К игровому театру* [*Towards a Theater of Play*], where he imparts how acting is a form of human expression not unlike play. Butkevich does this by deconstructing play into its core elements, which are similar to those of performance:

> The first characteristic of a game is *Drive*, i.e., the necessary enjoyment that all participants in the game experience. The game can't go on without this feeling: without the motor of the "drive," players will simply leave the game. The second characteristic is *Competition*, i.e., an opportunity to test each other's strengths, skills, and talent, inventiveness and foresight. The presence of *Structure* is the third characteristic of any game. A system of strict rules that regulates and defines the competition cements the game's identity. There must also be internal ramifications: not being able to leave the game before it is over; the ensemble of the team and the hierarchy of its players; the toolbox full of moves and preparation of tactical blocks. The fourth characteristic of the game is Risk.
> (Butkevich, 2002, p. 167)

All four of these characteristics connect to ensemble acting, and I will show how these four points are activated in the four staged dramas in which my language students put into movement their Russian skills. These four plays also echo the work of one of the most enduringly influential treatises on play, *Homo Ludens* (1938, Eng. 1944), by Dutch historian and play theorist Huizinga (1872–1945). Huizinga writes that play is a "voluntary manipulation of images taken from reality and placed by the imagination into a new, creative order of rules, freely accepted, outside the sphere of necessity or material utility" (p. 35). Building on Huizinga's formulation of play, what I call *deep play* is one's immersion into actions that are connected to a game or performance that is organized outside of everyday social practices (the social practices that we must do for necessity, to work and eat, and thus to exist).

Huizinga argues that play is a world secondary to reality, but it brings stimulation that is essential to life. Butkevich's and Huizinga's books are inspirations for finding meaning in play. It has been my experience that play in the forms of role-playing and drama brings necessary and pedagogically productive stimulation to my language classroom.

The idea of harnessing theater's structure of live communication built on meaningful dialogue is not new to language pedagogy (Alvarado, 2017), but there are few publications that share methods or a "how to" explanation of the process of integrating drama into the language classroom. The creation process of a performance in one's native language, let alone in a second language, is long and hard. Scholarship of Galante and Thomson (2017) brings science to it through controlled exercises during the theatrical-making process in teaching English as a second and foreign language. They established improvement in grammatical use and students' speaking skills after they studied theatrical performance and role-playing.

This chapter adds to the unfolding story the perspective of Russian as a foreign language by focusing specifically on theater in the Russian-language classroom. The method of interplay between staged performances and deciphering texts with lexical units (as well as grammar) could help instructors of Russian sustain student interest and – by extension – program longevity. This chapter demonstrates how a set of activities that are normally used in theater can be adapted to a classroom context. Tangible results of the lessons explained here include improved speech capabilities and comprehensibility and learning new language structures. Grammar learned within a dramatic performance leads to a high amount of retention achieved. Further, what is learned is often remembered for a long time because of the repetition of new words that rehearsal lends and because of the kinetic component of performance.

Since James Asher's seminal research in the 1960s on the powerful effect of movement for second language acquisition that he coined as total physical response (TPR), SLA studies have considered serious movement for the improvement of learning a second language. The performances that I directed show how theater can be incorporated into the semester not as an isolated content-based task but as an opportunity to use recently learned language structures and expressions in the authentic text of the drama. The dramas performed and the grammar lessons that grew out of them are described in an order that moves from dramas and lessons best suited for novice learners to advanced students of Russian. Describing the implementation of dramatic rehearsals as well as grammar lessons that connect to the grammar and syntax in the spoken dialogue of the play, this chapter explains how these lessons can be conducted in between textbook units or as supplementary material within a unit.

Master and Margarita: students exercising their identity and power through the second language

Theater is play and play is theater, according to Huizinga. He offers the following categorization of play in *Homo Ludens*: "Ludus covers children's games, recreation, contests, liturgical and theatrical representations, and games of chance" (Huizinga, 1971, p. 35). In preparation for a department evening of celebration of student talent, I directed my students (beginner Russian, second semester) at Dalhousie University in a dramatic production of *Master and Margarita*. Weeks before the event, I asked students if they had a play in mind that they would like to perform or a poem that we could adapt to the stage. One student suggested Bulgakov's *Master and Margarita*. Other students in the room confirmed this choice, and by popular demand, this performance went into the schedule for the Russian Major's Night. I wrote to one of my theater contacts in Moscow to ask for a dramatic adaptation of the novel and received the one that the director Sergei Zvenovach [Сергей Звеновач] used in his staging, which premiered in Moscow in 2017 (Звеновач [Zvenovach], 2017). Much of the Russian in this stage production was in fact appropriate for my students' level. More advanced syntax in the dialogue, I removed or retold in more basic sentences. While in the interest of time I did this task, it is also a task that can be assigned to students in the intermediate or advanced level, as it prompts them to do a *пересказ* [retelling] (*pereskaz*) – to retell the information into their own Russian. Each student was assigned a role. To engage students even more, I tried to connect those with talents such as dance skill and sewing to help with basic choreography and some costume-making. One student had been in a theater performance before; others had been in dance ensembles. When it came time for blocking or the addition of gesture and positioning onstage to the rehearsed dialogue, students readily took to their feet. Learners were no longer "non-native speakers" but, rather, "knowledgeable citizens" exercising their identity and power via the second language (Stoller, 2002). Drawing upon their natural creative talents in addition to their budding Russian language skills, the 15 students applied their abilities to the rules of time and space to embody a dramatic script. This is deep play in the Huizinga sense of it. And leading up until the night of the theatrical performance, the theater production became a game in the sense of Butkevich's third component of the structure of play: the impossibility of leaving the game before it is over, the ensemble of the team and the hierarchy of its players, and the toolbox full of moves and tactics. In a similar vein, Huizinga writes, "Play is an activity which proceeds within certain limits of time and space, in a visible order, according to rules freely accepted, and outside the sphere of necessity or material utility" (1971, p. 132).

It is in anticipation of such a performance – which can be viewed as a competition among the players to be in the spotlight – that the play-drive, an element critical in play, according to Butkevich, is felt among students. One of the reasons players of a game stay in the game is the enjoyment of playing. As Huizinga points out:

> The function of play . . . can largely be derived from two basic aspects under which we meet it: as a contest for something or a representation of something. These two functions can unite in such a way that the game "represents" a contest, or else becomes a contest for the best representation of something.
> (Huizinga, 1971, p. 38)

The motor of "drive" and competition can be stimulations in language acquisition. There is drive and impetus to be an excellent speaker of Russian, given the public performance when an audience will be watching and listening. The opportunity to steal the spotlight engenders yet another feeling inherent in deep play – competition. Students performed *Master and Margarita* to an audience of over 200 who were either connected to the university or to the Russian and Ukrainian émigré community in Halifax, Nova Scotia. Having a role and performing scenes from dramatic works of literature immersed students within the Russian text of their spoken dialogue and their task at hand: the embodiment of a character who speaks in Russian. "Play" itself comes from the word *spelian*, which specifically means "to represent somebody else" or "to take another's place" (Butkevich, 2002, p. 160). A point underlying the safety in risk-taking of public performances of Russian drama is the role, and improvement in pronunciation and confidence in speaking are the undercurrent of this chapter.

Theater for improved pronunciation and confidence in speaking in Russian

The process that I used for integrating students into a theater performance in the setting of a classroom (as preparation for a larger performance attended by faculty and other students) was somewhat similar to repertoire rehearsal. Our initial rehearsal resembled the traditional "round the table" setting, by which students read aloud their lines while seated, occasionally emphasizing meaning with gesture. The aim was to teach students to comprehend the meaning of the dramatic text and read with correct inflection. For about three weeks, we conducted rehearsals of *Master and Margarita* in class to prepare for a mid-March public performance, and our dramatic performance was not long in duration and appeared as a culminating act in a series of short musical acts in Russian by other university students in an evening of talent to share with the university and community. Over the weeks leading up to the performance, class would often first focus on a grammar lesson from the textbook for 25 minutes, and then, in the last half of the class, we would rehearse, with more time devoted to rehearsals the closer we came to the night of performance.

Scripted dialogue is a toolkit of ready-made sentences that equips students with support in speaking. Communicating in Russian, students express emotion, come face-to-face with a problem that is the action in the scene, and negotiate around it or conquer it. Repetition of spoken dialogue in rehearsal allows opportunities for the instructor to correct students' pronunciation and monitor improvements in pronunciation, since the text remains the same but the spoken execution of it is different in each rehearsal. Students are engaged in a structured assignment of presentational speaking, with the presentation being the night of the performance. By the time of the dress rehearsal – *прогон* – I assess the students' presentational speaking through a rubric with categories for which students could receive a maximum of 25 points each – pronunciation is one of these categories: I specifically pay attention to the even rate of speech and no blurring of the endings of nouns and verbs.

Anxiety, and the subsequent fear of speaking that it can produce, affects communication skills adversely. Woodrow (2006) recommends that anxious students benefit from repetition of both newly and previously learned material (p. 324). Rehearsal of spoken dialogue offers this type of supportive review. Of the many ways that theater leads to the improvement of second language acquisition, it is on pronunciation and confidence in speaking in the target language that a dramatic performance has the most impact. In speaking from the point of view of a character, self-conscious feelings are ameliorated. Concentration on the action of events in the play also allows one to overcome the inhibition dictated by Russian grammar, while mnemonic study of portions of the play helps enrich and widen students' vocabulary. Humor and comradery among classmates that arise in such a production as *Master and Margarita* also aid students in making the step from rehearsal to their oratory performance in public. Toward the end of this chapter, I include the outcomes of measured results in my performances and compare them to many other instructors' findings about using theater in L2 pedagogy.

Theater also provides the opportunity for movement, and studies show that movement-exercises, in particular when brought into the language classroom in a structured way, can reduce speaking anxiety among language students (Oflaz, 2019). Oflaz's studies have used the total physical response (TPR) method, by which vocabulary is taught as students physically move to react to verbal input. Developed by Asher (1966, 1969) in the Psychology Department at San Jose State University, TPR is linked to a memory theory in psychology named "the trace theory," and its premise is that the more often a memory relation is traced, the stronger a memory connection will be and the more likely it will be remembered. This can be done by oral repetition and/or by motor activity. Richards and Rodgers (2014) highlighted the approach of Asher in their volume on innovative and effective methods of language pedagogy because of Asher's unique insight into how learners best internalize language when they respond with physical movement to language input. More broadly, studies show that when learning is tied to movement, what is learned is remembered often for much longer than if the learned information were perceived in a sedentary way (Hrach, 2021).

It has been my experience that even upon returning to routine tasks in the classroom, there is improvement in students' speaking skills after they have participated in a drama in the target language. After demonstrating their ability to embody a character – to perform actions in the play while engaging in scripted dialogue in Russian before a large public – typical tasks connected to textbook learning that might have intimidated some of my students were embraced with less fear and more self-assurance by even the shyest of them when we met again back in the classroom after the public performance. The immediate results of implementing rehearsals and performing scenes are improved pronunciation and confidence in speaking in Russian. Ending the year of novice-level Russian on the high note of such performance gives students the motivation to enroll in intermediate-level Russian. But more recently, I have been staging performances earlier in the semester because the energy from the performance carries into subsequent weeks of learning and also because a performance always ignites students' speaking skills.

When rehearsing, I would often ask students which parts of speech they recognize. In the process of memorizing lines of scripted dialogue, students internalize Russian words and grammar. Rehearsal was interactive and joyful, and each of these classes, over the course of a few weeks, would always end on an upbeat note. This was my first dramatic production in a semester-long language course, and it is the one production in this article for which grammar lessons were mostly taught as separate from the language in the script so that I could complete unit tests (from *Golosa* textbook in my 2016 first-year Russian course) before the final exam in April. The experience led me to want to curate grammar classes in future performances around the syntax in the script.

Galante and Thomson (2017) examine the extent to which learners improve fluency, comprehensibility, and pronunciation in a study that compared how these skills were assimilated in drama-based activities to non-drama-based speaking activities in the context of English as a foreign language. Rehearsal for their drama-based activities was structured in a similar manner as mine. For example, when Galante and Thomson's lesson focused on particular lexical units, the dramatic activities would offer students opportunities to use the same linguistic items through role-playing or enacting given scenarios, but not in a public performance of a dramatic literary play. In a similar manner as when students rehearsed *Master and Margarita*, half of each class conducted by Galante and Thomson was taken up by a drama-based practice, with the remainder of the class devoted to a textbook exercise. Meanwhile, the non-drama-based classes encouraged both pair and group work, "but with no explicit focus on learner affect, nor rehearsal for a performance" (Galante & Thomson, 2017, p. 124). Students prepared oral presentations in that controlled group. The improvement in oral skills happened with more noticeable results among students who did the drama-based activities.

Connecting elementary, intermediate, and advanced Russian grammar lessons to rehearsal

A graduate institution of Middlebury College in Vermont, Middlebury Institute of International Studies (MIIS) in Monterey specializes in dual master's programs that require students to learn a foreign language in parallel to their master's areas studies. Only students who already have intermediate and higher levels of proficiency in a foreign language prior to the master's program can be admitted at the institute. It puts pressure on the quality of the Summer Intensive Language Program (SILP) that prepares prospective MIIS students to function in their chosen second language at the academic and professional level. My students began the summer at the novice level, and almost all students had never studied Russian before. The goal was that, at the end of eight weeks, they would perform at intermediate low or intermediate mid, ideally, according to ACTFL's proficiency standards. Some might perform at novice high in some skills.

SILP stands out from many intensive language programs because its rigorous teaching schedule (four hours a day, five days a week)[3] allows for time in the classroom to apply current second language teaching methodologies, in particular, the content-based approach that is based on authentic sources and that evaluates students' progress following ACTFL Integrated Performance Assessment model. My students at the Summer Intensive Language Program in 2019 at Middlebury Institute performed scenes from *Дальше . . . дальше . . . дальше . . .* [*Onwards . . . Onwards . . . Onwards . . .*] (1987) by Михаил Шатров [Mikhail Shatrov]. Since the original play is long, I abridged it. All students memorized their lines. Our abridged script still reflected the original plot: after Stalin is tried for his crimes by his victims and by Lenin (who all come back to life), he asks Lenin what to do next. Lenin answered that the Soviet people must go onward, onward. Many students in the MA program at MIIS are preparing for a career in international studies and diplomacy, and those students often are interested in Russian historical topics.[4]

A drama that immerses students in deep play for a few weeks ideally should be about a topic that connects to students' professional or academic interests. The *dramatis personae* of Shatrov's play were such historical figures as the Georgian Bolshevik and Soviet politician Sergo Ordzhonikidze, who refused to conspire with Stalin on campaigns related to the purges; Yakov Sverdlov, who was compliant anyway in Stalin's purge plans; one of the architects of Stalin's Terror, Felix Dzerzhinsky; Julius Martov, who was a mentor to Trotsky and close friend of Lenin; and Eino Rakh'ia, a commander during the Bolsheviks' attempts to invade Finland in 1918 past. Some audience members might not be aware of all these historical figures, and so when an actor playing the historical figures entered the stage, I projected on the wall the name of the student's character and two sentences about the character's historical significance. My Powerpoint slides that appeared in between scenes were similar to intertitles in Russian films of the 1920s and early 1930s.

On occasion, we rehearsed in the garden outside of our classroom so that students had more space to engage in group work in the target language and to enjoy the ocean air and, from certain areas of the garden, also ocean views.[5] One day, we met at the start of class, at 9:00 a.m., at the beach (a 15-minute walk from campus), and I asked students to say their lines to the ocean waves. The dramatic text brought onto the beach or in the garden helped immerse us in the deep play of preparing for a performance. Huizinga (1971) states, "In play there is something 'at play' which transcends the immediate needs of life and imparts meaning to the action. All play means something" (p. 1). Against the sound of the waves crashing, students could just get lost in the repetition of their lines until they felt they internalized the order of the words and stress on each one.

A play such as *Onwards . . . Onwards . . . Onwards . . .* about historical figures excited my students, but the language was complex, given that much of the dialogue was based on real documents from archives, including the letter of "Bukharin's Last Plea." When incorporating authentic texts in the classroom and, subsequently, confronting new words, a challenge can be the comprehensibility of individual words, phrases, or a literary plot. Nuss (2022) encountered this challenge when incorporating songs by Vysotsky in the language classroom. Her approach for overcoming the challenge brought on by the notorious Russian morphosyntax is to rephrase original text from the poetic to more common expressions: "As poetic language often employs patterns not typically used in regular communication, some phrases had to be given a more common appearance by rephrasing them" (p. 26). In a similar vein, when introducing to students Shatrov's original play – one that was based on historical archive material – initial rehearsals served the purpose of rewriting some difficult sentences in the dialogue into more direct and simpler words. I used *пересказ* [retelling] as a pedagogical tool. At some moments, when students struggled with some parts of their dialogue, I would ask them to retell [*пересказать*] the main idea of that area of dialogue.

This is a powerful interpretative task, and at ACTFL's intermediate level, students should be able to give a *pereskaz* of a paragraph length of text, but ACTFL also states that speakers at the intermediate-mid sublevel are able to handle successfully a variety of *uncomplicated communicative tasks in straightforward social situations*. These include personal information related to self, family, home, daily activities, interests, and personal preferences, as well as physical and social needs, such as food, shopping, travel, and lodging. Shatrov's play, based on authentic historical documents, does contain, in several areas of the play, historically specific content that is beyond the comprehension of intermediate-level readers and speakers. So I brought the resource of the dictionary into the classroom. Areas of high difficulty in the dialogue, students translated, working in pairs. I circulated the room to help answer questions. Some of the more difficult areas, I translated too, and as I mentioned earlier, I did abridge the play. Complex language, even if students knew the English equivalent, would be difficult to memorize. So the next task was to retell, or re-write, also with the use of a dictionary, some of the more complex parts of the original Russian into a more basic sentence structure, and students did this working in pairs (Table 8.1). In the interest of time, I completed what re-wording was needed if we did not finish this task over three to four classes.

Since the preceding text appeared in a letter by Bukharin, a student (who played the role of Lenin) read it aloud (and thus could deliver the text by reading it rather than speaking memorized dialogue). But the rest of the text in the play was spoken dialogue, memorized by my eight students. We had one performance only, and it was for the whole Summer Intensive Language Program, so audience members were program directors, all the instructors, and all the students, including those who were more advanced. This performance led us, thus, to the fourth characteristic of the game: risk. As Butkevich writes:

> Flipping a coin you are never sure what will turn out – heads or tails. Fate can abandon a team of champions to total defeat at the hands of amateurs. . . . Risk and chance constantly renew the game. They make a game dynamic, unexpected . . . anything but simple.

Table 8.1 An example *pereskaz* of Bukharin's letter in Shatrov's play

Bukharin's letter in Shatrov's play:	My students retold it the following way:
Обращаюсь к Вам, будущее поколение руководителей партии, на исторической миссии которых лежит обязанность распутать чудовищный клубок преступлений, которые в эти страшные дни становятся все грандиознее, разгораются, как пламя, и душат партию. Ко всем членам партии обращаюсь! В эти, может быть, последние дни своей жизни, я уверен, что фильтр истории рано или поздно **неизбежно сметет грязь с моей головы.** Никогда я не был предателем, **за жизнь Ленина без колебаний я заплатил бы собственной.** Любил Кирова, ничего не затевал против Сталина. Прошу новое, молодое и честное поколение руководителей партии зачитать мое письмо на пленуме партии, оправдать и восстановить меня в партии. Знайте, товарищи, что на том знамени, которое вы понесете победоносным шествием к коммунизму, есть и моя капля крови. Николай Бухарин.	Обращаюсь к Вам, будущее поколение. В эти последние дни моей жизни, я уверен, что фильтр истории **убирает грязь с моей головы.** Никогда я не был предателем, **за жизнь Ленина я сам бы умер.** Прошу новое, молодое поколение читать моё письмо. Знайте, товарищи, что на том знамени к коммунизму есть моя капля крови. Николай Бухарин. [I'm appealing to you, the young generation. In these final days of my life, I find certainty that the filter of history will clear the dirt from my head. I was never a traitor; I would have given my life for Lenin. I'm asking the new, young generation to read my letter. Please know, comrades, that on this flag of communism, there is a drop of my blood. Nikolai Bukharin]

Source: Shatrov and Li [Шатров & Ли] (1989, p. 60).

The meaning of the repetition of lines now had become justified. But we asked two audience members to be on book (follow the printed script and whisper to the actor their lines should the actor find themselves in a moment of loss of words). This support was used only once. Returning to class shortly after the performance to complete other written, speaking, and reading tasks for the final exit exam, that same sense of confidence and comradery that I could palpably feel in the classroom after *Master and Margarita*, I felt in the room at Monterey.

About three weeks into the fall 2021 semester at Sewanee: The University of the South of third-year Russian, with students whose speaking abilities ranged from intermediate high to advanced mid, rehearsals began for *The Blue Machinist* [*Синий слесарь*] by Mikhail Durnenkov. We rehearsed for almost a month, dedicating half of each class to it. This play premiered in 2007 in Moscow at the documentary drama venue Teatr.doc. The playwright Mikhail Durnenkov is one of the most prolific writers of the pioneering New Drama [*Novaia Drama*] movement. Before he moved to Moscow to study film and theater, he had worked at a factory in Tol'iatti, "the Detroit of Russia." Some expressions and anecdotes that he recalls from his own experience in Tol'iatti appear in the dialogue, and his play takes place in a contemporary factory near Moscow. While there aren't many stage directions, there's a lot of experimentation with language in the dialogue. The dialogue in this play offers contemporary mannerisms of Russian speech. The play includes haiku that the playwright weaves into dialogue. Several factory workers pass the time during work breaks by composing haiku. In between their performed dialogue, which students memorized, at least once each student approached a standing microphone to read aloud a haiku from the play. Opportunities for students to read aloud from the script now and then decrease the pressure brought about by live performance (Figure 8.1).

When making the abridged version of *Blue Machinist*, I selected only those scenes that had a clear action to perform in them, which would help the student actors, as well as the audience, make sense of the plot. Students were to memorize their lines so that the performances (five performances open to anyone at the college) would be electric. This performance would count toward students' major presentational speaking assignments in the course.

Using the opportunity of this performance to yoke tightly a grammar topic to the dialogue in the rehearsed play, I created a lesson that reviewed the imperative (command construction) with examples that drew directly from several of the students' memorized lines. I taught these grammar lessons in the space associated

Figure 8.1 QR code for the recording of the class with the *Blue Machinist* performance.

with where those lines were repeatedly spoken, in our performance space, the elegant Torian Room with excellent acoustics. The following instances from the text provided fruitful examples from which the advanced students could have a brief review of the imperative from the previous semester. I asked students to identify instances of the imperative in the text. Students pointed out the following examples:

Девочка-магнит: Моя Баб Валя как только узнала про мои магнитные способности, сразу сказала: "**Вези** её в Москву." [Magnit girl: When my Grandma heard of my magnetic abilities, she said instantly, "Take her to Moscow,"]

Геннадий: **Повторяйте** 96 раз [Gennadiy: Repeat 96 times].

Геннадий: Ренат и Андрей, **забирайте** стол [Gennadiy: Renat and Andrei, take away the table.]

Герой: **Присаживайся**. Хочешь выпить? [Hero: Take a seat. You want a drink?]

Based on my observation, often, when students learn and review the six grammatical cases in Russian, they learn both the most frequently used instances as well as the exceptions and rules that apply to more complex spelling rules. Through the years, the more frequent uses of grammar cases will be retained by language learners. But the less-frequent instances of it might not be retained in students' long-term memory. Some examples of seldom-occurring instances of the instrumental, for example, appeared in the dialogue of the play:

Девочка-магнит: Я приехала **с матерью** из Ярославля [Magnit girl: I came with my mother from Yaroslavl.]

Геннадий: **Пахнет** маслом машинным [Gennadiy: It smells like machine oil.]

The following examples of less frequently occurring instances of the Genitive case were used in the characters' lines:

Радио: Итальянские банды всегда начинались **с заводских бригад**. [Factory Radio: Italian gangs always started out as factory crews.]

Герой: Я не знаю **с чего** начать [Hero: I don't know how I should begin.]

The dialogue of *The Blue Machinist* provided an excellent opportunity to learn advanced grammatical constructions. I taught active present participles at a point during one rehearsal. First, we reviewed the relative pronoun который [which]. Each student was given a little collection of pieces of paper. On each paper was a clause. For instance, "Он говорит о друге [he is talking about a friend]." And then another piece of paper had written on it, "который всегда опаздывает [who is always late]." Students had to find two clauses that could be joined into a logical sentence through the correct use *of который*. I explained on the whiteboard how past and present active particles are formed, drawing from the textbook *Panorama* (Rifkin et al., 2017) or *Modern Russian* (Offord, 1993) to review their formation, and then switch the students' focus to the play's dialogue. The point was for students to try on their own to recognize in the dialogue at least one active participle in the present and in the past tense. Students spotted in the dialogue the following, spoken by the role of the Radio, which performs the function of a narrator. I gave one of my students the role of performing the Radio, and the student spoke from the side of the room to announce the lines of the Radio:

Радио [Factory Radio]: В то время множество японских эмигрантов, **ставшие** гражданами США, устраивались работать на конвейер, где трудились круглыми сутками за нищенское жалование, чтобы прокормить себя и многочисленную родню. [. . .] Принцип же, **основывающийся** на жестком самоограничении поэта, **придающий** весомость каждому слову. [At the time, many Japanese immigrants found employment at the conveyor belt and became citizens of the United States. In order to feed themselves and their large families, they worked twenty-four hour shifts for misery wages. These subtle Japanese poets reacted intuitively to their new surroundings. . . . The principle, however, remained the same: the poet exercises self-restraint and gives weight to every word.]

(Durnenkov, 2019)

I asked students to explain the meaning of sentences in English and then explain how they could be said in different ways in Russian using *который*. Such lessons in which grammar is explained alongside scenes of dramas can supplement grammar textbooks so that students have opportunities to see the grammar they study in the context of literature.

Students were also assigned to summarize [*пересказать*] some of the events and actions in the play into a paragraph of their own spoken Russian.[6] According to ACTFL proficiency guidelines for world-readiness, students' ability to retell in their own Russian a paragraph length of text is an advanced-/upper-intermediate-level language skill. I see *pereskaz* as a pedagogical tool to use when performing dramatic scenes in Russian, and I assessed their summary of the play's events along ACTFL's guidelines for advanced-mid speakers:

Advanced-mid speakers demonstrate the ability to narrate and describe in the major time frames of past, present, and future by providing a full account, with good control of aspect. Narration and description tend to relate relevant and supporting facts in connected, paragraph-length discourse.

(ACTFL, 2012)

Johan Huizinga states:

Play is an activity connected with no material interest, and no profit can be gained by it. It proceeds within its own proper boundaries of time and space according to fixed rules and in an orderly manner. It promotes the formation of social groupings which tend to surround themselves with secrecy and to stress their difference from the common world by disguise or other means.

Students moved outside the classroom into the performance space to apply their knowledge of Russian to the rules of time and space onstage, interacting with one another in Russian in the mindset of their characters, engaged in deep play. While my students' performance was in Russian, the gestures of the student-actors and the accompanying soundtrack (featuring Deep Purple and Grimes) helped convey meaning in the play to the audience, many of whom did not know Russian. Audience members had the choice of referring to English versions of the script. In the next semester, when I taught a contemporary Russian literature course in English, I included a translation of the play, and in our discussion of it, I showed the class the recording of the *previous class's* performance in Russian of the *Blue Machinist* in hopes that the non-Russian-speaking students, impressed by their peers, might want to achieve a similar feat in the target language and sign up for Russian in the fall. Here is the recording:

During the pandemic year, when the screen through which learning happened inhibited close contact between the instructor and students, and when a class was dependent on an Internet connection, thus increasing the tendency for disrupted attention,[7] deep play of theater and its way of absorbing students in an activity proved again to be a tool in language learning. If theater is deep play, then Ivan Vyrypaev's theater is an exercise of deep concentration. Ivan Vyrypaev is one of the leading playwrights of Russian New Drama [новая драма], a vibrant movement characterized by its innovations in post-dramatic, non-traditional theater since the 1990s. Vyrypaev is interested in theater as a structure that brings people together to focus on an issue in the play. The gathering of an audience whose focus is on actors as the actors cross into the chimerical realm of play creates a spiritual meeting for all sorts, and according to Vyrypaev (2022), by the end of the performance, the audience grows in their capacity for social understanding, in their sense of self, and in their spirituality. It is further apt to mention Vyrypaev's theater, as his plays have, in fact, been used in language pedagogy in the curriculum at the Russian Flagship Program at UNC–Chapel Hill. At a question-and-answer session with Vyrypaev, organized by Stanislav Shvabrin, Professor of literature and Director of UNC Russian Flagship Program, Vyrypaev remarked:

> In performance, there is absolute concentration and a show is a method of spiritual development. Engaging in dramatic dialogue on stage is a form of spiritual development. Theater is a philosophical thought about life. You read and then you embody what you read. In the theater the actors embody an image before an audience.
>
> (Vyrypaev, 2022)

To Vyrypaev (personal communication, May 11, 2013), watching a performance or an actor embodying a role is a form of meditation. In a similar vein, Huizinga in *Homo Ludens* describes play as "a free activity standing quite consciously outside 'ordinary' life as being 'not serious,' but at the same time absorbing the player intensely and utterly" (p. 2).

When the pandemic hit in March of 2020, the stage production of *Проект Сван*[8] [*Project SWAN*] – about a fictional/dystopian governmental agency that trains immigrants to speak in Russian poetry – that fourth-year students were rehearsing in a black box theater at Sewanee's Tennessee Williams Center was switched to Zoom. On this platform, students' acting was limited to "the neck up," and our production of Andrei Rodionov's and Ekaterina Troepolskaya's play[9] took on the form of a play-reading (known in Russia as читка [reading-through]) in April 2020. Zoom is a powerful device that allows for learning without a campus, but it does not recreate the *atmosphere* of the classroom ensemble. Instructors teaching on Zoom might ask, through habit, the entire class to repeat one phrase, only to catch a few seconds of how two students utter that phrase. To remedy this, students rehearsed in breakout rooms, and I would join the rooms to listen to students' fluency (natural flow of speech, prosody, no long pauses unless intentional). Then we would rejoin as a class on Zoom to perform individual scenes when we rehearsed between grammar lessons.

The setting for the play takes place in the near future, when the Russian Federal Immigration Office decides that citizenship will be given only after passing a Russian poetry exam. The entire play is written in verse. Students of advanced Russian were quite interested in political topics, and a few of them were double-majoring in international and global studies and Russian, and so the topic of immigration, albeit fictional, that was central to this play was of interest to my students. Students in this course performed at the advanced level according to ACTFL, and some had spent a semester or summer abroad. They could understand the complex phrasing in the play, but to make the dialogue easier for them to remember, we did a *pereskaz* of the areas in the dialogue with which some students struggled. By putting the ideas into their own words, the students could remember their lines better because they internalized the Russian text more easily. The Screen Share function of Zoom is conducive to close viewing of grammatical expressions on a shared Word doc (a replacement for a whiteboard). When rehearsing with students on Zoom, I shared on my screen the script, and below it, a Word document of some of the play's dialogue that we were rewriting in red font. Some of the lines, we rewrote into more basic sentences, which we used to remedy an additional challenge: the complexity of the language in the play. To illustrate, in the left-hand column in the following is the original text; on the right side is a sample of text that a student retold (Table 8.2). Students were assigned to retell in their own Russian at least ten sentences of dialogue from their role.

Even for advanced learners, *pereskaz* allows them to make use of their linguistic and cultural abilities and knowledge in a variety of ways and also to systematically improve them. By engaging in the interpretative act of *pereskaz*, students were working to meet ACTFL's guideline for advanced speakers:

> Advanced Mid speakers can handle with relative ease the linguistic challenges presented by an unexpected turn of events that occurs within the context of a routine situation. Their vocabulary is fairly extensive although primarily generic in nature, except in the case of a particular area of specialization or interest. Strategies such as circumlocution or rephrasing are often employed for this purpose.
> (ACTFL, 2012)

Table 8.2 An example *pereskaz* of an excerpt from Проект Сван [Project SWAN]

Молдакул:	Молдакул:
Все вы русские такие, в чем загадка вашего странного инстинкта? почему бы не сказать тихо, безыскусно: чем такая русская та твоя тропинка? и в буше австралийском, в джунглях Конго сырых и бразильской сельве никогда не приплетет человек прописку, даже если человек с лютого похмелья. [All of you Russians are like that What is the mystery of the Russian strange instinct? Why not say quietly, artlessly: Why is that path so Russian And in the Australian bush, In the jungles of the damp Congo and in the Brazilian selva A person will never be bond to a residence permit Even if the person has a severe hangover.]	Все вы русские такие: в чём загадка русского странного инстинкта? Почему эта загадка и не чёткие правила? В пустыне Австралии, в джунглях Конго и в бразильском лесу Даже там есть чёткие правила и не требуется сдать экзамен по поэзии, чтобы стать гражданином. [All of you Russians are like that: What is the mystery of the Russian strange instinct? Why this riddle and no clear rules? In the desert of Australia In the jungles of the Congo and the Brazilian forest. Even there there are clear rules. And you don't need to pass a poetry exam to become a citizen.]

Source: Rodionov and Troepolskaja [Родионов and Троепольская] (2017, p. 40).

The interpretative act of *pereskaz* in class also helps the instructor ensure that students understand the content of the dramatic play.

In review, for implementation of dramatic dialogue in the language classroom, when selecting an article or Internet blog to show in class, it is best to choose text that is at a level near students' level of proficiency. *Pereskaz* can aid the process of assimilating authentic material to various levels of proficiency. Performances of scenes build students' tolerance for reading and interpreting authentic texts, which sometimes has inverted word order and often includes words outside of the textbook. Dramatic performances are exercises for any level of Russian and will have the most effect on students' speaking and listening skills. In this sense, they can be considered excellent presentational assignments to help students prepare to use their Russian professionally. Presentations of dramatic scenes are bonding-inducing experiences that infuse the classroom with energy while providing supportive and encouraging steps toward professional public speaking (Figure 8.2).

172 E. Susanna Weygandt

Figure 8.2 QR code for the photographs of the students' performance.

The impact on oral proficiency

The following assessment instruments were given to students immediately after the performance of *Master and Margarita* and *The Blue Machinist*: a survey for evaluating students' motivation to learn the Russian language and an unofficial OPI test to measure their pre- and post-performance level of speaking skills. During the simulated OPIs (administered by myself, the instructor) on thematic topics recently studied before the performance, students could handle topics adequately and could complete the task; they needed longer to complete an answer before the performance than after. There were more serious grammatical mistakes in their speaking that affected meaning before the performance than after it. During OPIs after the performance, students were more resourceful with vocabulary and had more control of required grammatical constructions (which I credit to the confidence they achieved in their speaking). The discourse was more extended in the post-performance OPIs; students spoke in a less "choppy" way, with fewer pauses in between brief phrases.

I didn't incorporate these tests after *Project SWAN*, given that the pandemic hit two weeks before we had originally planned the live performance at the Tennessee Williams Center, nor did I include the evaluations for *Onwards . . . Onwards . . . Onwards . . .* because of the limited days of study in the intensive SILP schedule. Exit tests were administered instead for both students of SILP and those who had performed *Project SWAN*. In both of those courses, the play was performed after the midterm and before the final exams. At the midterm point, I did an unofficial OPI with each student and gave them a test designed to assess their grammar and mainly measure their listening and reading skills. The same skills (except for new grammar points) were tested during the final exam. The results for listening, reading, and speaking were higher at the final than at the midterm for all students. As a result of their participation in Russian theater, the students could often follow what they heard about events and experiences in various time frames (intermediate listening, according to ACTFL's metrics world-readiness standards). Several students could easily understand the main idea of texts aurally received that were about topics related to everyday life, personal interests, and studies (intermediate reading, according to ACTFL).

Similarly, students in fifth- and sixth-semester Russian demonstrated outstanding results in comparison to those in previous years, when theater was not part of the program. The students could easily understand the main idea in messages related to everyday life they heard in listening assessments, and they could understand the description of events and experiences in various time frames (advanced listening, ACTFL). As for their reading skills, they could certainly understand the fictional narrative of the drama we worked with – the main plotline and other subordinate details and plots – but I did not have room in the course to expose them to other extended fictional works.

The most significant improvement at all levels of Russian was in pronunciation, in speaking with more ease, with more confidence, with frequently correct emphasis on stressed syllables in words, evenness in the flow of speech, and with a wider range of vocabulary. In a questionnaire attached to official course teaching evaluations, students were prompted to provide anonymous feedback about whether they still had an interest in theatrical activity in the classroom after their performance of the *Blue Machinist* and whether they felt that participation in the performance improved their Russian. Improvement in speaking in the target language as a result of the performance was consistently mentioned. Here are some students' responses: "This play was extremely helpful in gaining confidence in speaking the language. I highly recommend this experience with other classes." "I think it did help me focus on pronunciation and understanding grammar." "I think it was good to be able to speak the language in a natural way." "It was an interesting experience going through the theater process in another language, and I think it helped give me more examples of the language in context." "Definitely helped me with speaking Russian. Highly recommended for all foreign language courses. I wish we had more than one play per semester."

Lessons learned

Today Russian language learners face challenges because of overwhelming access to technology as well as a surplus of information, in addition to the precarious political climate of Russia (its war against Ukraine) as well as COVID regulations. I urge instructors to incorporate a short performance early in the semester. Since confidence in speaking grows among students who participate in drama performances in the target language, with the most dramatic improvement in students who tend to be shy, the energy from the performance will carry into the classes and coursework in the rest of the semester.

I find theater to be a powerful tool in language pedagogy to help bring students' knowledge of grammar into interactive scenarios and spoken dialogue. My own research on Russia's dramatic canon and as it stretches into the twenty-first century has inspired me to connect drama to language pedagogy, in particular the use of contemporary Russian plays. Set in late- and post-Soviet Russia, the movement of Russian playwrights and directors, a group that is known as New Drama (*Novaya Drama*), represents the largest artists' circle in contemporary Russia who have produced hundreds of dramatic literary works each year (some have been awarded top national literary prizes). New Drama connects to themes of social critique that have influenced the social climate of the post-1989 transformation in the region, and theater and drama in general inspire some of my approach to language pedagogy. My research and ethnography inquiry seeks to examine what New Drama can teach us about post-socialism. Given the plays' insights into contemporary life and their use of contemporary speech and creative use of language (the embedded haiku in *The Blue Machinist*), they connect to students' interest in contemporary culture and Russian language. For this reason, I treat the new plays as not only cutting-edge artistic literature but also as key authentic texts to use in teaching the Russian language.

Notes

1 Princeton University's Slavic Languages and Literatures Department offered the upper-level *Russian Drama* course during Olga Hasty's professorship, which always culminated in a theatrical production in Russian. The Department of French Studies at Princeton offers L'Avant-Scène, which integrates language pedagogy with performance. It is directed by Senior Lecturer Florent Masse, who has directed more than 60 full-length productions of dramas from the French theatrical canon. In 2017, he was named Chevalier dans l'Ordre des Arts et des Lettres by French Minister of Culture Audrey Azoulay for his attachment to French culture and his action in favor of its promotion in America. Middlebury College's Summer Russian Language School annually stages a performance in Russian in which students and faculty members participate as part of the program's extracurricular activities offerings; the performance is not integrated into language pedagogy in the classroom. The University of Madison–Wisconsin offers a graduate-level course on the use of drama and theater in Russian language pedagogy.
2 For more information on the theatrical practice of Vasiliev's *verbal'naia tekhnika*, see Weygandt, "The Technique of Verbalizing: Anatoly Vasiliev and His Theater of Dissonant Dialogues." *The Russian Review*, 2023.
3 When creative activities are used, then more time is needed in the classroom. This can be challenging when language classes are limited to 50 minutes, and novice- and intermediate-level class schedules often are. This time frame limits the horizon of approaches that can be used in one session. SILP's language program, on the other hand, has a three-hour session each morning with a break, and thus, learning outdoors and content-based instruction can easily be used. At universities during the academic year, the fourth lab hour could be combined with a regular 50-minute class to generate at least one session a week

when students meet for a longer class period to learn outdoors or with a combination of methods in one session.
4 For more on tailoring content to learners' needs, see Long (2014).
5 Weygandt, S. (forthcoming) is on the topic of taking language instruction outdoors.
6 This assignment can be supplemented or initiated by the task of students writing their *pereskaz*.
7 "In the process of teaching during the pandemic, instructors of the program found new forms of interaction through learning in the context of emergency remote instruction; however, we are under no illusion that the program's efforts to build community through the activities and affordances described above [in the Zoom platform] are always successful. Students still feel stressed and isolated, deprived of the spontaneous encounters and social activities that form a vital part of campus life. Students still report a preference for in-person language courses" (Evans-Romaine et al., 2021, p. 35).
8 Project SWAN refers to a fictional/dystopian governmental agency that trains immigrants to speak in Russian poetry verse in order to receive Russian citizenship. As the drama describes, it is "where ugly ducks/Are turned into civic cygnets."
9 English translation of this play is available in Weygandt and Hanukai (2019).

References

ACTFL. (2012). *ACTFL performance descriptors for language learners*. www.actfl.org/resources/actfl-proficiency-guidelines-2012/russian

Alvarado, J. (2017). The use of theater and drama techniques to foster speaking skills in English. *Class Revista de Lenguas Modernas, 26*, 305–317.

Asher, J. J. (1966). The learning strategy of the total physical response: A review. *The Modern Language Journal, 50*(2), 79–84. https://doi.org/10.1111/j.1540-4781.1966.tb03573.x

Asher, J. J. (1969). The total physical response approach to second language learning*. *The Modern Language Journal, 53*(1), 3–17. https://doi.org/10.1111/j.1540-4781.1969.tb04552.x

Butkevich, M. [Буткевич, М.]. (2002). *Towards a theatre of play. K Igrovomy teatru: liricheskii traktat* [К игровому театру: лирический трактат]. GITIS.

Durnenkov, M. (2019). The blue machinist (A. Aizman, Trans.). In M. Hanukai & S. Weygandt (Eds.), *New drama: An anthology* (pp. 221–222). Columbia University Press (Original work published in 2007).

Evans-Romaine, K., Murphy, D., Tumarkin, A., Marshall, L., & Almuratova, A. (2021). Connecting through language and culture learning during the COVID-19 pandemic: The University of Wisconsin-Madison Russian Flagship Program. *Russian Language Journal 71*(2), 23–38.

Galante, A., & Thomson, R. I. (2017). The effectiveness of drama as an instructional approach for the development of second language oral fluency, comprehensibility, and accentedness. *TESOL Quarterly, 51*(1), 115–142. https://doi.org/10.1002/tesq.290

Hrach, S. (2021). *Minding bodies how physical space, sensation, and movement affect learning*. West Virginia University Press.

Huizinga, J. (1971). *Homo ludens: A study of the play-element in culture*. Beacon Press.

Kohonen, V., Jaatinen, R., Kaikkonen, P., & Lehtovaara, J. (2014). *Experiential learning in foreign language education*. Routledge.

Kolb, D. (1984). *Experiential learning: Experience as the source of learning and development*. Prentice Hall.

Long, M. (2014). *Second language acquisition and task-based language teaching*. Wiley-Blackwell.

Nuss, S. V. (2022). Morphology acquisition research meets instruction of L2 Russian. In S. Nuss & W. Martelle (Eds.), *Task-based instruction for teaching Russian as a foreign language* (pp. 15–35). Routledge. https://doi.org/10.4324/9781003146346-2

Offord, D. (1993). *Modern Russian: An advanced grammar course*. Bristol Classical Press and Duckworth.

Oflaz, A. (2019). The foreign language anxiety in learning German and the effects of total physical response method on students' speaking skill. *Dil Ve Dilbilimi Çalışmaları Dergisi*, *15*(1), 70–82. https://doi.org/10.17263/jlls.547616

Richards, J. C., & Rodgers, T. S. (2014). *Approaches and methods in language teaching*. Cambridge University Press. https://doi.org/10.1017/9781009024532

Rifkin, B., Dengub, E., & Nazarova, S. (2017). *Panorama: Intermediate Russian language and culture*. Georgetown University Press.

Rodionov, A., & Troepol'skaja, E. [Родионов, А., и Троепольская, Е.]. (2017). *Optimism. Poetic plays* [Оптимизм. Поэтические пьесы.]. Novoe literaturnoe obozrenie.

Shatrov, M. [Шатров, М.]. (1988). *Further . . . Further . . . Further . . .* [Дальше . . . Дальше . . . Дальше . . .]. Znamja, 1.

Shatrov, M., & Li, G. [Шатров, М., и Ли, Г.]. (1989). *Further, further, further: Discussion around one play: Based on press materials and readers' letters* [Дальше, дальше, дальше: дискуссия вокруг одной пьесы: по материалам печати и читательским письмам]. Knizhnaja palata.

Stoller, F. (2002). Project work: A means to promote language and content. *Methodology in Language Teaching: An Anthology of Current Practice*, *10*, 107–119.

Swain, M. (2005). The output hypothesis: Theory and research. In E. Hinkel (Ed.), *Handbook of research in second language teaching and learning* (Vol. 3, pp. 495–508). Routledge.

Vyrypaev, I. (2022, May 27). *A conversation with Ivan Vyrypaev, Polish-Russian dramatist* [Address]. UNC Chapel Hill, Department of Germanic and Slavic Languages and Literatures.

Weygandt, S. (forthcoming). *From gesture to coded knowledge: Rediscovering TPR when teaching Russian in an outdoor classroom* [Unpublished manuscript].

Weygandt, S., & Hanukai, M. (2019). *New Russian drama: An anthology*. Columbia University Press.

Woodrow, L. (2006). Anxiety and speaking English as a second language. *RELC Journal*, *37*(3), 308–328. https://doi.org/10.1177/0033688206071315

Zvenovach, S. [Звеновач, С.] (2017). *Schizophrenia in two acts* [Шизофрения в двух частях]. Live performance at the Studio of Theater Art, Moscow.

Chapter 9

"I like brown, eyes, potatoes"
Gamified poetry for beginners

Polina Peremitina

CHAPTER SUMMARY

This chapter discusses existing scholarship on utilizing creative writing tasks and activities in a foreign language curriculum. Research shows that such practices engage and motivate students, improve writing and communication skills, and encourage learner autonomy and creativity. As instructors strive to create a student-centered learning experience, poetry writing offers a way to expand traditional classroom practices. In this light, I describe a creative writing exercise in the form of a poetry game conducted with a paper-cut poetry kit, with words and expressions taken from a vocabulary list for a unit in the textbook. Initially created for a vocabulary review, the game can be adapted for various classroom needs, including language assessment.

Краткое содержание главы

В этой главе рассматривается использование творческих письменных заданий в учебной программе по русскомы как иностранному языку. Исследования показывают, что такие задания мотивируют учащихся, улучшают их навыки письма и речи и поощряют самостоятельность и творческое отношение к изучению языка. Для преподавателей, стремящихся создать учебный процесс, ориентированный на учащихся, написание стихов может стать еще одним способом расширения традиционных методов языковой практики. Далее я описываю упражнение по творческому письму в форме поэтической игры, проводимой с набором стихов, вырезанным из бумаги, со словами и выражениями, взятыми из словаря главы учебника. Первоначально созданная для повторения изученных слов и выражений, игра может быть адаптирована для различных педагогических задач, включая оценку владения языком.

In what follows, I offer a description of a poetry game and the prompt for elementary-level Russian-language students in tertiary context based on vocabulary from the *Beginner's Russian* textbook (Kudyma et al., 2010). I conceptualize and detail a poetry-based language exercise that can motivate students to acquire and

DOI: 10.4324/9781003369721-13

retain vocabulary by incorporating target lexical items into creative autonomous tasks. Learners make the language their own by experimenting with the form and meaning-making process. Before offering a description and critical evaluation of the game, I will briefly review the theoretical premises behind the exercise.

Learner autonomy and creative writing

Leaver and Campbell (2020) describe the ongoing paradigm shift in language pedagogy from communicative language teaching (CLT) to transformative language learning and teaching (TLLT) as a movement toward greater learner autonomy. Personal transformation is at the core of this educational philosophy, with students ultimately in charge of a predominantly self-directed, self-regulated learning experience (p. 147). This philosophy of transformation emphasizes the self-directed study and learner-centered forms of content; a language instructor's role in this scenario is to serve as an advisor who guides student learning. Under the TLLT paradigm, it is expected that students assume a more self-directed and self-regulated approach to their studies.

The idea behind designing a poetry game that generates individualized outcomes (as opposed to a linear mechanical exercise in which a student must produce one objectively correct answer or word form) lies in shifting from a teacher-led review session to a student-led exercise facilitated by an instructor. The value of a student-centered approach to learning is well-established. For instance, Martin and Nuss show that this concept may draw students to the study of Russian and help them maintain their motivation to continue learning the language (Martin & Nuss, 2022a). Writing on the importance of student-centered task-based instruction, Baer and McIntyre (2022) concentrate on online assessment and point out that every assignment is ultimately a learning opportunity. As students work on creative assignments, they acquire new knowledge about the content of their studies and (perhaps more importantly) about themselves if the tasks are designed holistically and in a student-centered manner. Baer and McIntyre conclude that assessments should showcase and encourage student growth that goes beyond acquiring language skills. Furthermore, for instructors who teach online or hybrid classes, creative assignments can boost student engagement, as these types of assignments perform well in a remote modality: surveying student engagement in the Ukrainian as a foreign language learning in the remote classroom, Sivachenko and Nedashkivska (2021) show that students "stressed the importance of individualized and creative projects, with some expressing a preference for group projects that would lead to elevated interest in the learning process" (p. 68).

The use of creative writing assignments in a foreign language classroom is not a new pedagogical intervention. Allen (2018) makes a compelling argument for including more writing elements in foreign language instruction. Noting the gap between the significance of "soft" communicative skills and focus on different modalities of writing in the foreign language, Allen urges instructors to "integrate linguistic, sociocultural, and cognitive dimensions of writing instruction and, therefore, fully reflect the complex nature of FL [Foreign Language] writing." Arshavskaya (2015) found that students in her study spoke of creative writing assignments as "both enjoyable and beneficial for the development of their writing" (p. 68). Introducing creative writing assignments into the course to engage less-motivated students, Arshavskaya based her work on Paulo Freire's pedagogy of liberation (Freire, 2020), which advocates for classroom democracy and a continuous dialogue between the instructor and the students. Perhaps more interestingly, the study shows that creative writing assignments present a slightly different opportunity for the instructor to engage with student work: focusing on the content "creates a non-threatening environment for L2 learners to express and develop their ideas in writing" (p. 68–69). We must then view the language classroom as a safe space for creative experimentation.

In the same vein, Martin and Nuss (2022b) call for normalizing "linguistic discomfort as a sign of growth" and talking to students openly, explaining that this discomfort is in fact quite normal. Working on a creative writing exercise, some students will inevitably feel that, although they have plenty of thoughts or ideas to express in response to the prompt, the task pushes them to say more than they feel they can at their level. An assignment of this sort will therefore push students out of their comfort and proficiency level, which stimulates them to experiment and to expand their language skills – for instance, by using vocabulary clusters related to a current lesson topic. Finally, from a holistic standpoint, instructors should consider talking to students about additional strategies that help embrace the discomfort and turn it into a rewarding experience: Martin and Nuss suggest risk-taking as one such strategy (p. 198–99) that teachers must not only promote to students but also support in instruction and grading practices with fidelity.

It should be separately articulated that poetry writing as an activity resembles gaming in that there are rules to follow, especially depending on the prompt: for example, would you want your students to rhyme? Within these rules, students might find their own style to achieve "the goal," their creative project. Wordplay and imaginative metaphors are encouraged, and there are endless possibilities for exploring different identities in writing, especially for students who might be shy to express themselves.

Writing poetry in L2 settings

Writing poetry in the language classroom goes far and beyond the immediate task of language learning. Developing the concept of meaningful literacy, Hanauer (2012) suggests that poetry writing as a methodology both humanizes the language classroom and creates space for students to focus on emotions as a part of their language learning experience. The opportunity to reflect and act on one's own subjectivities thus centers the individual student in the process of their own learning, and here Hanauer finds a solution to the difficulty of making language learning truly individualized and contextualized. Reviewing metaphors students provided for learning language, Hanauer notes that this process "would seem to be embodied in the physical, intellectual and emotional life of the individual language learner." Writing poetry, therefore, serves as an ultimate outlet for such reflections.

Piscayanti and Yuliasri (2021) further advocate for using poetry writing in a foreign language classroom as a tool to practice mindfulness as a part of the learning experience. The results of their study conducted with a narrative inquiry method show that "poetry writing can represent [the] voice of [a] L2 learner's identity; their new perspectives of the world, reflection and sensitivity to context" (p. 79). Hanauer (2012) also discusses the importance of poetry as a genre, noting that it holds a significant place in many cultures and thus weighs accordingly in student understanding of writing tasks. As instructors, we have a unique opportunity to invite students to bring the experience of their culture into the classroom, thereby diversifying what could have been an ordinary writing assignment.

Similarly mindful of the student learning experience, Tay (2014) applies Paulo Freire's seminal work *Pedagogy of the Oppressed* to the nature of creative writing. As Freire advocated for the authenticity of one's language, Tay argues that poetry writing frees language from being treated as an object to be acquired. "There is a need to depart from the prosaic and instrumentalist attitude as discussed previously and instead to approach language not with the agenda of mastery but with a degree of openness that allows for difference" (p. 111). It is important to emphasize as well that poetry writing in a foreign language classroom should not make strict accuracy its ultimate goal. Instead, writing poetry should be radically differentiated from any other type of writing students are required to do in the class. Therefore, when designing a poetry game, an instructor must explicitly state that students have the creative freedom to express themselves and explore the language, albeit within introduced scaffolding limits. Wichadee found that clear and well-received instructions for self-directed learning can challenge "learners to be prolific writers, particularly when writers are able to interact" (as cited in I-Ju Tu, 2021). The benefit is twofold: to successfully work on creative writing assignments, students must rely on self-directed learning skills and strategies; at the same time, students will hone these skills while working on creative assignments. Giving creative writing assignments in a foreign language classroom, therefore, stimulates and encourages students' transformation into direct owners of their language-learning experience.

Feedback and assessment

The goal of foreign language education is to build communicative skills, which are often supported by writing – just like speaking, writing encourages self-expression and presumes an audience (e.g., Manchón & Williams, 2016; Vasylets, 2017). Anderson and Walsh (2020) note that non-traditional writing assignments such as research-based Internet writing projects give students the opportunity to both create and review each other's projects, thus allowing them to communicate with each other in the target language in a realistic situation that involves giving and receiving feedback. Poetry writing can be viewed as a non-traditional writing assignment with multiple opportunities for self-expression and conveying of feelings. The dialogical nature of creative writing and peer learning component can be further enhanced by accompanying poetry writing with a role-play, in which students give each other feedback: a follow-up assignment can invite students to write an "editorial note" to a peer poem.

Writing poetry can work for both formative and summative assessment. For example, formative assessment may involve reviewing and deploying vocabulary items to help students evaluate their progress and identify the directions for improvement. Likewise, a poem or similar creative writing exercise could fall under the umbrella of summative assessment if offered as a final project at the end of the semester. These assessments could also be broken down into smaller parts – initial writing, editing, annotating, rehearsing, and presenting – and discussed with students in advance. Gunn (2021) recommends that instructors not only explicitly state learning objectives in the syllabi but also "discuss all assessment expectations" and "encourage students to make connections between content covered in class and the assessment" (p. 263). Every assessment, accordingly, should clearly state its purpose in the assignment description.

Martin and Nuss (2022b) point out that while we encourage students to take risks in their language studies, we must similarly rethink the way we grade. A large part of the creative writing's appeal lies in the fact that, while rules and expectations exist, there are also no strictly right or wrong answers and no rigid norm against which the teacher judges the student. Instead, students have a task – in this case, a vocabulary review – and they reach the goal individually with an instructor's guidance and support. With writing tasks in particular, it is crucial that students know how they will be evaluated: to ease potential anxiety, an instructor should emphasize that students will not be assessed for their creativity but, rather, if the goal is to review target language, their use of vocabulary. Martin and Nuss call for "a way to gather documented evidence of growth such that we can justify assigning individual grades within the traditional framework of our institutional contexts" (p. 199). A portfolio of creative assignments could offer a useful and effective alternative to traditional grading systems, with students showcasing their genuine individual achievements.

Language assessment is often associated with performance anxiety (Ritonga et al., 2022). Activities that promote playful learning (and poetry writing is one example of such activities) effectively alleviate performance anxiety by approaching failure as an intrinsic part of the learning process, provided that students have a safe space to play and take risks. Nørgård et al. (2017) cite the "magic circle" (a metaphor drawn from game studies) to illustrate the "liminal space between the rule-bound and the free-form" (p. 271), and it is in this circle that students and teachers may rethink "the managerialism and consumerism of higher education" and learn playfully. Nørgård et al. (2017) conclude the discussion of their research by admitting the paradoxical nature of playful learning: students both value the assessment and are stressed by it, which in turn "undermines the creation of a safe and comfortable environment" (p. 279). With this in mind, an instructor might consider omitting quantitative evaluation for the gamified creative writing exercise altogether in hopes that this approach would serve pedagogical purposes better than orienting toward a formal grade or offer a participation pass/fail grade if they must.

On the process

The proposed poetry writing activity was inspired and made possible by the Magnetic Poetry kit. Originally developed by songwriter Dave Kapell in an attempt to overcome writer's block, Magnetic Poetry quickly won the hearts of poetry fans. Magnetic Poetry has now sold over three million kits all over the world; it has a version for kids and various languages. With Magnetic Poetry, the concept of wordplay gained a new meaning: the literary technique of manipulating a limited set of words to arrive at unexpected and amusing connotations. The main charm of Magnetic Poetry is that the game is inclusive and accessible by all sorts of players, not only poets. It can be played solo or collaboratively in pairs and groups; players can also compete against each other to produce the best poetic text possible.

Отдыхать
   Жить
      Слушать
         Музыка
Куда? Море

The highly customizable nature of the game and the multitude of outcomes make it a suitable pedagogical tool for language learners. In my classroom, the goal of the poetry writing game is to review previously covered vocabulary, although the game can be adapted to various needs, such as practicing grammatical patterns or even introducing new material (see Finch, 2003, for more ideas). The game was presented to 15 students of a first-year Russian course who met five times a week for 50-minute sessions in addition to less-formal class meetings, during which this game was implemented. Up to five students were present at each session, creating a more close-knit environment particularly conducive to creative tasks. The students were native speakers of English, although some had native or near-native proficiency in Japanese, Portuguese, or another language. The poetry game was introduced to the students in the first month of the second semester of Russian instruction. Students had an hour to write their poems (individually, although I was available to help), and they could continue writing them at home. After the study session, students shared their poems with their main language instructor, who left feedback on their writing. It should also be noted that basic principles of poetry writing were not introduced, so this exercise adopted a broad, loose definition of "poetry." Although some students inquired whether their poems should rhyme or follow formal conventions, the task did not demand poetic meter and rhyme. Instead, students were invited to focus on imagery and creative connections between randomly chosen vocabulary words.

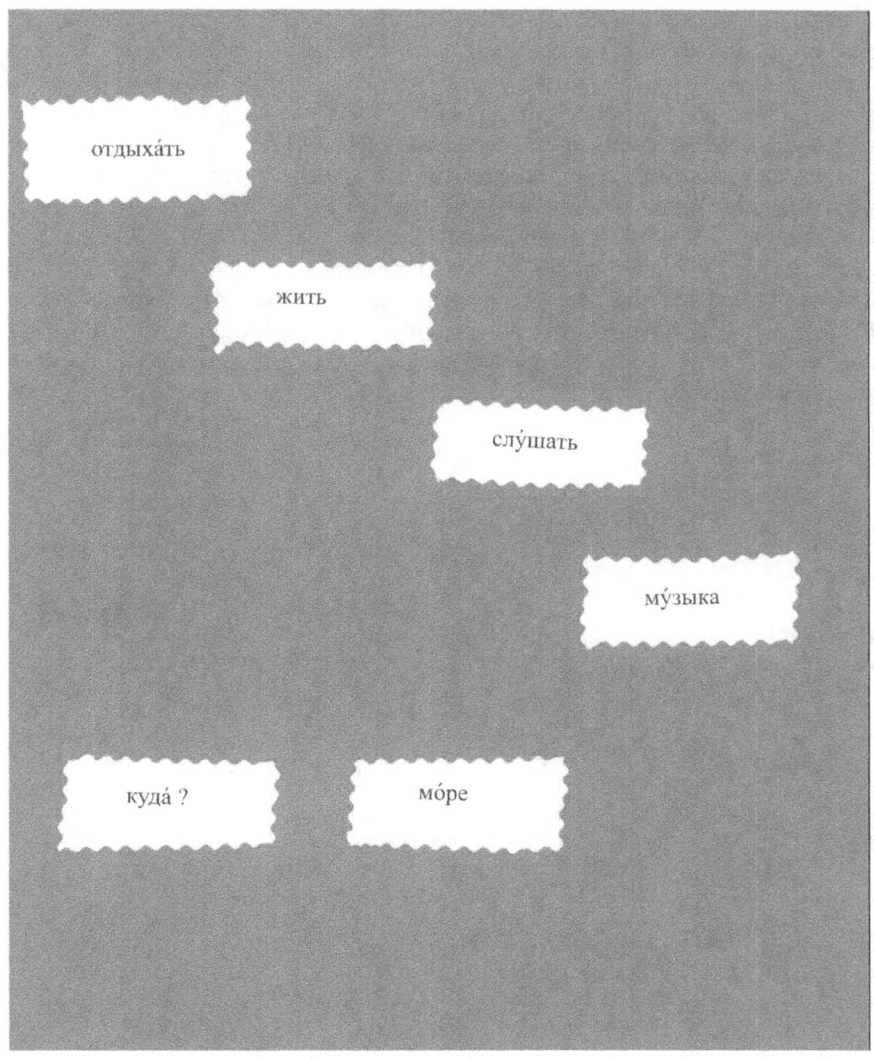

Figure 9.1 University of Illinois at Chicago, October 2022, free prompt.

Beginner's Russian (Kudyma et al., 2010) offers comprehensive vocabulary lists at the end of each chapter and carries accompanying online flashcards with these lists. For this exercise, we aimed to review the vocabulary from the previous 13 chapters studied throughout the first and ongoing second semesters, including topics like university and home life, free time, family, food and dining out, and personality traits.

In the introduction to the game and its rules, I explained these premises and encouraged students to incorporate as much covered material as possible during the poem-making process. In the preparation stage, I printed vocabulary lists for chapters the students covered with the lead instructor and then cut these lists into single-word elements, mixed the pieces, and offered them to students along with paper, glue sticks, and scissors: students picked and chose words from a bowl and a hat, randomizing the word review. They asked each other about word meanings if they did not remember and exchanged pieces that they wanted to use. Some students preferred working with the pieces independently, and some preferred writing their poems on paper that they later presented to the instructor for feedback. When I repeated this game later at the University of Illinois at Chicago, I left feedback on their poems via email and Blackboard, helping them reach grammatical accuracy and praising the content.

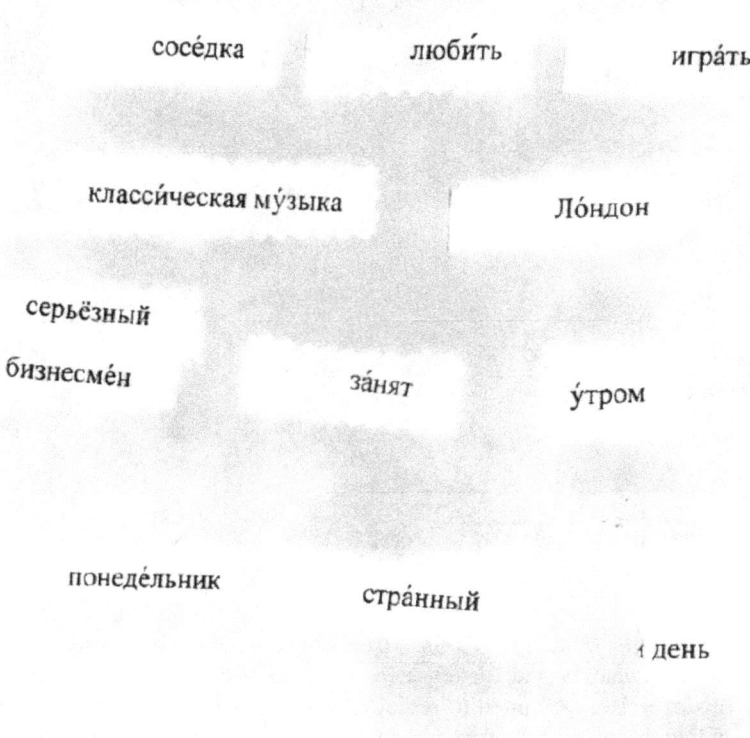

Figure 9.2 University of Illinois at Chicago, October 2022, free prompt.

To gamify the activity, I introduced several rules that served as a guidance and also eased students' anxiety by narrowing down the poetic choices. I was mindful of the chapter topics, and these limitations targeted specific vocabulary groups and grammar parts that were up for review. To start, I required that students begin with the "I like/I dislike" construction [*мне нравится* or *мне не нравится*]. This opening phrase thus constituted a theme for the entire project, which could be nearly any subject of student-author's (dis)liking. In choosing this theme structure, I additionally hoped that students' work would be as individual and self-referential as possible. Other similarly open-ended prompts might include "I want . . ." [*я хочу*] or "Tomorrow, I will . . ." [*завтра, я . . .*]. Next, I requested that students use at least one adjective to describe color, as this category was among the class review topics. I also suggested that somewhere in the poem, students use the word "eyes" [*глаза*] (also on the vocabulary review list) and a number spelled out in Russian. Stylistically, I requested that somewhere in the poem students use a two-word line. These rules sparked students' creativity and introduced a sense of competition that further gamified the exercise.

At first, not all students were enthusiastic about the game: some were hesitant to try, sharing that the task felt daunting and somewhat impossible. As a session facilitator, I saw that some of the students were hesitant either to express themselves creatively in Russian for the first time or to write creatively altogether. Some students, however, enthusiastically reacted to the task. The comic element also helped release some of the aforementioned difficulties. For students struggling with the task, I suggested an additional gamification element – that they could adopt a persona and write a poem from their point of view.

Lessons learned

After conducting the exercise and looking through the student submissions, the need for higher flexibility and customization became apparent. For example, *Magnetic Poetry* kits sold in English, German, French, Dutch, Italian, Spanish, Swedish, and Norwegian account for grammatical structures of these languages and therefore provide additional separate pieces that, for instance, help with differentiating verbal forms. The German kit features cores of verbs (like *geh-*) and includes a number of endings that would allow a player to create grammatically correct sentences. Additionally, the kit includes single-letter and two-letter fragments with prefixes.

Writing the prompt for the exercise, I relied on the implicit understanding that the words given to students are presented in their dictionary forms and therefore require modification based on the context of the poems. While this assumption

Table 9.1 Example of the German Magnetic Kit incorporating the German morphosyntax

| die | Sonne | schein | t | im | scho | en | blau | en | Himmel |

186 Polina Peremitina

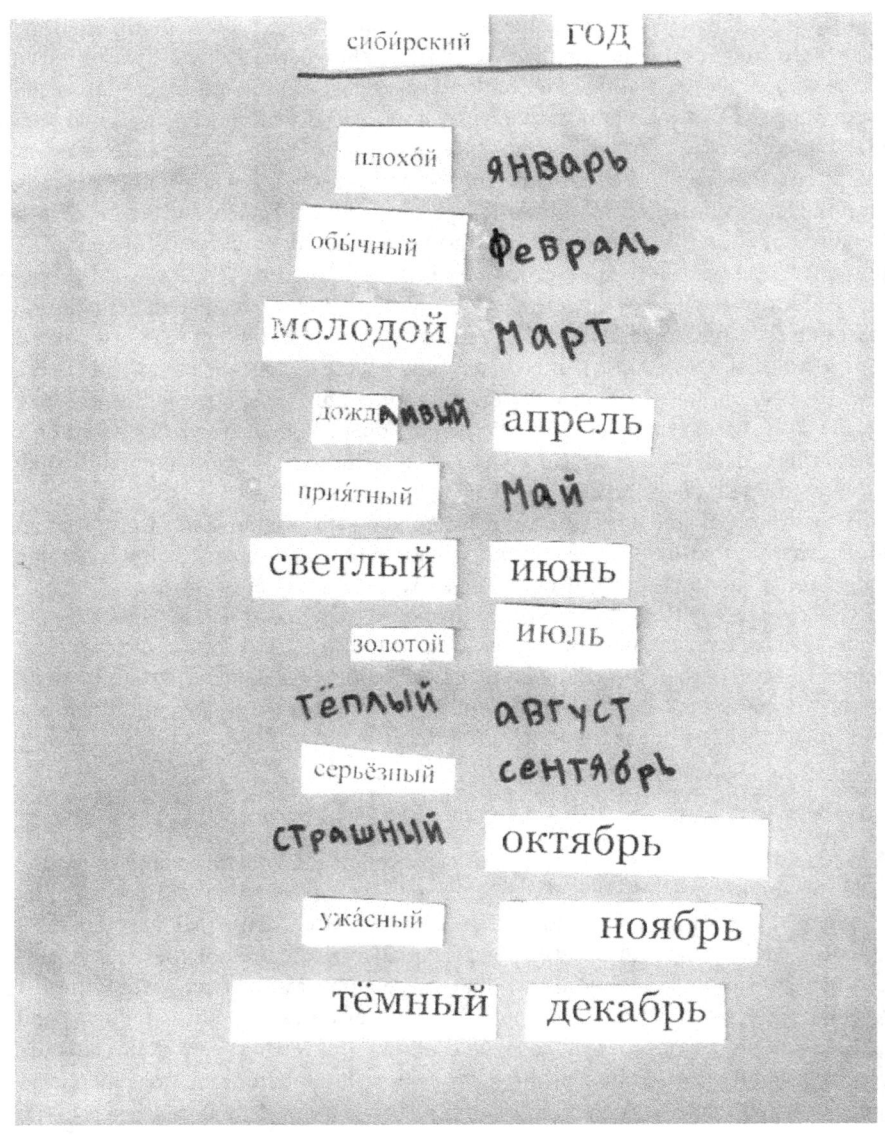

Figure 9.3 University of Illinois at Chicago, October 2022, free prompt. Notice that the student made an adjective "rainy" [дождливый] out of the noun for "rain" [дождь].

Table 9.2 Possible way to integrate the Russian endings into the game

я	ид	у	в	нов	ую	библиотек	у

could work with students of higher standing in the Russian language programs (as this understanding itself is a major principle that learners must acquire), I would include additional elements for lower-level students that could scaffold the writing process. In my session, some students realized the need to choose endings for plural nouns and would use pens and markers to fix the words of their choice. To highlight the need for such modifications, I would recommend adding more scaffolding elements, especially if they relate directly to the writing project's specific language goal(s). For Russian-language students, such elements could include additional cards for plural endings of nouns, gendered and plural endings of adjectives, conjugated verb endings, and prefixes, among others. These elements can be glued directly on top of the original dictionary word forms.

Furthermore, I would make game directions as concrete and explicit as possible. For example, if students should work with plural nouns, that stipulation should appear within the prompt: for example, "in your poem, use at least one plural noun and at least one plural adjective." Similarly, if this assignment falls under the category of purely creative writing that aims to make students more comfortable with the language, I would lift or ease formal limitations and instead encourage independent exploration of the topic, possibly requiring students to create their kits around the topic they would like to write about. Creating and distributing thematic word lists could also be a potential extension for this project.

Because this game has the potential to be used for a variety of learning purposes, I recommend that the card for each given word indicate its part of speech. As students spend time arranging their words into a poem, these pieces of text could potentially become flashcards for students to reuse later in the class. In my version, I did not include translations for offered words, but if the transformation of the word pieces into flashcards is the goal, I would add translations and examples of the words in context.

Additionally, as with any creative writing activity, but especially in a foreign language, humor should be allowed and encouraged whenever possible. As students make the language their own, it is inevitable that early attempts at poetry writing, especially at lower levels, would result in misunderstandings and lighthearted laughter. For students with higher levels of proficiency, potential prompts could incorporate more nuanced, explorative topics.

In conclusion, poetry writing games offer students opportunities to express themselves in Russian creatively while they review previously covered vocabulary. Instead of reviewing vocabulary in a teacher-centered manner, students took charge of the task and approached it in a manner that benefited their own learning trajectory. Students also read their poems aloud to each other at the end of the sessions, sharing the diverse outputs they generated from one exercise. From a facilitator's standpoint, it felt liberating to loosen control over students' learning practice and to provide them with a safe space for playful experimentation.

References

Allen, H. W. (2018). Redefining writing in the foreign language curriculum: Toward a design approach. *Foreign Language Annals, 51*(3), 513–532.

Anderson, C., & Walsh, I. (2020). Research-based Internet writing projects in the Russian curriculum. In E. Dengub, I. Dubinina, & J. Merrill (Eds.), *The art of teaching Russian* (pp. 431–454). Georgetown University Press.

Arshavskaya, E. (2015). Creative writing assignments in a second language course: A way to engage less motivated students. *InSight: A Journal of Scholarly Teaching, 10*, 68–78.

Baer, B. J., & McIntyre, T. (2022). Bringing task-based instruction online: Challenges of remote language assessment. In S. V. Nuss & C. L. Martin (Eds.), *Student-centered approaches to Russian language teaching: Insights, strategies, and adaptations*. Routledge.

Finch, A. (2003). Using poems to teach English. *English Language Teaching, 15*(2), 29–45.

Freire, P. (2020). Pedagogy of the oppressed. In P. Kuppers & G. Robertson (Eds.), *The community performance reader* (pp. 24–27). Routledge.

Gunn, Y. (2021). Assessment design in online Russian language courses: Lessons from COVID-19. *Russian Language Journal, 71*(2), 13.

Hanauer, D. I. (2012). Meaningful literacy: Writing poetry in the language classroom. *Language Teaching, 45*(1), 105–115.

Kudyma, A., Miller, F. J., & Kagan, O. (2010). *Beginner's Russian with interactive online workbook: A basic Russian course*. Hippocrene Books.

Leaver, B. L., & Campbell, C. (2020). The shifting paradigm in Russian language pedagogy: From communicative language teaching to transformative language learning and teaching. In E. Dengub, I. Dubinina, & J. Merrill (Eds.), *The art of teaching Russian* (pp. 147–162). Georgetown University Press.

Manchón, R. M., & Williams, J. (2016). L2 writing and SLA studies. In R. M. Manchón & J. Williams (Eds.), *Handbook of second and foreign language writing* (p. 567). Walter de Gruyter GmbH & Co KG.

Martin, C. L., & Nuss, S. V. (2022a). Student-centered teaching of Russian: From principles to practice. In S. V. Nuss & C. L. Martin (Eds.), *Student-centered approaches to Russian language teaching: Insights, strategies, and adaptations* (pp. 3–17). Routledge.

Martin, C. L., & Nuss, S. V. (2022b). Reflections on practice, additional considerations, and the importance of institutional support for teachers. In S. V. Nuss & C. L. Martin (Eds.), *Student-centered approaches to Russian language teaching: Insights, strategies, and adaptations* (pp. 192–202). Routledge.

Nørgård, R. T., Toft-Nielsen, C., & Whitton, N. (2017). Playful learning in higher education: Developing a signature pedagogy. *International Journal of Play, 6*(3), 272–282.

Piscayanti, K. S., & Yuliasri, I. (2021). Inventing voice of identity through L2 poetry writing: A construct of mindfulness-based strategy in remote learning. *Language Circle: Journal of Language and Literature, 16*(1), 71–80.

Ritonga, M., Farhangi, F., Ajanil, B., & Farid Khafaga, A. (2022). Interventionist vs. interactionist models of dynamic assessment (DA) in the EFL classroom: Impacts on speaking accuracy and fluency (SAF), foreign language classroom anxiety (FLCA), and foreign language learning motivation (FLLM). *Language Testing in Asia, 12*(1), 1–21.

Sivachenko, O., & Nedashkivska, A. (2021). Student engagement in a remote language learning environment: The case of Ukrainian. *Russian Language Journal, 71*(2), 4.

Tay, E. (2014). Curriculum as cultural critique: Creative writing pedagogy in Hong Kong. In D. Disney (Ed.), *Exploring second language creative writing: Beyond Babel* (Vol. 19). John Benjamins Publishing Company.

Tu, I. J. (2021). Developing self-directed learning strategies through creative writing: Three case studies of snowball writing practice in a college Chinese language classroom. *Thinking Skills and Creativity, 41*, 100837.

Vasylets, O. (2017). *Task-modality effects: A study of task complexity effects in speech and writing* [Unpublished doctoral dissertation]. Universitat de Barcelona, Spain.

Chapter 10

Playing at conversation
Chatbots in Russian language teaching

Daria Dornicheva and Sandra Birzer

CHAPTER SUMMARY

Total digitalization has become an everyday occurrence and is changing language teaching and learning. The models of language teaching and learning are constantly being reshaped accordingly. When new tools and formats are introduced, it is important that they are in harmony with the Internet, its logic, and the digital culture that is developing from it. This chapter discusses the use of chatbots for L2 Russian conversational practice. At present, teaching tools in the chatbot format form an emerging field for the teaching of Russian as a foreign language (RFL). In the first section of this chapter, we report on the use of four different types of chatbots: general and social chatbots capable to converse on any topic, specialized chatbots used mainly for different types of (customer) service, and educational chatbots designed for teaching English as a second language and discuss the transferability of the underlying didactic ideas to teaching RFL. In the second part, we introduce the Russian general chatbot *roBot*, some specialized chatbots (among others, for booking different services and for planning trips), game-bots, and humbots (providing psychological assistance) and suggest possible applications of these tools for training L2 Russian conversational skills. Finally, we propose criteria for developing Russian educational chatbots and formulate further research questions regarding the use of chatbots in teaching Russian.

Краткое содержание главы

Тотальная дигитализация, ставшая будничным явлением, меняет, среди прочего, и всю систему преподавания и изучения языков. Соответственно, модели преподавания постоянно переосмысливаются, идет поиск новых инструментов и форматов, гармонирующих с интернетом, его логикой и развивающейся на его основе цифровой культурой. В главе рассматривается использование чат-ботов для разговорной практики. Поскольку в данный момент использование формата чат-бота как учебного инструмента представляет собой новую область в преподавании русского языка, в первом разделе главы мы рассказываем об использовании различных типов чат-ботов в преподавании английского языка и обсуждаем возможность переноса дидактических идей, лежащих в их основе, на преподавание русского языка. Мы рассматриваем общие и "социальные" чат-боты, способные вести беседу на любую тему, специализированные чат-боты, используемые в основном для различных видов обслуживания (клиентов) и образовательные чат-боты. Во второй части мы описываем, как существующие на русском языке чат-боты могут быть использованы для обучения разговорным навыкам: нами представлены социальный чат-бот *pBot*, некоторые специализированные чат-боты (в том числе для бронирования различных услуг и планирования путешествий), игровые боты и гибридные боты, оказывающие психологическую помощь. Наконец, мы предлагаем критерии для разработки образовательных чат-ботов и формулируем дальнейшие исследовательские вопросы, касающиеся использования чат-ботов в обучении русскому языку.

Communication in L2 classroom

Communication is a vital process of language acquisition (Richards & Rodgers, 2001; Swain & Lapkin, 1995). While practicing communication in the target language (L2) plays a crucial role in second language acquisition, it is quite challenging for many reasons. First of all, the learner should be willing to communicate in the target foreign language, be mentally ready to engage in conversation, and actively take part in it despite language barriers, which are even higher in morphologically complex languages such as Russian (Gilabert & Castellví, 2019; Mikhaylova, 2018; Nuss, 2022), and of possible misunderstandings due to these barriers, as well as cultural differences. Moreover, learners should be familiar with the topic of discussion, be capable of developing and organizing their own ideas on the topic and of transforming them into persuasive arguments. Finally, the arguments should be framed in understandable sentences, which requires appropriate vocabulary and grammatical structures as well as pragmatic knowledge. The ability to ask appropriate questions and to give situation-adequate backchannels (Yngve, 1970)[1] to express feelings and emotions is no less important. Non-linguistic factors, such as speaking anxiety and self-confidence, also play a significant role in communication (MacIntyre et al., 1998). These concepts are also closely related to learner identity (Norton, 1995; Pavlenko & Norton, 2007).

The acquisition of the linguistic system does not automatically lead to the development of communicative skills: conversation practice is needed. In second language learning, the role of the communication partner is usually assigned to the teacher, who is capable of correcting and commenting on errors, or to peers, that is, other learners or language tandem partners. While live communication is very important for learners, varying communicative skills – due to differing target language proficiency and personality traits – pose a challenge in the classroom. In the case of Russian, this is even more pronounced, as learner groups usually include both foreign language learners and heritage speakers with specific learning needs (Bergmann & Brüggemann, 2021; Brehmer & Mehlhorn, 2018a; Carreira & Kagan, 2018; Dubinina & Kisselev, 2019; Polinsky, 2018).

Consequently, conversational practice in the classroom that is useful for some learner types may be completely unsatisfactory for others due to differences in cognitive styles or learning strategies (Bondarenko & Kogan, 2021). To meet learners' needs, a more differentiated instructional approach (e.g., different research tasks in text corpora for subgroups of learners) has been used in the teaching of Russian in recent years, including in relation to conversational practice (Mehlhorn, 2014; Nuss & Martin, 2022; Steinbach & Birzer, 2014, Wapenhans, 2016). The rapidly growing popularity of chatbots offers new opportunities for teaching and learning Russian in a more learner-centered way. Used as a stand-alone tool or as part of blended learning settings (Spasova & Welsh, 2020), chatbots allow for differentiated approaches and can be used for training various aspects of communicative competence: for example, fluency, accuracy, or pragmatics. Thus, they can be used as a gateway to a conversation at lower proficiency levels and for refinement at higher levels.

This chapter discusses the use of chatbots in L2 Russian classrooms. First, we provide a brief review of studies on using chatbots for L2 teaching and learning and clarify what using chatbots has to do with the gamification of L2 teaching. In the second part, we discuss different ways of employing conversational chatbots in heterogeneous learner groups of Russian and propose starting ideas for developing educational chatbots. Finally, we present the insights based on our teaching experience and lessons learned.

Literature review

Chatbots as communication partners in L2 teaching

Since the label *chatbot* is associated with very different things, we will start with a definition: for us, chatbots are software tools that fulfill the role of humanlike digital conversational assistants and interact with users in real time and natural language, using text or voice.[2] This definition encompasses a wide range of tools that can be classified alongside two dimensions, namely, technical construction and content.

Rule-based chatbots and AI chatbots

The conversations of template-based or rule-based response mechanisms are based on pre-scripted material and on response options that can be selected from a menu.[3] Consequently, their range of topics and reactions is restricted. Chatbots based on artificial intelligence, such as *Cleverbot* or *Elbot*, can converse on a broader range of topics and give individualized responses to each user. Nonetheless, communication with AI chatbots has distinct limitations: the set of topics they can manage is still limited, and conversation is not entirely casual and humanlike. Although many AI chatbots demonstrate high-quality speech recognition, semantic analysis, and speech synthesis, they fail in the most important feature of interaction – recognizing the content of whole discourses, which is significant for fully fledged communication (Dokukina & Gumanova, 2020). The problem can be seen in the following example analyzed in (Mazzilli (2021):

1. NutzerIn: Do you have friends?
2. Cleverbot: Not really.
3. NutzerIn: Why not?
4. Cleverbot: Because I don't like math that much. (Mazzilli, 2021, p. 97)

As we can see in this example, the response of *Cleverbot* – an AI chatbot considered to be one of the best ones in chatbots-landscape, which passed one of the key tests of artificial intelligence, the Turing test, with 59.3% votes – is formally correct, but as it does not correspond to the general topic of the conversation and actually does not answer the question, the communication act between the person and the machine fails. The technical reason for the semantic inconsistency of the bot's answer is the fact that *Cleverbot* does not retain information; it doesn't "remember" any statement of the current conversational session but searches for its answering utterances among billions of responses ever given in similar conversational situations.

Furthermore, AI chatbots are not able to use common ground and do not create truly coherent conversations (Lotze, 2016).

General and specialized assistants

On a content level, we may distinguish between general[4] and specialized[5] assistants. It is not too surprising that AI chatbots with their broad range of topics are employed mostly as general assistants. Social chatbots, or virtual companions in terms of Grudin and Jacques (2019), are AI chatbots that form a specialized subtype of general assistants whose specific goal is communication with the user.[6]

Specialized chatbots are designed for certain purposes, often in the realm of customer service, for example, making reservations for restaurants or hotels, managing complaints, etc. Chatbots specifically designed for education also form a subset of specialized chatbots.

Chatbots and gamification

There are a number of characteristics that chatbots and games share in common.

From the various definitions of *gamification*, we would like to draw on Deterding et al.'s definitions of gamification stating that *gamification* is "the use of game design elements in non-game contexts" (2011, p. 1) and on Hidayatulloh et al.'s definition as "the application of a game's design, in whole or in part, to real-world issues" (2021, p. 73). The usage of chatbots for language learning oscillates between the two aforementioned definitions, depending on the setting. For example, if a specialized chatbot for selling shoes or making reservations is used in the classroom, we are dealing with a (mock) real-world issue, whereas educational chatbots rather fall under Deterding et al.'s definition.

As gamification is considered to have positive effects on motivation, game design elements have been tested for their motivational potential (see Schöbel et al. (2020) for a very comprehensive evaluation of elements, Sailer et al. (2017) for effect sizes of motivation, and Sailer et al. (2013) for the different aspects of motivation).

In general, chatbots provide the following motivational factors considered typical for gamification:

- The chatbot's answer is "immediate feedback in form of positive and negative reinforcement" and should depend on the adequacy of the learner's question.
- Interactions with chatbots may be used with "a clear and achievable goal" and "foster . . . mastery orientation regarding goals," which results in the "feeling of competence" on the students' side.
- Since learners interact with the chatbot independently from their co-students, chatbots provide "the feeling of autonomy."
- Chatbots – especially when they are used for preparing discussions in class – may help "decrease . . . negative feelings like fear, envy, and anger." (Sailer et al., 2013, pp. 33–34)

These motivational effects are achieved by the following game design elements, whose implications we will discuss extensively in the sections that follow:

- In many cases, the communicative tasks students have to solve by interacting with the chatbot resemble gaming quests (Sailer et al., 2013, p. 35; Endarto & Tanojo, 2018, p. 131). If students are, for example, asked to make a reservation in a restaurant by interacting with a specialized chatbot, the process of making the reservation may be considered a quest.
- The product achieved by interaction with the chatbot, that is, reservation, as such may be considered the reward (Endarto & Tanojo, 2018, p. 132).
- As the interaction (at least) with non-educational chatbots replicates real-life situations likely to be encountered in Russian-speaking communities, it can be considered as a *meaningful story* (Sailer et al., 2013, p. 35; Endarto & Tanojo, 2018, p. 132; Schöbel et al., 2020, p. 657).[7]

Non-educational conversational chatbots for language learning purposes

We will now discuss the application of both non-educational and educational chatbots for language learning. First, we will focus on non-educational conversational chatbots, then on educational ones specifically designed for language learning purposes.

Since dialogue is a very natural form of language use (Lee et al., 2009), L2 learners will want to practice it, and it seems quite effective to use conversational chatbots for this purpose. The possibility of delegating at least some conversations to automated dialogue systems can be a relief for both the instructor, who is freed from repetitive work, and the student, providing him with an opportunity for conversations with tireless assistants at any time, at any place, not bound to any specific setting (Huang et al., 2021, p. 238). The only limiting factor for introducing chatbots into language classes seems to be their availability in the respective target language. In reality, however, even for English, the technically most advanced conversational chatbots do not compare to human interlocutors with regards to understanding learners' speech and adapting to their proficiency levels: they are not able to handle some word forms due to vocabulary limitations, fail in recognizing the content of whole discourses, cannot therefore recognize some natural human speech constructions, such as elliptical constructions, and can only create the illusion of coherence (see Lotze (2016) on linguistic analysis of communication with AI chatbots).

Considering these limitations, it is not surprising that students deem conversation with human interlocutors to be not fully replaceable by chatbot conversations. Gallacher et al. (2018) report an experiment in which English L2 learners performed spoken interviews with both AI and human partners in alternating sessions and considered the AI chatbot an unreliable interlocutor. Unfortunately, the paper does not give any information whether there is a correlation between students' perception of the chatbot and their language proficiency level: one would expect advanced students to have a higher threshold of tolerance for communication failures and a better error-handling ability. In case of an interactional pitfall or misunderstanding, they are able to reformulate their question, to change the topic of conversation, etc. However, some studies suggest that social chatbots are useful at the initial levels of learning and that problems due to communication failures arise on advanced levels (Dokukina & Gumanova, 2020). Thus, the correlation between learners' proficiency, successful communication with the chatbot, and the learning progress resulting thereof will be a rewarding research question in the future.

Gallacher et al. (2018) also pointed out that their student participants considered the chatbot rather a novel technology than a communication partner or a legitimate language-learning tool. The *novelty effect* as a possible reason for short-term positive effects of employing chatbots in L2 teaching was also discussed in other studies. Fryer et al. (2017), in their 12-week experimental study aimed to test the longer-term effects of chatbot technology on students' task and course interest, show that students' interest in conversation-based tasks already drops significantly after the first task if the interlocutor is a chatbot. The authors attribute this to the novelty effect of chatbots, which does not occur in the communication with a human partner.[8]

Nonetheless, there are many examples of successful use of conversational chatbots for L2 learning. As shown by Kim (2018), communication with voice-based general assistants can be useful for training partial competences involved in the interaction and enhance listening and comprehension skills (also Dokukina and

Gumanova (2020)). As shown by Mazzilli (2021), text-based social chatbots can be successfully integrated in the L2 learning process to achieve specific learning goals when using the potential of their most "critical" aspects. In her German course, Mazzilli used *Elbot*, a general chatbot, as a problematic interlocutor to train conflict-solving skills in the L2. *Elbot* provided a stress-free environment, resulting in participants perceiving the setting as motivating and feeling "more confident while dealing with conflicts with the chatbot than while facing them with humans" (Mazzilli, 2021, p. 110).[9]

Narrowly focused specialized digital assistants can be integrated into traditional learning settings to train conversation patterns in a limited set of topics, such as weather, restaurants reservations, booking flights, etc. (Dokukina & Gumanova, 2020, p. 544). Still, we were unable to find publications describing the experience of using them in the classroom.

To sum up, conversational non-educational chatbots of different types can be used for conversational practice only to a limited extent and only under certain conditions. The teacher needs deliberate strategies when giving chatbot-based tasks, by either preparing students for the challenges of "free" communication with a machine or relieving those difficulties through very narrowly worded learning tasks or using a combination of both.[10] Both teacher and learners should be aware of the technical restrictions imposed on conversing with a chatbot, such as inconsistency of communication, the machine's inability to recognize elliptical syntactic constructions natural to human interaction, the limited vocabulary of the machine due to its ignorance of the rules of morphology that prevents them from recognition of creative word formations (Lotze, 2016). This will prevent communicative failures resulting thereof in decreased learners' motivation. To reduce the risk of conversational failures, a conversation should touch upon a limited number of topics, as constant changes of topic makes inappropriate answers more likely.

Combining the skills of different types of conversational chatbots – intelligent general and specialized assistants and social chatbots – is a desideratum in order to provide the possibility of free conversation which meets users' expectations (Grudin & Jacques, 2019). Another desideratum is designing educational versions of existing chatbots to adapt them to special learners' needs (Cai et al., 2021; Mazzilli, 2021), which, however, seems to be rather unlikely for less-commonly taught languages.

Language learning with educational chatbots

Conversational chatbots designed specifically for language learning purposes are another opportunity for students to practice conversation. The basic principle of all educational chatbots, which can also be defined as *intelligent tutoring systems*, *special learning assistants* (Dokukina & Gumanova, 2020), or *learning support tools* (Goda et al., 2014), is dividing up the language learning process into small steps: learning objectives define the individual steps, which are then implemented as tasks for an appropriate conversational tool.

Quite expectedly, the vast majority of chatbots developed to date are made in more commonly spoken and taught languages, primarily in English. Similarly, most studies on this topic consider educational chatbots for teaching English.

Many online schools that rely on online learning incorporate chatbots in their mobile apps. The offer has an especially wide range for beginners: learning chatbots can help with practicing simple dialogues on real-life, everyday scenarios, such as making an acquaintance or ordering drinks (*Mondly* or *Babbel*, to mention just a few ones).

In the realm of conversational practice, Ayedoun et al. (2016, 2019) designed an embodied conversational agent fostering students' motivation and *willingness to communicate* (McCroskey & Baer, 1985).

Specialized educational chatbots are also used for preparing students for live discussions in the classroom, by covering various learning objectives, such as organizing ideas, building a line of argumentation, or finding appropriate vocabulary. Jia (2004) developed a chatbot that aimed to help students organize their thoughts and learn some expressions that could be used in the following conversation in the classroom, which make students feel more prepared. The modern form of this multifunctional web-based instruction system for English learning enables dialogue simulations, including role-play (Jia, 2015).

Goda et al. (2014) point out that a group discussion can be affected in a positive way through a preceding conversation with a chatbot. For their experiment, a learning chatbot reflecting the Socratic inquiry method based on Eliza-bot was developed. The results of the first case study show an increase both in the number of contributions to conversations in class and the number of conversations in which the students participated (ibid. 6). In the second case study, it was shown that conversing with the Socratic chatbot-inquiry as a pre-discussion activity could affect factors of the individual critical thinking, such as "awareness of critical thinking" and enable them to form an "inquiring mindset."

The topic never ceases to be relevant: the number of chatbots and research on their use is growing. Aware of the limitations of existing non-educational conversational chatbots, universities are bringing together developers, researchers, and language educators to program new conversational chatbots for L2 learning (Cai et al., 2021), which gives an opportunity to improve the functionality of chatbots and meet various educational purposes. A recent meta-study by Huang et al. (2021) examines the use of both educational and non-educational chatbots for different areas of language learning in order to discover technological, pedagogical, and social affordances of using chatbots in language learning and to identify possible challenges.

Russian conversational chatbots and their usage in teaching Russian

For less-commonly taught languages such as Russian, teaching tools in chatbot format form an emerging field. For the time being, the few educational bots developed for the Russian language focus on vocabulary training, grammar, and spelling. For instance, *MyRUSkey* training bot is designed for beginner-level learners of Russian and offers its users daily 1 of 100 most frequent words of the Russian language in a minimal context, with comments, questions, and tasks (Bikkulova & Ivkina, 2021). The short conversations offered by this bot are based on pre-scripted material written in a flashcard format. More examples can be found on the chatbot platform *Learning Snacks*, developed to provide teachers with easy-to-use freeware to develop small game-based interactive learning units in the form of text-based chatbots for their students. The chatbots use the IRF exchange structure (initiation-response-feedback, also called follow-up), which is considered to be an essential teaching structure (Edwards & Westgate, 1994). The chatbots developed on the platform offer a new outer design for familiar exercise types, such as multiple choice, gap filling, odd-one-out, etc. For spelling, tools such as the *@grammarnazibot* in Telegram and Twitter exist.

We will first focus on how Russian conversational chatbots originally developed for other purposes can be applied to teaching Russian.

Language evaluation, search for wording, practicing free conversation: social chatbots

Some famous chatbots, such as *Cleverbot* or *Eviebot*, have Russian versions, but the quality of the Russian language in translated bots is unsatisfactory in most cases. *pBot* can be used as a social chatbot for Russian. *pBot* is a text-driven AI social chatbot with open learning, allowing every user to contribute by correcting *pBot*'s answers and adding new answer variants. Since input data is controlled by humans, inappropriate utterances, namely, senseless answers, insults, obscene language, or advertising, are deleted from the knowledge base, whereas "interesting, kind or funny" answers are prioritized in upcoming conversations (http://p-bot.ru/en/learning.html). *pBot* demonstrates a live cross section of current and authentic Russian language. It provides a broad range of vocabulary with a large number of colloquial elements. The communication style varies from neutral to colloquial. Some example dialogues with the bot can be found here: http://p-bot.ru/dialogs.html.

pBot or other Russian social chatbots can be used to train advanced students' ability to engage in free conversation and to maintain it by asking different types of questions. Students at the beginner level may be presented with small-scale tasks, such as planning a short dialogue, asking questions on a specific issue, reformulating questions, giving thanks for information or accepting thanks, saying goodbye, and arranging a new meeting. Intermediate-level students, on the other hand, can converse with the bot on more demanding topics according to a conversation plan developed by the instructor or by the student. For technical reasons, it is necessary to prepare for conversations with chatbots. Since chatbots have technical restrictions in speech recognition and cannot handle a number of natural human speech constructions, such as elliptical constructions or some word forms due to vocabulary limitations, this must be taken into account when planning the students' interaction with them. The planning can take different forms, depending on the proficiency level of the group or the proficiency levels of students within the group. For example, for upper-intermediate and advanced students and speakers of Russian as a heritage language, it is sufficient to provide instructions or rules of communication with a chatbot, after which they can enter into a free communication with a chatbot on the planned topic.

At the mid-intermediate level, it may be advisable, in addition to the list of rules, to ask students to formulate questions for the chatbot as part of their preparation for communication. Discussing these pre-prepared questions in class prior to conversing with a chatbot will enable the instructor to dictate the direction in which the conversation will proceed, whether it conforms to the rules, and, if necessary, to make adjustments. The third option, which can be used with low-intermediate-level students, can be the formulation of questions by the instructor. In this case, students will communicate with a chatbot using questions from a ready-made list. The focus, in contrast to the first two options, will be the training of reading and comprehension skills. Depending on the students' level and the purpose of the lesson, the instructor can decide what form of planning is most appropriate. It should be noted that the only time-consuming experience in communication with chatbots is the initial planning. As chatbots enter the classroom and become part of the learning routine, students will no longer need to explicitly state the rules and can prevent potential communication difficulties on their own.

pBot's vote-option for good and bad answers offers the possibility to reflect on the thematic, pragmatic, and/or stylistic appropriateness of *pBot*'s answers and to correct them if necessary. This option can be used for partner work or work in small teams of advanced-level and/or heritage language students. For example, students collect a list of questions on a certain topic, present them to the bot, and discuss the answers. If the students deem an answer off-topic, stylistically inappropriate, or unsuccessful, they shortly describe the insufficiency(ies) and offer their own answer(s). The results can be saved as a screenshot and presented in class, accompanied by reasons for their decisions.

An authentic environment for real-life tasks: specialized digital assistants

On the beginner and lower-intermediate level, narrowly focused specialized digital assistants can be used for engaging learners in simple conversations on everyday topics. Specialized assistants provide immersion in an authentic language environment to achieve a specific goal: booking a table or booking a ticket for a concert, getting information on the best flights to the desired destination (for example, with the Telegram-based *MetaMetaBot*), finding fellow travelers (for example, with the Telegram-based *DublwayBot*, which helps search hitchhikers – both drivers and passengers – when traveling in Russia), etc. Some chatbots offer attractive additional options: for example, the Facebook chatbot Россия из дома/*Russia from home* (http://russiafromhome.ru/), devoted to traveling in Russia, not only advises users on the destination but also provides links to Russian-language travel blogs, photos by Russian photographers, etc.

Most specialized chatbots can be recommended for the elementary level, for example, as an additional task after the corresponding topic has been covered in the classroom.

Instructors should be aware that bots of this type are rather short-lived and change constantly (so check the availability before repeating a lesson); the Russian-language register (and grammatical correctness) also varies.

Having fun: game-chatbots

AI games can be an inviting way to prepare for a conversation. While most chatbot games were developed in most commonly taught languages and, for the time being, are either not translated into Russian or show poor quality of language in translation, there are some exceptions. For instance, the Russian version of the popular game *Akinator*, released in 2007 by the French company *Elokence*, has a high-quality translation. During gameplay, the fictional character, the genie Akinator, attempts to determine what fictional or real-life character the player is thinking of by asking a series of questions. The player answers with "Yes," "No," "Probably," "Probably not," or "Don't know." The question structure used in Akinator can prepare students for similar conversational games in class (https://ru.akinator.com/game).

If it's getting serious: humbots

The purposes of human bots or humbots are to sell goods, provide customer support, or provide psychological support. Since human beings serve at the back end of humbots, their exploitation in language learning raises ethical issues. For ethical reasons, we do not consider vendor and customer service humbots here.

However, situations may arise that justify working with humbots providing psychological support. Cultural identity is often an issue for speakers of heritage Russian (Brehmer & Mehlhorn, 2018b). The oscillation between majority and heritage culture is one issue that has been discussed rather intensively (Dietz & Roll, 2017; Isurin, 2011, 2017). Among Russian heritage speakers, (inter-generational) conflicts may arise due to different political standpoints, often influenced by propaganda. Russian aggression in Ukraine has added new complications: some students are fearing for their relatives in Ukraine, others speak about conflicts with relatives heavily influenced by Russian television propaganda, and some students report being addressed as "Russians" in public spaces and being forced to take on responsibility for the Russian war in Ukraine, regardless of their own political opinion.

For those students, it can be of great importance to maintain a safe, anonymous environment away from accusations, foreign attributions of identity, or propaganda distortions. This can help them express their thoughts and feelings about current events in their family language and also to learn to set boundaries when talking about such topics if they feel that their identity is being challenged. Chatbots such as Telegram-based *Бот службы поддержки/@HelpdeskMediaBot*, founded by the Helpdesk Media (https://helpdesk.media/), can be highly recommended for these purposes. After some general questions posed by a real chatbot, a user can chat with a volunteer. As a rule, these support bots are founded by non-profit organizations and financed from independent foundations, that is, they are in no way connected with state propaganda of the Russian Federation or any other state.

Working on specific learning objectives: Designing chatbots for learners' needs

As stated earlier, currently, no specialized educational chatbots are available for training communication in the Russian language. In this section, we will formulate some starting ideas for developing such educational chatbots.

An educational chatbot can support learners in mastering skills that are important for conversational interaction. Since, as mentioned earlier, communicating exclusively with chatbots has a negative impact on students' motivation, the use of any chatbot should be restricted to the intermediate steps between announcing the topic of conversation/debate and the live exchange of statements in the face-to-face learning phase. Figuratively speaking, chatbots serve as "springboards" to live/real communication, which give students the opportunity to prepare for a subsequent conversation in class.

Accordingly, educational chatbots may support learners in achieving the following goals:

- Introducing the topic of conversation or discussion/debate (topic-immersion chatbots)
- Structuring students' thoughts on the topic (inquiry chatbot)
- Developing and elaborating on their own arguments (debate role-play chatbot)[11]
- Vocabulary work (vocabulary-relief chatbot elements)
- Identifying appropriate syntactic structures for expressing their thoughts (sentence structure chatbot or chatbot elements)
- Expanding their vocabulary for structuring discourse, for example, connectives, discourse markers, etc. (connection creator chatbot)
- Acquiring appropriate reactive and proactive backchannels (backchannels-training chatbot or chatbot elements)

For obvious reasons, educational chatbots should take into account the specific problems encountered at different proficiency levels and of heritage vs. foreign language students. This can be accomplished either by creating separate chatbots for different proficiency levels or by differentiating between levels within one chatbot. Since learner groups are often heterogeneous (and variation can be observed even if all students are on the same proficiency level), it seems advisable to install "complexity branching" of the chatbot, which assigns students to different complexity levels depending on their answers. However, it should be kept in mind that additional branches are technically challenging and time-consuming to create, thus making it important to assess which of the two ways is more appropriate in each case.

To the best of our knowledge, there have been no experimental studies on Russian educational chatbots, which opens up several research questions for future work:

- Do educational chatbots have a positive effect on students' "willingness to communicate" (MacIntyre et al., 1998) outside of the chatbot context, and which factors (e.g., students feel better prepared) explain this effect?
- How do students rate the effect of different types of chatbots on their motivation/readiness to communicate? (For operationalized factors, see MacIntyre et al. (1998).)
- How do instructors rate the effect of different types of chatbots on students' motivation/readiness to communicate?
- How do students rate the training effect of different types of chatbots on their conversational skills?
- How do instructors rate the training effect of different types of chatbots on students' conversational skills?
- How do students' and instructors' ratings correlate, and what does this tell us about the benefits of employing chatbots in language teaching?
- Can a passive way of using backchannels in a chatbot setting animate students to use them in conversations outside the digital environment?

Conclusions and lessons learned

Since chatbots are a rather new technology, there still are many open questions and uncertainties regarding the conditions under which non-educational chatbots can be useful learning tools and regarding the basis for creating educational ones. As shown above, under certain conditions (clear frameworks, deliberate strategies by using them), chatbots can provide a stress-free and motivating learning environment.

The Institute for Slavic Studies at the University of Bamberg is currently developing educational chatbots for the Russian language, based on the principles mentioned earlier. They are conceptualized as a part of the learning materials designed for blended learning settings for heterogeneous groups of students, developed in the project "Developing Digital Cultures of Teaching" (*Digitale Kulturen der Lehre entwickeln*).[12] The first trial chatbots were tested in winter semester 2022/2023 by three groups of students at different proficiency levels (A1 to B2, heritage speakers being part of two of three groups) at Universities of Bamberg and Leipzig, Germany. We would like to thank the teachers who agreed to try out the chatbots for their cooperation.

Characteristics of trial chatbots:

Type: Rule-based educational chatbots
Software: Landbot
Type of interface design: Web-based chatbots, mobile chatbots
Pedagogical use: Interlocutor
Type of use: Developed for individual learning activities (students communicate with one chatbot via an individual channel) as a part of blended learning settings
Context: Higher education
Language proficiency levels: proficiency levels A1–B2 and heritage speakers; at the moment, no additional internal differentiation through "complexity branching"

In all groups, chatbots were offered for autonomous learning as part of homework.

The first test group consisted of students of the proficiency level A1 of the University of Bamberg. They were asked to repeat the learning material of the first two lessons of the textbook *Jasno! Neu. A1-A2* (Brosch et al., 2020). The chatbot was developed on the basis of the material students have worked through and simulated an acquaintance with a photographer from Russia. The chatbot contained vocabulary-relief chatbot elements, sentence structure chatbot elements, and backchannels-training chatbot elements. The students who gave feedback pointed out the attractiveness of the format, which gives a considerable measure of freedom in choosing the place and time of the lesson and allows review material in a non-conventional and natural form. All the interviewed students indicated that the proposed format was well suited to vocabulary work, giving them a good opportunity to repeat words they already knew and to learn some new ones, guessing them from the context or consulting the dictionary. Some students indicated that they would welcome more technical possibilities – in particular, more possible answers (instead of the two or three programmed in the proposed version of the chatbot), which would give them more room to maneuver.

The second test group consisted of students of B1 proficiency level of the Language Center at the University of Bamberg. They tried out a topic-immersion chatbot with vocabulary-relief chatbot elements, based on an interview with Alexei Vasiliev, a photographer from Yakutia. The purpose of its use was to prepare for a conversation about Russian regions. Students indicated that this form of preparation increased their interest in the topic and their desire to talk about the topic in class, and that they felt better prepared for the conversation. It was also noted in this group that this form of work added a welcomed variety to the learning process. In addition, the opportunity to practice using the Russian keyboard was positively noted.

The third test group consisted of students of the proficiency levels B1.2 to B2, Slavic studies, and teacher's degree students who are training for teaching Russian as a foreign/second language from the University of Leipzig. In this group, an advanced version of a topic-immersion chatbot with vocabulary-relief chatbot elements, based on an interview with the photographer Alexei Vasiliev, was used. Students were asked to prepare for a conversation about Russian regions and Russian documentary photography. After the chatbot session and conversation in the class, students were asked to write a letter to the chatbot developers to inform them about positive and negative sides of the experience. In addition, those students who were preparing to become Russian teachers themselves were asked whether chatbots could be used in school classrooms and in what contexts.

As feedback showed, the students were enthusiastic about the new format. Many of them noted the attractive design, the opportunity to talk about serious "textbook" topics in a playful way, the opportunity to repeat familiar words and learn new colloquial words and expressions from a "live" context, which was perceived by many students as an authentic conversation.

Most students indicated that they would like to have more than two or three answer-options (cf. feedbacks from the first test group). When asked if chatbots could be used in school classrooms, most students answered affirmatively, specifying in their answer that the tool could be used for introducing the topic or for repeating the material and reinforcing the vocabulary introduced.

Heritage speakers in both first and third groups were particularly positive about the opportunity to practice using the Russian keyboard on their cell phones, indicating that one of the important goals of the Russian language course for them is to correspond with Russian-speaking family members via WhatsApp and other messengers.

The teachers of all three groups noted that the students really enjoyed the format of work with the chatbot and readily described and discussed their experience with it. Teachers in groups 2 and 3 noted that the students did indeed come out in speech much easier after working with the chatbot, and that it was noticeable that the words and expressions on the topic were activated.

Two of three teachers expressed the belief that at lower levels, the chatbot can be a great tool for mastering the Russian keyboard as well as for repeating and summarizing material, while at advanced levels, it may be especially effective for introducing new topics.

In concluding the chapter, we would like to emphasize that chatbots are definitely not a one-size-fits-all format and have clear limitations. The opportunity for learners to practice speaking in class is still very important. Chatting with a bot should therefore only be seen as part of a learning scenario, a useful tool that gives students the possibility to review previously learned material in an entertaining way or make learners more prepared and less anxious when speaking in class after the chat session. Given a significant measure of conventionality, conversation with a chatbot should not be compared with a conversation with a human partner – and the expectations should be lowered accordingly: it should be seen as a simulation, or playing at conversation.

Note from the authors:
This chapter was written prior to the introduction and widespread use of ChatGPT, so the features of this language model could not have been considered. A separate study should be conducted to explore the growing functionality of ChatGPT and its potential applications in language teaching, including Russian, within the field of didactics.

Notes

1 The term *backchannels* was introduced by Victor H. Yngve in 1970 in his paper "On Getting a Word in Edgewise" to refer to meta-conversational signals which convey the listener's attention, comprehension, and/or interest. The idea caught on, and today there are some other terms for this phenomenon, such as "signals of attention," "accompaniment signals," etc. (Ayedoun et al., 2019). We prefer the term *backchannels* because it implies different functions they may perform in spontaneous dialogues, which appears to be especially important in light of recent research. For instance, the study by Tolins and Fox Tree (2014) shows that backchannels are not purely reactive phenomena; rather, some types are proactive and collaborate in narrative development.
2 Depending on the goal, other definitions and bot taxonomies are also possible. For the purposes of this chapter, we will only consider conversational bots.
3 Many educational and media chatbots are based on this principle. For example, the mobile app *Vasya*, which is designed for Russian-speaking learners of English and provides instruction for beginner level (Guriev, 2020). Another example are in-article chatbots by BBC, which aim to give readers the ability to find out more about the topic in an individualized way, such as this one: www.bbc.com/news/world-us-canada-42872231.
4 The most technically advanced are Apple's *Siri*, Microsoft's *Cortana*, Google's *Google Assistant*, Amazon's *Alexa*. They give information and send notifications on a broad range of topics but keep conversations short.
5 Innumerable narrowly focused "specialized digital assistants" (Meisel, 2016), or task-focused chatbots (Grudin & Jacques, 2019), are developed to handle simple requests, like weather forecasts, booking flights, or buying shoes. They are designed to perform tasks and maintain brief goal-oriented conversations.
6 In most studies, social chatbots constitute a separate type of chatbots that "engage on any topic and keep a conversation going" (Grudin & Jacques, 2019, p. 3). The first one, called *ELIZA*, was developed at the Artificial Intelligence Laboratory in Massachusetts by Joseph Weizenbaum in the 1960s. They became widespread in recent years as a result of mass use of social media. One of the greatest successes along the way is considered to be the development of the empathetic social chatbot *XiaoIce* – the most "human" AI in the world, developed by Microsoft in 2014 (Moioli, 2019; Shum et al., 2018).
7 However, Sailer et al. (2017, p. 377) show that the motivational effect of meaningful stories is lower than that of other game design elements.
8 This is also supported by Følstad and Brandtzaeg (2020), who analyzed users' experiences with chatbots in non-educational contexts and also report that chatbots "may be perceived as boring once the novelty wears off" (Følstad & Brandtzaeg, 2020, p. 10).
9 This is also in line with the work of Wegerif (2004), who stated that in human–machine conversation, the combination of a humanlike ability to ask questions with a machine-like patience and lack of judgment had positive effects for children with autism spectrum disorders, who often feel uncomfortable in human interaction. The use of automated dialogue systems can also alleviate difficulties experienced by some students, especially by *low input generators* (Seliger, 1977), such as fear of making mistakes, fear of "stupid" questions or "stupid" answers, internal blockage when discussing "problematic" topics, or the general unwillingness to communicate.
10 Some examples can be found in the second part of the article.
11 cf. the BBC project *Crossing divides* http://crossingdivides.bbcnewslabs.co.uk/.
12 The project is funded by the Foundation "Innovation in University Teaching" (*Stiftung Innovation in der Hochschullehre*).

References

Ayedoun, E., Hayashi, Y., & Seta, K. (2016). Web-services based conversational agent to encourage willingness to communicate in the EFL context. *The Journal of Information and Systems in Education, 15*(1), 15–27. https://doi.org/10.12937/ejsise.15.15

Ayedoun, E., Hayashi, Y., & Seta, K. (2019). Adding communicative and affective strategies to an embodied conversational agent to enhance second language learners' willingness to communicate. *International Journal of Artificial Intelligence in Education, 29*(1), 29–57. https://doi.org/10.1007/s40593-018-0171-6

Bergmann, A., & Brüggemann, N. (Eds.). (2021). *Herkunftssprache Russisch in Deutschland. Zu linguistischen Grundlagen und didaktischen Prinzipien des Unterrichts.* Slavic Language Education 1. https://doi.org/10.18452/23202

Bikkulova, O. S., & Ivkina, M. I. (2021). Chatbot v metodike prepodavanija RKI. *Mir russkogo slova, 1*, 91–96. https://doi.org/10.24412/1811-1629-2021-1-91-96

Bondarenko, M., & Kogan, V. V. (2021). "Shouldn't we do more grammar?" Learners' perspectives on the communicative approach in the Russian L2 classroom. *DiSlaw – Didaktik Slawischer Sprachen, 1*(1), 30–47. https://doi.org/10.25651/3.2021.0001

Brehmer, B., & Mehlhorn, G. (2018a). *Herkunftssprachen*. Tübingen: Narr Francke Attempto.

Brehmer, B., & Mehlhorn, G. (2018b). Unterricht in den Herkunftssprachen Russisch und Polnisch – Einstellungen und Effekte. In G. Mehlhorn & B. Brehmer (Eds.), *Potenziale von Herkunftssprachen. Sprachliche und außersprachliche Einflussfaktoren* (pp. 259–292). Stauffenburg Verlag. https://doi.org/10.1515/infodaf-2020-0053

Brosch, M., Burdukowa, G., Ossipova-Joos, N., & Verbitskaya, V. (2020). *Jasno! Neu A1–A2. Russisch für Anfänger*. Klett Sprachen GmbH.

Cai, A., Konstantopoulos, D., Davis, R., Zheng, Y., & Liu, D. (2021, August 31). Let's code for lLanguages: Integrating AI chatbots into language learning. *The FLTMAG*. Retrieved August 12, 2022, from https://fltmag.com/ai-chatbots/

Carreira, M., & Kagan, O. (2018). Heritage language education: A proposal for the next 50 years. *Foreign Language Annals, 51*(1), 152–168. https://doi.org/10.1111/flan.12331

Deterding, S., Khaled, R., Nacke, L., & Dixon, D. (2011). Gamification: Toward a definition. *Proceedings of the gamification workshop (CHI 2011)* (pp. 12–15), Vancouver, Canada. http://gamification-research.org/wp-content/uploads/2011/04/CHI11_Workshop_Gamification.pdf

Dietz, B., & Roll, H. (2017). Ethnic German and Jewish immigrants from post-Soviet countries in Germany: Identity formation and integration prospects. In L. Isurin & C. M. Riehl (Eds.), *Integration, identity and language maintenance in young immigrants: Russian Germans or German Russians* (pp. 41–68). John Benjamins Publishing Company.

Dokukina, I., & Gumanova, J. (2020). The rise of chatbots – New personal assistants in foreign language learning. *Procedia Computer Science, 169*, 542–546. https://doi.org/10.1016/j.procs.2020.02.212

Dubinina, I., & Kisselev, O. (2019). *Rodnaya Rech': An introductory course for heritage learners of Russian*. Georgetown University Press.

Edwards, A. D., & Westgate, D. P. G. (1994). *Investigating classroom talk* (2nd ed.). Routledge.

Endarto, I. T., & Tanojo, K. L. (2018). Gamifyinganguage testing through web-based platforms. *Atlantis Press, Advances in Social Science, Education and Humanities Research, 145*, 130–134. https://doi.org/10.2991/iconelt-17.2018.29

Følstad, A., & Brandtzaeg, P. B. (2020). Users' experiences with chatbots: Findings from a questionnaire study. *Quality User Experience, 5*(3), 1–14. https://doi.org/10.1007/s41233-020-00033-2

Fryer, L. K., Ainley, M., Thompson, A., Gibson, A., & Sherlock, Z. (2017). Stimulating and sustaining interest in a language course: An experimental comparison of Chatbot and Human task partners. *Computers in Human Behavior, 75,* 461–468. https://doi.org/10.1016/j.chb.2017.05.045

Gallacher, A., Thompson, A., & Howarth, M. (2018). "My robot is an idiot!" – Students' perceptions of AI in the L2 classroom. In P. Taalas, J. Jalkanen, L. Bradley, & S. Thouësny (Eds.), *Future-proof CALL: Language learning as exploration and encounters – Short papers from EUROCALL* (pp. 70–76). Research-publishing.net. https://doi.org/10.14705/rpnet.2018.26.815

Gilabert, R., & Castellví, J. (2019). Task and syllabus design for morphologically complex languages. In J. W. Schwieter & A. Benati (Eds.), *The Cambridge handbook of language learning* (pp. 527–549). Cambridge University Press. https://doi.org/10.1017/9781108333603

Goda, Y., Yamada, M., Matsukawa, H., Hata, K., & Yasunami, S. (2014). Conversation with a Chatbot before an online EFL group discussion and the effects on critical thinking. *The Journal of Information and Systems in Education, 13*(1), 1–7. https://doi.org/10.12937/ejsise.13.1

Grudin, J., & Jacques, R. (2019). Chatbots, humbots, and the quest for artificial general intelligence. *Proceedings of the 2019 CHI conference on human factors in computing systems* (pp. 1–11), Glasgow, Scotland. Association for Computing Machinery. https://doi.org/10.1145/3290605.3300439

Guriev, V. (2020). Znakom'tes', Vasya – virtual'nyy uchitel' angliyskogo. *Skyeng Magazine,* 24th September 2020. Retrieved July 29, 2022, from https://magazine.skyeng.ru/meet-vasiliy/

Hidayatulloh, I., Pambudi, S., Surjono, H. D., & Sukardiyono, T. (2021). Gamification on chatbot-based learning media: A review and challenges. *ELINVO Electronics, Informatics, and Vocational Education, 6*(1), 71–80. https://doi.org/10.21831/elinvo.v6i1.43705

Huang, W. H.-Y., Hew, K. F., & Fryer, L. K. (2021). Chatbots for language learning – Are they really useful? A systematic review of chatbot-supported language learning. *Journal of Computer Assisted Learning, 38*(1), 237–257. https://doi.org/10.1111/jcal.12610

Isurin, L. (2011). *Russian diaspora: Culture, identity, and language ghange.* De Gruyter Mouton.

Isurin, L., & Riehl, C. M. (Eds.). (2017). *Integration, identity and language maintenance in young immigrants: Russian Germans or German Russians.* John Benjamins Publishing Company.

Jia, J. (2004). CSIEC (Computer Simulator in Educational Communication): A virtual context-adaptive chatting partner for foreign language learners. In Kinshuk, C.-K. Looi, E. Sutinen, D. Sampson, I. Aedo, L. Uden, & E. Kaehkoenen (Eds.), *Proceedings of ICALT (International conference on advanced learning technology by IEEE computer society)* (pp. 690–692). IEEE Computer Society Press.

Jia, J. (2015). The web-based intelligent English instruction system CSIEC. In *Intelligent web-based English instruction in middle schools* (pp. 60–103). IGI Global. https://doi.org/10.4018/978-1-4666-6607-8

Kim, N.-Y. (2018). A study on chatbots for developing Korean college students' English listening and reading skills. *Journal of Digital Convergence, 16*(8), 19–26. https://doi.org/10.14400/JDC.2018.16.8.019

Lee, N., Mikesell, L., Joaquin, A. D. L., Mates, A. W., & Schumann, J. H. (2009). *The interactional instinct: The evolution and acquisition of language*. Oxford University Press, Inc.
Lotze, N. (2016). *Chatbots. Eine linguistische analyse*. Peter Lang GmbH Internationaler Verlag der Wissenschaften.
MacIntyre, P. D., Clément, R., Dörnyei, Z., & Noels, K. A. (1998). Conceptualizing willingness to communicate in a L2: A situational model of L2 confidence and affiliation. *The Modern Language Journal*, *82*(4), 545–562. https://doi.org/10.1111/j.1540-4781.1998.tb05543.x
Mazzilli, F. (2021). Chatbots for action-oriented language learning: Using Elbot to enhance conflict-solving skills in learners of German as a foreign language. *EL.LE*, *10*(1), 95–116. http://doi.org/10.30687/ELLE/2280-6792/2021/01/005
McCroskey, J. C., & Baer, J. E. (1985). Willingness to communicate: The construct and its measurement. *Paper presented at the annual convention of the speech communication association*. https://files.eric.ed.gov/fulltext/ED265604.pdf
Mehlhorn, G. (2014). Sozialformen und Differenzierung. In A. Bergmann (Ed.), *Fachdidaktik Russisch. Eine Einführung* (pp. 241–252). Narr Verlag.
Meisel, W. (2016, July 27). *Specialized digital assistants and bots expected to generate over $600 billion in revenue by 2020*. CISION PR Newswire. Retrieved August 5, 2022, from www.prnewswire.com/news-releases/specialized-digital-assistants-and-bots-expected-to-generate-over-600-billion-in-revenue-by-2020–300304454.html
Mikhaylova, A. (2018). Morphological bottleneck: The case of Russian heritage speakers. *Journal of Language Contact*, *11*, 268–303. https://doi.org/10.1163/19552629-01102005
Moioli, F. (2019, April 3). Xiaoice: The most "human" AI in our world?. *LinkedIn*. Retrieved July 29, 2022, from www.linkedin.com/pulse/xiaoice-most-human-ai-world-fabio-moioli
Norton Peirse, B. (1995). Social identity, investment, and language learning. *Teachers of English to Speakers of Other Languages, Inc. (TESOL) Quarterly*, *29*(1), 9–31. https://doi.org/10.2307/3587803
Nuss, S. V. (2022). Morphology acquisition research meets instruction of L2 Russian: A contextualized literature review. In S. V. Nuss & W. W. Martelle (Eds.), *Task-based instruction for teaching Russian as a foreign language* (pp. 15–35). Routledge Russian Language Pedagogy and Research.
Nuss, S. V., & Martin, C. (Eds.). (2022). *Student-centered approaches to teaching Russian: Insights, strategies, and adaptations*. Routledge Russian Language Pedagogy and Research.
Pavlenko, A., & Norton, B. (2007). Imagined communities, identity, and English language learning. In J. Cummins & C. Davison (Eds.), *International handbook of English language teaching* (pp. 669–680). Springer Science+Business Media, LLC. https://doi.org/10.1007/978-0-387-46301-8
Polinsky, M. (2018). *Heritage languages and their speakers*. Cambridge University Press. https://doi.org/10.1017/9781107252349
Richards, J., & Rodgers, T. (2001). *Approaches and methods in language teaching*. Cambridge University Press.
Sailer, M., Hense, J. U., Mandl, H., & Klevers, M. (2013). Psychological perspectives on motivation through gamification. *Interaction Design and Architecture(s) Journal*, *19*, 28–37. www.researchgate.net/publication/278672057
Sailer, M., Hense, J. U., Mayr, S. K., & Mandl, H. (2017). How gamification motivates: An experimental study of the effects of specific game design elements on psychological need satisfaction. *Computers in Human Behavior*, *69*, 371–380. http://doi.org/10.1016/j.chb.2016.12.033

Schöbel, S. M., Janson, A., & Söllner, M. (2020). Capturing the complexity of gamification elements: A holistic approach for analysing existing and deriving novel gamification designs. *European Journal of Information Systems*, *29*(6), 641–668. https://doi.org/10.1080/0960085X.2020.1796531

Seliger, H. W. (1977). Does practice make perfect?: A study of interaction patterns and L2 competence. *Language Learning*, *27*(2), 263–278. https://doi.org/10.1111/j.1467-1770.1977.tb00122.x

Shum, H.-Y., He, X., & Li, D. (2018). From Eliza to XiaoIce: Challenges and opportunities with social chatbots. *Frontiers of Information Technology & Electronic Engineering*, *19*, 10–26. https://doi.org/10.1631/FITEE.1700826

Spasova, S., & Welsh, K. (2020). Mixing it up with blended learning. In E. Dengub, I. Dubinina, & J. Merrill (Eds.), *The art of teaching Russian* (pp. 405–430). Georgetown University Press. https://doi.org/10.2307/j.ctv18sqxnd.23

Steinbach, A., & Birzer, S. (2014). А у вас щас времени нету, да? Mündliche Sprache und ihr Wandel [Zur Bewertung mündlicher Leistungen im Russischunterricht]. *Praxis Fremdsprachenunterricht-Russisch*, *5*, 7–9.

Swain, M., & Lapkin, S. (1995). Problems in output and the cognitive processes they generate: A step towards second language learning. *Applied Linguistics*, *16*(3), 371–391. http://doi.org/10.1093/applin/16.3.371

Tolins, J., & Fox Tree, J. E. (2014). Addressee backchannels steer narrative development. *Journal of Pragmatics*, *70*, 152–164. https://doi.org/10.1016/j.pragma.2014.06.006

Wapenhans, H. (2016). Rasskaži, čto . . . – Einen Monolog im 2. Lernjahr bewerten. *PRAXIS Fremdsprachenunterricht Russisch*, *1*, 10–11.

Wegerif, R. (2004). The role of educational software as a support for teaching and learning conversations. *Computers & Education*, *43*(1), 179–191. https://doi.org/10.1016/j.compedu.2003.12.012

Yngve, V. H. (1970). On getting a word in edgewise. *Proceedings of the Chicago linguistic society, 6th meeting* (pp. 567–578), Chicago, IL, USA. The University of Chicago.

Part V

Are the games worth the candle?

Chapter 11

Playing while learning

Are the games worth the candle? Reflections on practice and future directions

Vita V. Kogan and Svetlana V. Nuss

CHAPTER SUMMARY

The chapter analyzes the themes and challenges of teaching with games that were discussed in the volume's chapters. The authors see game-based teaching of Russian as a student-centered practice and provide advice on how to integrate games into instruction, specifically addressing the diversity of cultural backgrounds, the need for time in game design, and the difficulties in evaluating game effectiveness, among others. Connections between real-world tasks and games are explored in relation to needs assessment and transfer of learning. The chapter offers a table with an actionable framework for integrating games into the instruction flow and detailed advice on how to ensure the transferability of learning. We further discuss the role of a teacher in game-based language learning and pedagogy of game integration, focusing on methodology, materials, and mediation. The chapter concludes with a call to the field of teaching RFL to explore teaching with games as a way to offer our learners a world of positive emotions, curiosity, and adventure, reshaping the current discourse about the Russian language from a "hard" language to study into "fun" instead. The chapter positions the volume as a multifaceted reflection on post-pandemic teaching and the shifting pedagogical paradigm from cognitive to affective factors in language education and beyond. Game-based teaching accommodates this changing mindset particularly well by bringing a powerful potential to transform one's emotive state, boost motivation, and engage, in addition to providing educational value.

КРАТКОЕ СОДЕРЖАНИЕ ГЛАВЫ

В данной главе анализируются темы и проблемы обучения с помощью игр, которые обсуждались авторами книги. Авторы рассматривают игровое обучение русскому языку как как ориентированную на студентов практику и дают советы о том, как интегрировать игры в образовательный процесс, учитывая культурные факторы и оценку эффективности игры, в числе прочих. Исследуется связь между целевыми заданиями и играми, особое внимание уделяется оценке потребностей студентов и проблеме трансфера знаний с таблицей, облегчающей интеграцию игр в процесс обучения. Обсуждается педагогика интеграции игр с акцентом на методологию, материалы и роль учителя. Глава завершается призывом к использованию игр как способ вызвать положительные эмоции и дух приключений у студентов, изменяя существующий дискурс о русском языке с "трудного" на "увлекательный". Глава позиционирует данный том как шаг ведущий к смене установок педагогической парадигмы с когнитивных на аффективные как в языковом образовании, так и за его пределами. Использование игр при этом играет особую роль, поскольку обладает мощным потенциалом для передачи человеческого эмоционального состояния и повышения мотивации в дополнение к своей образовательной ценности.

In this volume, we have attempted to link game-based learning and gamification with specific challenges of the acquisition of Russian as a foreign, heritage, and second language. There were many questions to answer: What role do games play in instructional settings? How can one balance entertainment with educational content and ensure that students learn what they are intended to learn? How does the teacher fit into the picture? What are the relationships between various game types and proficiency levels? What are the different roads to game design? And of course, what are the students' attitudes toward the gamified classroom? In terms of the Russian language, we were particularly interested in exploring how games can support the acquisition of Russian's rich morphosyntax, what sociocultural components can be conveyed via games, and how speaking in the language can be facilitated and enhanced with games. We believe that some of these questions were answered with the scholarship presented here, and some questions would constitute items on our agenda for future research.

Each chapter of this volume reflects on the professional experience of teaching L2 Russian in a tertiary setting. As the work progressed, many authors had to adjust their initial ideas when those ideas met real classrooms with real people in them. There was also learning taking place as the teachers were developing and fine-tuning the game mechanics and dynamics. Chapter 1 establishes the need for pedagogical cohesion in the integration of games into the instruction of foreign languages and discusses research advances that may help teachers of foreign languages shape their approaches. It provides practical considerations for balancing research and practice when designing student experiences and implementing games in language teaching. The chapter analyzes the volume's contributions based on the context of instruction, the kind of games and gamified teaching they offer, the affordances of various games, and the student-centered nature of teaching language with games and argues for the necessity of shifting the instruction of RFL to be more human-centered and empathy-driven. Chapter 2 provides a brief overview of the history of play in language education and offers our definitions of game-based learning and gamification. The volume then presents a showcase of classroom cases that expand the reader's pedagogical repertoire and supply them with relevant theory. Our goal was to focus on the unique learning profile of the Russian language and the unique challenges of the L2 Russian learner. To briefly illustrate, analysis of the research on L2 Russian morphology acquisition indicates that:

> There is currently no definitive answer regarding the mechanics of L1-like systems of L2 acquisition development by L2 learners [of Russian] as they acquire multimorphemic words. . . . Teachers, therefore, continue to look for effective instructional strategies to develop the learner's ability to form a system of inflection expectancy and morphological fluency.
>
> (Nuss, 2022a, pp. 32–33)

This focus on L2 Russian learners compels us to translate the existing game-based research to applicable classroom activities that promote best teaching practices and maximize learning outcomes for our students. In so doing, we aim to integrate game-based initiatives in teaching RFL into a rich pre-existing discourse of game-based and gamified education, with a final product serving as guidance and inspiration for Russian-language researchers and practitioners as well as the wider language teaching profession. The pedagogical accounts detailed in the chapters of this volume may serve as an additional resource in moving forward the overall practice and research of teaching languages with games. It is clear to us that current thinking in the field of second language acquisition integrates well with gaming and gamification. However, the primacy of pedagogy in teaching languages with games has yet to become a widespread reality, and it is especially true for Russian, a less commonly taught and underexplored language in SLA research.

We are convinced that games are a universal tool of learning: they stimulate similar attitudinal, cognitive, and behavioral changes as those which take place in response to real-world experiences. Many tenets of games are described and discussed critically in this volume, but one aspect seems to be particularly important for education: games instantly convert students into active participants of the learning process. It is hard to think of another educational activity that would serve as an equally effective trigger to roll up one's sleeves and dive into learning. Games open opportunities for the authentic application of knowledge and skills, the experience of a feeling of success or failure, and readily present the results of learning for further reflection. This magic cycle, repeated many times, transforms the language classroom and the learner.

Many of our readers are already convinced of the benefits of incorporating games into their academic curriculum but may be unsure about the workload that this endeavor might entail. Indeed, when a game is incorporated into the class flow, it is replacing some other activity that was planned in the existing syllabus: by making time for one activity, we are taking away from another. Even more so if the game involves the use of an unfamiliar technology. Which activities must yield their space in the workflow to make room for a game, and why?

The experience shows that teachers do not need to have all the answers before beginning to implement games in their practice, but there are some pedagogical, cultural, and linguistic considerations and choices to be made. The cases presented in this volume demonstrate that it is not necessary for the teacher to navigate the elaborate philosophical nuances of the theory of a game or dedicate all their time to game design and planning for the transformational effects of gaming and games to take place. Games are incredibly versatile and provide a wide range of pedagogical interventions: from an entire semester of gamified learning – *systemic mode*, when an entire syllabus or institutional program is built and sequenced based on games and gamification of instruction – to a short review exercise at the end of class – *incremental mode*, when teachers use games as an increment of instruction, more or less cohesively integrating them in otherwise non-game-oriented coursework, to include the use of games for assessment (definitions of *systemic* and *incremental modes* of instruction with games are based on definitions put forward in Nuss and Whitehead Martelle, 2022, p. 1, pertaining to teaching language with tasks). The authors of this volume:

- Use existing authentic games – games that native speakers of Russian use, such as *dominoes* in Leontyeva and Schnittke (Chapter 5).
- Adapt existing educational games from other languages, such as *Pick the Lie* by Pavlenko and Pastushenkov (Chapter 7).
- Create a game and then recycle it in many different ways, as Bondarenko does with her author game *Я гуляю по Москве* [*Walking the Streets of Moscow*] (Chapter 6).
- Incorporate only certain game elements as opposed to a full-scale game, as in mingling games by Kotelnikova and Bogomolova (Chapter 3) or poetry writing by Peremitina (Chapter 9).
- Use their knowledge of other disciplines and fields to gamify the learning: Weygandt (Chapter 8) brings her expertise in the theater to the classroom, Khotimsky (Chapter 4) incorporates history and sciences into a trivia game format, and Dornicheva and Birzer (Chapter 10) introduce chatbots to their students.

Teachers use games as a short warm-up activity (e.g., Kotelnikova and Bogomolova, Chapter 3), as one of the PPP (presentation-practice-production) components and as other classwork (e.g., Leontyeva and Schnittke, Chapter 5; Weygandt, Chapter 8), as homework (e.g., Dornicheva and Birzer, Chapter 10; Khotimsky, Chapter 4), as an extracurricular activity (e.g., Peremitina, Chapter 9; Weygandt, Chapter 8), and as an assessment tool (e.g., Bondarenko, Chapter 6; Khotimsky, Chapter 4; Pavlenko and Pastushenkov, Chapter 7). Games can be played in large classes, in small groups, in pairs, and solo. Games can be employed to introduce and practice grammatical structures, improve speaking skills (including pronunciation), and fuel writing and reading. The versatility of games does not end there. Besides supporting the development of linguistic skills, games are a unique pedagogical vehicle for mastering aspects of language learning that are not immediately obvious: confidence in speaking, interpersonal competence, creativity, linguistic, cultural, and metalinguistic awareness, and an improved sense of new language identity.

Addressing these factors in a holistic and safe way truly makes games a very effective instructional device.

Student-centered nature of teaching with games

Certainly, game-based learning and gamification are not without shortcomings, especially when implemented with fidelity on a larger scale. For example, in their recent paper, York et al. (2022) propose moving away from gamification strategies as focusing too much on rewards by employing behaviorist strategies to influence – or "trick," in York and colleagues' terms – the learner. In response, we bring the conversation back to the student-centered nature of the educational process that modern society aspires to develop with its human-centered discourse, where:

> Learners are consistently seen as reflective and metacognitively aware agents responsible for one's learning with a voice in designing one's learning path, where learning is valued more than its result and is considered in its societal connectedness and mutual influence.
>
> (Nuss, 2022b, p. 26)

Here, learner autonomy, self-directed learning, and self-efficacy come into play, as students need to realize how playing a game can advance their language skills, rather than be manipulated into performing certain activities and favoring certain behaviors. The teachers should explicitly discuss metacognitive learning strategies to ensure that students know exactly what is expected of them and how they stand to benefit from participating in the activity, not only in terms of language and content, but also including larger issues of personal identity and interpersonal communication.

It may be tempting to "simplify" the teacher's life by narrowing down instructional approaches (teaching with games, task-based language teaching), tools (use of technology: devices, certain platforms), and affordances (gamification), labeling some of them as *student-centered*; however, when such attempts meet practice, their superficial nature reveals itself. Task-based instruction can serve as an example here: despite its student-centered reputation in the field of language teaching, practice shows that it may or may not be conducted as a student-centered learner experience when task design is not balanced. Consider, for example, what happens to student performance if check-in points (progress-tracking individual conferences with the teacher) are not placed at appropriate intervals of task development or if, instead of a low-key formative assessment, a formal summative evaluation is planned. Either one of these situations is capable of causing unnecessary pressure, sending students the wrong message and derailing learning.

We believe that whichever teaching methodology and tools we use, it is essential to approach a student as a human being and an individual, as opposed to a passive recipient of knowledge, a human being whose "empowered engagement is called on to play a central role in enabling learners to co-author their learning" (Nuss,

2022b, p. 28). With this attitude, games and gamification will always serve us right. In the follow-up section, we explore some other concerns that the authors of this volume shared in their chapters and the lessons they learned while playing.

Common concerns of integrating game-based teaching practices

Games may distract from learning

The complexity of some games (visuals, plot, rules), as well as linguistic complexity involved, could occupy most of the learner's cognitive capital, leaving little room for learning. Non-educational games, games that we play in our native language for the joy of it, are created to keep us engaged and therefore might come across as rather intense for language learners. Even educational games that are meant specifically for the purpose of language learning often have distracting elements which are particularly salient when introduced for the first time. Students might need to spend some time processing and exploring a new learning medium. Various types of pre-play effectively address this issue. For example, Leontyeva and Schnittke (Chapter 5) point out that some games are best played initially in the students' first language before attempting them in L2 Russian. Some games require a step-by-step walk-through when the teacher and students critically examine the rules together and "marinate" in a new setting; watching somebody else play first also helps (e.g., a video of other students playing).

In preparation for play, Pavlenko and Pastushenkov (Chapter 7) suggest instructing students on how to give each other effective feedback and correct recurring mistakes. For team-based games, Khotimsky (Chapter 4) points out that lower-level learners might benefit from concrete models of possible exchanges during the game: phrases for moderating the game and discussing and reflecting on choices. We can add the peer language of moral support and encouragement to this list (e.g., *Молодец!* [Good job!], *Хорошо сказал!* [Well said]). Khotimsky recommends using a handout or a slide with key phrases that are helpful for sustaining the group conversation in Russian.

Gamified environments (online social spaces or physical quests and escape rooms) can also be rather overwhelming for educational purposes and require a gradual warm-up. For example, holding a virtual class in Gather.town is challenging the first time around as students are mesmerized by the new world and its features and pay little attention to the academic purpose of the context. In this case, pre-play might constitute homework activities completed on the same platform, which would allow students to spend as much time as they wish exploring the world and familiarizing themselves with its mechanics.

Games are good for speaking but may not be good for grammar

When we think about games in the classroom, we first consider the icebreakers and warm-up activities that are so popular within the communicative approach to language teaching and serve as conversation starters. Yet games have much more to offer: thanks to their intrinsically repetitive and restrictive nature, they constitute perfect practice for grammatical forms and structures. In fact, one of the most exciting lessons all of us in this volume have learned is that games – authentic and educational alike – are an irreplaceable tool when the notorious Russian grammar has to be conquered. We are all too familiar with the mind-numbing grammar drills and fill-in-the-blank exercises that our students have to struggle through, sometimes for hours at a time. The volume's chapters demonstrate that only minimal manipulations may be required to convert any textbook activity into an engaging, meaningful game that would instantly motivate students and maximize time on task. Leontyeva and Schnittke (Chapter 5) go as far as proposing to substitute all grammatical drills with games. We cannot agree more! Again, games do not have to be intricate, visually stimulating box editions: simply cutting phrases into pieces and asking students to match them could spark joy and engagement in the classroom.

Teachers have to constantly come up with new games

We already observed that games can be incredibly versatile. Just like the linguistic output of the same task can be tailored to various language proficiency levels, the same game can be played with beginner or advanced students alike. For example, Bondarenko's *Я гуляю по Москве* [*Walking the Streets of Moscow*] works well with zero-beginner learners, when the players simply move from location to location and read the names of the locations aloud; the next level would be adding the prepositional case for *Я в Московском Государственном Университете* [*I Am at the Moscow State University*], etc. The same game works great when the verbs of motion are introduced, and even very advanced learners benefit from walking around Moscow by engaging in a complex narration in different tenses and expanding their journey to cultural and pragmatic references. Bondarenko (Chapter 6) points out that besides speaking, the game can help integrate and develop other skills: after "the walk," students may be invited to write a short report on the places they visited or check out the websites associated with featured landmarks, or complete additional tasks (e.g., purchase a ticket on the Bolshoi Theater website).

Using the same game throughout the semester serves as a thematic leitmotif and reduces the time spent on introducing new mediums and rules. Playing the same game several times – even if it is played the same way – has positive effects on mastering the skills, building learner confidence, and possibly more, similar to task repetition (Bygate, 2018).

Students may not be used to playing games

The value of game-based learning and a game's potential impact on language learning may be contested by participants. It is not uncommon to observe hesitation and even resistance in class when games are first introduced. In fact, adult language learners express distinct overall dissatisfaction with games in language-learning classes when they cannot clearly identify learning goals and do not realize the specific learning outcomes that playing games helps them achieve (Annamalai et al., 2021). This fact alone clearly speaks of the importance of placing the proverbial pedagogical horse in front of the educational wagon altogether, with gamification and game-based language learning being but a small sliver of the language learning pie. Some students are not convinced games are a valuable educational tool, while others feel intimidated by the game mechanics (e.g., mingling games can be challenging for shy and introverted learners), and others still believe that games infantilize the classroom and somehow undermine students' adult identity. Kotelnikova and Bogomolova (Chapter 3) suggest communicating the objectives of each game clearly and explicitly explaining learning gains beforehand; in extreme situations, the word "game" can be replaced with more academically familiar words "task" or "activity." Generally speaking, it is enough to introduce a game once or twice in class for students to warm up to the idea and start paying attention. And again, the questions of student agency and student ownership of learning come forward as necessary elements of a student-centered environment where learners are viewed, in Dewey's terms, as objects of educational effort and artists of their own education as opposed to its subjects.

Additionally, some students might simply be shy to play because the instructions are vague. Peremitina (Chapter 9) gives examples of how to give concrete and actionable instructions: it is particularly important for her poetry-writing activity because of the creative and open-ended nature of the task.

Diversity of cultural backgrounds may interfere with playing

Qualitative research on analog games, particularly games of a mingling nature, reveals some issues that are unlikely to come up in a digital space. Some of these issues are not related to language learning per se but may hinder it. The teaching profession continues to trip over differences in cultural backgrounds, obvious for some and opaque for others, particularly issues of personal space and bodily attitudes – a well-described phenomenon in a language classroom (Habók et al., 2021; Oxford, 1996). This can be cultural differences in attitudes and willingness to participate in activities that involve close body contact and other culturally sensitive areas of human interaction. Not surprisingly, some participants would resent using other people's clothes (for example, shoes) to construct a "tower" or would not be willing to place paper between different body parts (Annamalai et al., 2021). While the teaching of RFL has a rich tradition of respecting learners' cultural differences, every teacher has to negotiate these nuances of human interaction in real time and usually with no time to prepare. The more important are pedagogical accounts of how various challenges of engaging learners whose cultural background differs from that of the teacher and/or the learning environment in the activities they perceive as less traditional and not productive (Kotelnikova & Bogomolova, chapter 3).

Teachers do not know how to play

Understanding game mechanics, how specific games can fit into the lesson plan and academic curriculum, what skills are activated, and what caveats are waiting around the corner develop better when we, teachers, start playing games with friends and family. Gamification is a state of mind and even a life philosophy. In her bestseller *Reality Is Broken: Why Games Make Us Better and How They Can Change the World*, Jane McGonigal posits a question: What if we started living our real lives as gamers? She explains how games excel at optimizing the human experience and organizing collaborative communities of practice. Playing at life a little – either through actual games or by gamifying certain aspects of daily activities (e.g., ChoreWars.com) – has the potential to unlock a new layer of meaning in our existence. Or perhaps simply make us better at teaching with games.

Leontyeva and Schnittke (Chapter 5) advise trying new games with colleagues or family members first. It is not uncommon that the volume of game material (e.g., cards) has to be adjusted to fit a specific time slot or to stimulate the dynamic. When repurposing games from other languages, it is crucial to make sure they work well with the specific linguistic features of the Russian language, as Peremitina (Chapter 9) discovered with her poetry-writing game. As her students were putting poems together, it became obvious that Russian morphology should be taken into account. In the same way, playing *Monopoly* in Russian might feel and sound very different from playing this game in other languages – for example, the players have to manipulate the intricate complexity of number declension and number–noun agreement (*У меня нет ста шестидесяти рублей*. [*I don't have a hundred sixty rubles*]). Oftentimes, by playing games, we discover affordances and learning opportunities beyond those originally built into game design and planning. In Leontyeva and Schnittke's version of *Memory*, learners get to practice *мне нужно* [*I need*] structure, which is not the immediate learning goal of this game. This delicious educational twist is only discoverable when teachers themselves are avid gamers.

There is no time for game design

Students can design, find, and bring games to class too! The recent pedagogical turn toward a more horizontal and egalitarian classroom has demonstrated how powerful and beneficial the student-centered curriculum can be. Not only are students knowledgeable citizens who actively contribute their diverse and rich identities to the educational process, but they are also an indispensable source of creativity and imagination. While introducing *Trivia*, Khotimsky (Chapter 4) suggests involving students in every step of game design and implementation: from the search for game material (content, mechanics, rules, etc.) to evaluation and reflection. Allowing students to contribute to the organic development of a game or a game repertoire that they use in class ensures that the resulting game material will be tailored to these specific students' objectives and interests. Such division of labor benefits students and teachers alike.

Evaluating game effectiveness is not easy

Many authors in this volume report instances where students continue playing an educational game after the lesson is over and even borrow the game from the teacher to play it in their spare time. This is the best feedback the teacher can receive. If a game does not engage students and they stop playing it immediately after the class is over, perhaps it is not the best game to play with these specific students. Being in tune with one's students and watching them keenly instead of getting carried away with one's own favorite game ensures the constant evolution of the teacher's game repertoire. Only the fittest games should survive.

Another question we are naturally concerned with is, *Did the game work?* At the end of the day, the goal of educational gaming is learning, and if it does not happen, such games serve very little purpose. Under the umbrella of learning, we include both cognitive (skill, knowledge) and affective factors (motivation, confidence) that help students succeed in the acquisition of Russian. Wrapping up and evaluating the results of a game can be done in a variety of ways: from asking students directly (as Dornicheva and Birzer, Chapter 10, do with chatbots) to following up the game with a short quiz or simply observing the class performance. Standardized and institutional tests can help measure the impact that game-based instruction has on student language proficiency, as well as offer a way to compare a gamified classroom with a traditional one, as Weygandt (Chapter 8) does with the help of the ACTFL proficiency testing. It is imperative that the field engages in this intentionally and regularly, not only to fine-tune the approach, but also to provide class-based evidence for future research.

From games to real-world tasks: needs assessment and transfer of learning

In his classic educational psychology text, Klausmeier (1961) asserts, "The main reason for formal education is to facilitate learning in situations outside school" (p. 352). Transfer of learning – the application of the learning experiences acquired from games to novel contexts – constitutes a topic of heated debate in educational gaming. Previous research on transfer of learning has shown that it cannot be taken for granted that learning will transfer, or indeed that any learning will necessarily occur from a given set of experiences (Barnett & Ceci, 2002; Detterman, 1993). Lost in play, it is easy to lose sight of the big picture: What are students learning through this particular game? How will it contribute to their language development? Is this the best way to learn it? In other words, do we necessarily need to gamify this aspect of learning, or are there better ways to learn about it? In his upcoming paper, deHaan (2023) discusses the goals of ludic language pedagogy (teaching with and around games; York et al., 2021) and formulates the following question: "How can [pedagogical] methods, materials, and mediation transform students and classrooms and society?" He proposes explicitly discussing this question with students at the beginning of the semester. Based on the answers received, deHaan describes an activity during which the teacher and the students brainstorm the learning roadmap together by drawing connections between games, game skills, and possible real-world projects that students can accomplish. Students reflect on their current identity and skillset, what skills they want to acquire in the future and what dream projects they would like to attempt that require these skills. This reflection, realized as a collaborative mind map drawn on the whiteboard or a poster, serves as the needs analysis data for the teacher to draw on when outlining the list of language skills and related games (see Table 1 for a quick actionable overview).

One example from deHaan's paper features a student whose dream is to become a translator and work on movie subtitles. There are a number of games that support the practice of translation (e.g., Weygandt, Chapter 8; Kotelnikova and Bogomolova, Chapter 3, of the present volume), but more important is how these skills would be connected and integrated into a real-world project – the last piece of a pedagogical puzzle that the teacher has to put together. deHaan and the students brainstorm possible projects and decide on creating subtitles for an existing and publicly available YouTube video (e.g., a TED talk). Not only would such a project showcase the evidence of student learning at the end of the semester, but it would also contribute to a real-world cause (the community of YouTube watchers) and could be displayed as a representative work sample in the student's résumé/professional portfolio to show future employers. deHaan emphasizes that the process of needs-game-project connection does not have to be a long, laborious process with the teacher designing and assigning an individual project to each student. With his 30+ students in a typical class, he dedicates only one classroom session to needs assessment and transferability, pushing the students to the center of the action and making them responsible for their learning. As much as students are free to pick any project they feel motivated to accomplish, it is preferable that the chosen projects are related to students' future careers or personal aspirations as opposed to fantasy projects detached from reality. In his earlier paper, deHaan (2019) observes:

> If the purpose of education is to develop students' interests and abilities to participate, as they wish, in various private, public and professional areas of life, then games, if used at all, should directly facilitate students' reaching this goal.
> (deHaan, 2019, p. 4)

The following table offers an actionable framework for integrating games into the instruction flow and details practical advice on how to ensure the transferability of learning.

A final reflection on students' projects can take various formats and serve as a conclusion for the course, at which point students should have a clearer picture of how their needs and objectives were met throughout the semester and how the undertaken pedagogical activities (games!) contributed to this process. We personally believe that an end-of-semester exposition where students can present their projects and reflect on them through questions and feedback from peers and other visitors is an effective way to summarize and celebrate the acquired knowledge. Such an exposition can take place in-person or online via socializing platforms like Gather.town or Topia.io, synchronously or asynchronously. The latter option can be implemented through Google documents or Flipgrid, where students can view and comment on each other's work.

Table 11.1 Ensuring transferability of learning

When	What	How	Comments and tips
Before or during the first class of the semester	Needs analysis Narrowing down the list of language skills to acquire and games to practice them	Collaborative mind map activity Anonymous survey with Google Forms or Socrative.com	Keep it short (3–5 questions). See Appendix A for a needs analysis example survey and responses from students.
Before or during the first class of the semester	Needs integration into an existing curriculum	Finding the overlaps between students' needs and the existing curriculum Adjusting the curriculum accordingly (e.g., more focus on speaking or specific content)	Teachers have the right to contribute too! Essentially, a perfect syllabus is where all *four* come together: the teacher, the students, the institution, and societal imperatives.
Before or during the first class of the semester	Game design Translating skills into games	Levels of gamification: • Warm-up • Stand-alone exercise • Entire-lesson activity • Entire-semester project • Homework • Assessment	Include students in the process of game creation to save time and maximize engagement.
At the midpoint of the semester	Transition to the real world	With an eye on needs analysis and ongoing language development, brainstorm possible projects to complete by the end of the semester.	Final projects can be used as a summative assessment if the institutional settings allow it.
At the end of the semester	Reflection	Reflections can be done either as an entire-class discussion in students' native language or as a homework assignment/part of a course evaluation survey.	A self-assessment questionnaire can be used to help students substantiate their learning and evaluate progress.

Note: The actionable framework for integrating games into the instruction flow summarized in this table is inspired by deHaan (2023).

Methodology, materials, mediation: pedagogy of game integration

In the following section, we analyze the pedagogical accounts of game-based teaching practices comprising this volume and offer a summary of practices the authors of the chapters describe and implicate in their case studies. This **analysis of teaching practices involved in facilitating language acquisition via the use of games and affordances of gamification** lends strong evidence to York et al.'s (2021) conclusion that pedagogy of language teaching is crucial for language acquisition of learners to occur in this context, and that mere student engagement with games is not enough on its own for language learning to take place. We offer this preliminary lineup of teacher involvement activities to illustrate the extent of teacher influence as the learning experiences unfold.

Methodology

In relation to methodology, the authors of the present volume create student learning experiences and demonstrate their mastery of methodology as they:

- Determine the appropriateness of the learning experience considering student background and level of proficiency
- Scaffold the necessary language and produce required supporting materials
- Individualize student learning experience and differentiate support
- Establish the reason for conducting the activity and help students understand the purpose of the game as a language learning activity
- Model game mechanics, moves, and interactions language- and content-wise
- Facilitate noticing of form/meaning connections
- Formatively assess and check student comprehension and both factual and perceived progress
- Offer connections for language transfer, actively integrate cultural realities and content-based areas of special student interest
- Cultivate student agency by inviting student voice and allowing student creation of learning content
- Are mindful of real-life connections in organizing instruction, making learning relevant to students
- Promote student self-reflection and learner autonomy
- And, above all, facilitate the meaningful use of language with a purpose greater than simply *use of language*

Materials

Developing and adopting materials for their games and gamified learner experiences, the authors:

- Scaffold the necessary language and produce required materials
- Develop and perfect directions for the activities

- Produce essential formative and summative evaluation materials
- Produce materials to help facilitate connections for language transfer
- Create and supply game materials and games as such (cards, boards, dice, and more)
- Choose the required technology
- Develop student reflection and feedback forms

Mediation

The authors of the chapters featured in this volume engage in the following mediation practices as they arrange student learning experiences:

- Teachers mediate student overall success.
- Individualize student learning experience and differentiate supports.
- Brainstorm and discuss steps and strategies.
- Facilitate understanding and dynamics of game mechanics.
- Establish and promote game literacy – to include digital literacy.
- Enable and empower students' appreciation of learning taking place via games – adult learners and children alike benefit from explicit information about the purpose of employing games in instruction (just like the purpose behind their engagement with any other activity).
- Provide with comments that help students stay focused on language learning.
- Provide emotional support during games.
- Encourage exploration of new content- and culture-based contexts.
- Facilitate student access to the technology involved in the learning experience.
- Organize student reflection on learning and learner feedback to the teacher.

Missing from this lineup of teachers' activities is the professional development and research efforts teachers invested in discoveries of the games they wanted to incorporate into their instructional workflow. It is certainly convenient to view "methodology" as a tenet already in a teacher's possession, just as it is certainly unrealistic to assume that all teachers acquire this tenet in their professional training prior to entering their teaching context. Then again, who are our language teachers at universities, and how do they acquire the pedagogy of language teaching? While it is practically impossible to teach in a K–12 setting without having gone through a specialized professional program, tertiary institutions often dismiss the pedagogy component completely or place it in the background when recruiting their faculty with language teaching in their workload. It is high time that the approach to hiring language teaching professionals regards their teaching with a renewed respect to skillful pedagogy. Not every outstanding historian, poet, or literature specialist who speaks the language of their area of expertise can facilitate language acquisition and "teach language" – in our case, Russian. The process is in slow reversal, with many language departments developing specialized language pedagogy faculty, but the overall approach lacking attention to language pedagogy prevails.

> Just as we cannot force students into holistic learning by simply physically placing them in our classrooms or in front of the screen of the computer, we cannot force teachers into nourishing teaching by simply giving them teaching assignments. Pedagogy must be cultivated.
>
> (Nuss, 2022b, p. 20)

Playing nice together

This volume directly responds to the call of York and colleagues (2021), who strongly advocate for a sharp change in the research vector of the use of games in language teaching. Even though the pedagogical accounts presented here are not framed by the authors as teacher action research (Manfra, 2019), each of the contributing authors acted as a teacher-researcher when they planned and conducted game integration into their teaching practices. Many of them took meticulous notes on the experience and measured and recorded the impact their instruction had on student performance and language acquisition. The authors engaged in deep professional reflection by first thoroughly reviewing the existing literature on their particular game or gamification affordance, compared their own experience with what was reported previously, and responded with systematic analyses and personal observations. Every one of these case studies can be re-framed as a qualitative research contribution.

Here, of course, the issue of institutional support of teachers in language learning emerges in full bloom, and we raise the issue of institutional support of language teachers yet again (Anderson et al., 2020; Martin & Nuss, 2022b; Nuss, 2022a; Spasova & Welsh, 2020; Whitehead Martelle & Nuss, 2022). From having paid time available to plan instruction to being able to afford quality professional development without sacrificing enormous amounts of personal time – there is room to grow in how society and institutions can better support the language teaching profession. The need for such support becomes even more urgent when we consider the unprecedented challenges the world of education faces today, where teachers have to respond to the post-pandemic student- and human-centered shifts of societal discourse and new demands to the teaching profession (Martin & Nuss, 2022b).

The volume we offer to the reader reflects on post-pandemic teaching and the shifting pedagogical paradigm from cognitive to affective factors in language education and beyond. Games accommodate this changing mindset particularly well by bringing a powerful potential to transport one's emotive state, boost motivation, and engage – in addition to supplying educational value – to teachers and learners alike.

Dynamic Teaching of Russian: Games and Gamification of Learning presents an inspiring portfolio of implementing games and gamification in the context of teaching L2 Russian. We think of *inspiring* as the keyword here: introducing the theory and practice of play, this volume is also an invitation into the world of positive emotions, curiosity, and adventure. As history unfolds itself, the Russian language teaching profession is witnessing difficult times. Playing nice together and supporting each other through games while exploring the language and the culture behind it is as important today as ever.

The authors would like to thank the three anonymous reviewers as well as Nicholas Brazones, Christina Nuss, Olesia Pavlenko, and Wendy Whitehead Martelle for their insightful comments, masterful editing suggestions, and respect for the author's voice. All remaining shortcomings are our own.

Appendix A

An example of a needs analysis form (Kogan, 2022)

Student survey

Your answers to the following questions will help me make sure our class is what you want or need it to be. Please answer in as much or little detail as you think necessary.

1. What other subjects besides Russian are you studying this year, and what profession are you working toward?

2. What do you love to think about?
   For example, how people "tick," the newest Apple gadget, your next road trip, how effective democracies work, movements for positive social change, cross-cultural (mis)understandings, black holes . . .

3. By the end of this academic year, what do you want to be able to DO in Russian? For example, "I'd like to be able to discuss my professional goals with a potential employer in a Russian-speaking country," "I'd like to be able to negotiate with Russian speakers at the local farmers market," "I'd like to be able to listen actively and respond empathetically to someone's concerns in Russian," "I'd like to be able to sell an idea in Russian to friends/colleagues/boss/public," and so on. Try to be specific here.

4. Are there games that you particularly like to play or watch? Table games, sports, TV games?

5. Any special request/wishes for the upcoming semester?

An example of responses from students (Kogan, 2022):

2. **What do you love to think about?**
For example, how people "tick," the newest Apple gadget, your next road trip, how effective democracies work, movements for positive social change, cross-cultural (mis)understandings, black holes . . .

History.

Russian literature and thought.

Political activism, media analysis (art, music, film, etc.), anthropology, archaeology.

Military, sport, languages, and cultures (the way countries get on, how international politics works), linguistics (like specifically grammar itself, inter-language connections), travel. Cooking too – as of recently.

History, sports, world news/politics.

I really enjoy political problems and policy issues as well as current affairs.

How we would be able to further regulate the Internet and introduce cyberlaw.

It's a cliché, given my course, but I suppose political issues and current events; also, as a hobby, folklore/history and folk music.

References

Anderson, C., Mikhailova, J., & Tumarkin, A. (2020). Russian language readiness in graduate teaching assistants: Implications for teaching and learning. In E. Dengub, I. Dubinina, & J. Merrill (Eds.), *The art of teaching Russian* (pp. 72–94). Georgetown University Press.

Annamalai, N., Kabilan, M. K., Rashid, R. A., Oleskevicience, G. V., & Vaičiūnienė, V. (2021). English language learning through non-technology games: A case study of international students at a Lithuanian university. *The Qualitative Report, 26*(10), 3261–3278. https://doi.org/10.46743/2160-3715/2021.4986

Barnett, S. M., & Ceci, S. J. (2002). When and where do we apply what we learn? A taxonomy for far transfer. *Psychological Bulletin, 128*(4), 612–637. https://doi.org/10.1037/0033-2909.128.4.612

Bygate, M. (2018). *Learning language through task repetition*. John Benjamins Publishing Company.

deHaan, J. A. (2019). Teaching language and literacy with games: What? How? Why? *Ludic Language Pedagogy, 1*, 1–57. https://doi.org/10.55853/llp_v1Art1

deHaan, J. A. (2023). *Methods, materials and mediation for student-centered transformation and social participation* [Unpublished manuscript]. University of Shizuoka.

Detterman, D. K. (1993). The case for the prosecution: Transfer as an epiphenomenon. In D. K. Detterman & R. J. Sternberg (Eds.), *Transfer on trial: Intelligence, cognition, and instruction* (pp. 1–24). Ablex Publishing Corp.

Habók, A., Kong, Y., Ragchaa, J., & Magyar, A. (2021). Cross-cultural differences in foreign language learning strategy preferences among Hungarian, Chinese and Mongolian University students. *Heliyon, 7*(3), e06505. https://doi.org/10.1016/j.heliyon.2021.e06505

Klausmeier, H. J. (1961). *Educational psychology. Learning and human abilities*. Harper.

Kogan, V. V. (2022). *Needs analysis form for Russian* [Google Forms]. University College London. https://forms.gle/NBwQRRckTCiEa9va9

Manfra, M. M. (2019). Action research and systematic, intentional change in teaching practice. *Review of Research in Education*, *43*(1), 163–196. https://doi.org/10.3102/0091732X18821132

Martin, C., & Nuss, S. (2022b). Reflections on practice, additional considerations, and the importance of institutional support for teachers. In S. Nuss & C. Martin (Eds.), *Student-centered approaches to student-centered approaches to Russian language teaching: Insights, strategies, and adaptations*. Routledge.

McGonigal, J. (2011). *Reality is broken: Why games make us better and how they can change the world*. Penguin Books.

Nuss, S. (2022a). Morphology acquisition research meets instruction of L2 Russian: A contextualized literature review. In S. Nuss & W. Martelle (Eds.), *Task-based instruction for teaching Russian as a foreign language* (pp. 15–35). Routledge. https://doi.org/10.4324/9781003146346-2

Nuss, S. (2022b). History of student-centeredness, its modern vision in education, and what this means for teaching L2 Russian today. In S. Nuss & C. Martin (Eds.), *Student-centered approaches to student-centered approaches to Russian language teaching: Insights, strategies, and adaptations*. Routledge.

Nuss, S., & Whitehead Martelle, W. (2022). Task-based instruction for teaching Russian as a foreign language: Perspectives and practice. In S. Nuss & W. Whitehead Martelle (Eds.), *Task-based instruction for teaching Russian as a foreign language*. Routledge. https://doi.org/10.4324/9781003146346-1

Oxford, R. L. (Ed.). (1996). *Language learning strategies around the world: Cross-cultural perspectives*. University of Hawaii Press.

Spasova, S., & Welsh, C. (2020). Mixing it up with blended learning. In E. Dengub, I. Dubinina, & J. Merrill (Eds.), *The art of teaching Russian* (pp. 405–430). Georgetown University Press.

Whitehead Martelle, W., & Nuss, S. (2022). TBLT in Russian classrooms: Reflections on practice and future directions. In S. Nuss & W. Whitehead Martelle (Eds.), *Task-based instruction for teaching Russian as a foreign language* (pp. 206–217). Routledge.

York, J., deHaan, J., Childs, M., & Collins, M. (2022). How is gamification like being trapped in the Matrix? And what is the "real-world" of game-based learning? *Digital Culture & Education*, *14*(3), 35–54. Retrieved December 28, 2022, from www.digitalcultureandeducation.com/volume-14-3

York, J., Poole, F. J., & deHaan, J. W. (2021). Playing a new game – An argument for a teacher-focused field around games and play in language education. *Foreign Language Annals*, *54*(4), 1164–1188. https://doi.org/10.1111/flan.12585

Index

4A Games 140, 142

AAA Games 139–140, 149
academic curriculum 21, 23, 215, 220
ACTFL Proficiency Guidelines 168, 170
active participles 72, 168
adjectival endings 103, 104
affect 152, 197
affective factors 213, 222, 227
affordances (of board games) 107–109, 124, 131
Among Us 141
arguments 144, 190, 200
artificial intelligence (AI) 191, 192, 194, 197, 199; *see also* chatbot
authentic application of knowledge 215
authentic environment 108, 198
authentic games in RFL classroom 81–97
authentic materials 132, 171

backchannels 190, 200–202, 204
behavioral theories 18
blended learning 191, 201, 202
brain plasticity 19, 25
Bring Home the Beaver 145

CD Projekt Red 140, 142
challenges 6, 10, 17–18, 170, 173, 195–196, 213–215, 220, 227
chatbot 189, 191–204; educational 189, 191, 193, 195–196, 200–201
classroom community 67–68, 77
Code Names 84
cognition 112
cognitive linguistics 107, 110, 112–113, 131
collaborative/collaboration 22, 23, 40, 69, 109, 131, 221, 223–224
collaborative learning 69, 109

communication 12, 24, 26–27, 39–42, 54, 65, 67–69, 74, 76–77, 109, 124, 140, 158, 160, 164, 190–200, 217
communicative: approach 40, 83, 88, 218; methods of language pedagogy 155, 156
competition 41, 54, 69–71, 74, 82, 109, 157, 159–160, 185
comprehensive input 23, 28
computer-assisted learning 24
computerized adaptive testing 22
confidence in speaking 42, 155–156, 160–161, 173, 216
construction 69, 72, 89, 97–98, 112, 130, 144, 166, 185, 191
constructivist theories 18–19
content-based instruction 174
conversation 4–5, 8–9, 41, 70, 73, 75–77, 83, 97, 146, 189–204, 209, 217–218
conversational: assistant 191; practice 189, 191, 195–196
cooperative learning 39, 40
corpus 69, 132
corrective feedback 29, 89, 97, 126, 131, 139
creativity 8, 20, 177, 182, 185, 216, 221
cultural background 106, 213, 220; differences 190, 220
Cyberpunk 2077 142, 148

deep cognitive encoding 130
dialogue 23, 69, 106–197, 139, 141–142, 149, 155–171, 174, 179, 194, 204
differentiating 185, 200
digital culture 189
digital literacy 226
discussion 7, 9, 17, 29, 30, 44–45, 51, 65,

70–74, 77, 98, 132, 138, 169, 181, 190, 196, 200, 204
discussion-based classes 70
discussions 9, 72–73, 76, 143, 193, 196
diversity 11, 213, 220
drama 95, 155–163, 166, 169, 173–175
drill 10, 11, 19, 88, 109, 219

educational chatbots 189, 191, 193, 195–196, 200–201
elementary level 162, 177, 199
emergency remote instruction 175
epic context 21–22, 26

feedback 19, 22, 25, 28–30, 39, 71, 76, 89, 97, 139, 141, 149, 173, 180–184, 193, 197, 202, 203, 218, 222, 223, 226
find the person who 43, 46, 55
Flagship Russian Program 5, 69, 169
Flipgrid 223
focus of form 28
foreign language students 200
formative assessment 12, 86, 181, 217
form-focused games 67, 75, 76
functional language use 27

game: complexity 124, 218, 221; design 5, 17–23, 90, 192, 193, 204, 213, 214, 221, 224; effectiveness 213, 221; evaluation 70, 178, 181, 221; meaning focused 49; mechanics 17, 20–21, 23–25, 81, 85, 87, 90, 214, 220, 225, 226; recycling 30, 42, 87, 216; repetition 30, 219; traditional 10, 138, 139, 142
Game-Based Learning (GBL) x, 138–141, 146, 148–149, 214; and multimodality 138, 140, 141
general chatbots 189, 195
genitive case 144, 147, 167
gerunds 70–72
goals 14, 21, 70, 87, 89, 97, 108, 193, 195, 200, 203, 219, 222, 229
grammar: drills 10, 11, 219; rules 40, 41, 112
grammatical accuracy 81, 83, 184
group work 21, 42, 71, 73, 162–163

Have You Ever 28, 145
heritage language students 190, 198–203, 214

heterogeneous 191, 200, 201
higher cognitive skills 19
history 27, 29, 70–76, 81, 165, 214, 216, 227, 230
holistic 26, 179, 217, 227
humbots 189, 199

identity 29–30, 157–159, 180, 190, 199–200, 216, 217, 220, 222
imperative/command form 166–167
improvement in pronunciation 160
incremental mode 216
independent practice 86, 88
individual differences 20
inherently repetitive tasks 85, 109, 129–131
inner speech 83, 85, 89, 98, 105, 106
inquiry-based study 180
instructional settings 214
instrumental case 53, 72, 81, 90, 145, 167
Integrated Performance Assessment 163
interactionist perspectives 139, 141
interactive: board 189; dialogue 155, 156; learning 197
interlocutor 194–195, 202
intermediate 25, 26, 67–68, 76, 88–94, 103, 107, 110, 121–123, 144–145, 156, 159, 161–166, 168, 173–174, 197–200
interpersonal 27, 216–217
interpretation 18

Jeopardy 68, 70, 75–76

Kahoot 138–140, 146–149
keyboard 202–203

language assessment 177, 181
language pedagogy 4, 69–70, 155–156, 158, 161, 169, 174, 178, 222, 227
Language Related Episodes 141
language transfer 225, 226
learner: autonomy 177, 178, 217, 225; empowerment 13, 217, 226; engagement 8, 18–19, 42, 69, 178, 219, 225; motivation 24
learning outcomes 20, 21, 26, 215, 219
less-guided practice 90
listening 42, 70, 141–142, 159, 171, 173, 194
List Game 143
Lost on a Deserted Island 143

low-stake environment 19
ludology in language teaching 83

Mafia 29, 30, 141, 149
manageable obstacles 22
Master and Margarita by Mikhail Bulgakov 156, 158–162, 165, 172
meaningful interaction 23, 27, 28, 83
meaningful speaking activities 39
metro 127, 139, 141, 148
mingles 42, 49
mingling games 39, 40–43, 49–50, 53–54, 216, 220
modal constructions with нужно [need] 81, 89, 103, 106
motivation 7, 8, 24, 29, 40–41, 50, 82, 97, 109, 140, 161, 172, 178, 193, 195–196, 200–201, 213, 222, 227
multimodal 139, 148, 149
multimodality 138, 140–141

narrative-communicative frames 107, 113–115
narrative games 26
needs assessment 213, 222–223

online: activities 183, 218; games 5, 54, 68–75, 138, 141, 147–149, 218; instruction 9, 67, 178, 196; learning spaces 23, 89, 196, 223
open educational platforms 24
oral proficiency 26, 155, 172

Padlet 89
participles 70–74, 77, 167
partner 42, 46, 47, 52, 54, 144, 190, 194, 198, 203
peer: communication 39; interaction 23, 76, 139, 143; teaching 23
pereskaz (retelling) 159, 164–165, 168–171, 175
The Perfect Fortune Teller 144
performance 22, 28–29, 155–169, 172–174, 181, 217, 222, 227
Pick the Lie 142, 216
positive emotions 19, 22, 213, 227
post-pandemic teaching 213, 227
pre-play 86, 98, 218
project-based learning 68, 131; tasks 70, 76

questionnaire 45, 173, 224

reading 7, 42, 46, 49–50, 72, 141–142, 155–156, 164–165, 170–173, 198, 216

real-world tasks 26, 213, 222
recording homework 28
recycling vocabulary 42, 46
review activities 70, 72
Roblox 147–149
role-play 25–26, 42, 69, 126, 140–142, 148, 156, 158, 162, 181, 196, 200
roll-and-move game 107, 109, 113, 124, 130–132
rubric 160
rule-based 191, 202
Russian: beginner 142, 143, 146, 158, 197, 218; elementary 162, 177, 199; grammar instruction 65, 155; language instruction 11–12, 68, 156, 175, 178; learner 81, 90, 93, 139, 143, 145, 148, 215
Russian as a Foreign Language (RFL) 3–4, 6, 8–9, 11, 40–42, 68–71, 74, 76, 81, 83, 85, 88, 156, 189, 213–215, 220
Russian verbs of motion (RVoM) 107, 110, 142

safe failure 21, 23
science 27, 70–73, 76, 158
self: -assessment 22, 26–27, 224; -efficacy 8, 217; -regulated learning 178
self-confidence 42, 66, 190
semantic labeling 12, 107, 110, 113–116, 129, 132
service-based learning 22
single-player games 27, 148
situated language 27
small group work 45, 71, 73, 76, 145
social: chatbots 189, 192, 194–197, 204; connectivity 22, 26, 41
Space Crew 145
speaking: accuracy 39, 41, 46; anxiety 29–30, 109, 161, 190; fluency 29, 39, 41–42, 46, 49
specialized assistants 192, 195, 198
specific learning objectives 195, 200
storytelling 113–114
student: agency 11, 86–87, 220, 225; -centered curriculum 221; -centered learning 12, 67, 177; -centeredness 11, 13; engagement 69, 178, 225; feedback 39, 76, 126, 131, 141, 149, 173, 202, 203; retention 20, 158; survey 27, 172, 224, 229
systemic mode 216

tandem learning 23
task-based language teaching (TBLT) 85, 88, 97–98
teaching: morphologically rich languages 82; syntax 159
technology-mediated tasks 5, 9
textbook 22, 25, 46, 89, 129, 155, 158, 160–162, 167, 171, 177, 197, 202–203, 219
third-year classroom 70–71, 76, 165
token 107, 109
Total Physical Response (TPR) 131–132, 158, 161
transfer/transferability of learning 26, 213, 222, 225–226
translanguaging 141
Trip to Russia 143–144
trivia game 67–70, 75–77
Two Halves Make a Whole 142

Я гуляю по Москве [Walking the streets of Moscow] 107–110, 117–124, 129–132, 216, 219
warm-up 46, 69, 71, 216, 218, 224
Werewolf 141

The Witcher 140, 142, 148

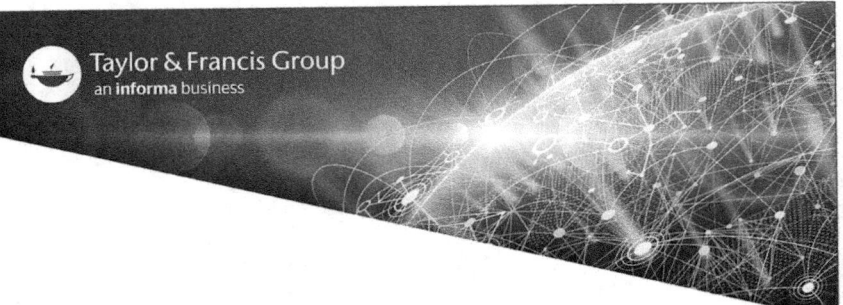

For Product Safety Concerns and Information please contact our EU representative GPSR@taylorandfrancis.com
Taylor & Francis Verlag GmbH, Kaufingerstraße 24, 80331 München, Germany